UNIVERSITY OF WALES SWANSEA
PRIFYSGOL CYMRU ABERTAWE
LIBRARY/LLYFRGELL

Classmark   HD38.5 H1367 2005

Location   Bay Library

1006033849

Logistics
Management
and Strategy

PEARSON
Education

We work with leading authors to develop the
strongest educational materials in logistics,
bringing cutting-edge thinking and best
learning practice to a global market.

Under a range of well-known imprints, including
Financial Times Prentice Hall, we craft high quality print and
electronic publications which help readers to understand
and apply their content, whether studying or at work.

To find out more about the complete range of our
publishing, please visit us on the World Wide Web at:
www.pearsoned.co.uk

Logistics Management and Strategy

Second Edition

Alan Harrison

Remko van Hoek

FT Prentice Hall
FINANCIAL TIMES

An imprint of **Pearson Education**
Harlow, England • London • New York • Boston • San Francisco • Toronto
Sydney • Tokyo • Singapore • Hong Kong • Seoul • Taipei • New Delhi
Cape Town • Madrid • Mexico City • Amsterdam • Munich • Paris • Milan

Pearson Education Limited
Edinburgh Gate
Harlow
Essex CM20 2JE
England

and Associated Companies throughout the world

Visit us on the World Wide Web at:
www.pearsoned.co.uk

First published 2002
Second edition published 2005

© Pearson Education Limited 2002, 2005

The rights of Alan Harrison and Remko van Hoek to be identified as authors
of this work have been asserted by them in accordance with the Copyright,
Designs and Patents Act 1988.

All rights reserved. No part of this publication may be reproduced, stored in
a retrieval system, or transmitted in any form or by any means, electronic,
mechanical, photocopying, recording or otherwise, without either the prior
written permission of the publisher or a licence permitting restricted copyright
in the United Kingdom issued by the Copyright Licensing Agency Ltd,
90 Tottenham Court Road, London W1T 4LP.

All trademarks used herein are the property of their respective owners. The use of
any trademark in this text does not vest in the author or publisher any trademark
ownership rights in such trademarks, nor does the use of such trademarks imply any
afflliation with or endorsement of this book by such owners.

ISBN 0273-68542-2

British Library Cataloguing-in-Publication Data
A catalogue record for this book is available from the British Library

Library of Congress Cataloging-in-Publication Data
A catalog record for this book is available from the Library of Congress

10 9 8 7 6 5 4 3 2 1
08 07 06 05 04

Typeset in 9.5pt Stone Sans by 3
Printed and bound by Ashford Colour Press, Gosport

The publisher's policy is to use paper manufactured from sustainable forests.

To Nick, Katie and Ticho, with love.

Contents

Part Four CHANGING THE FUTURE

10 Logistics future challenge 273

FOREWORD

It is a real pleasure to introduce such a quality text as *Logistics Management and Strategy*, which helps to enhance our understanding of such an important area of business today. It is an area that is rapidly gaining importance and focus as businesses like Reckitt Benckiser address the challenge of meeting increasingly demanding customer expectations in all five continents.

Reckitt Benckiser is rightly famous for the excellence of our products – but product excellence must be supported by logistics excellence so that our broad range is always available for the end-consumer to buy. One challenge is obviously to ensure this availability to the consumer while complying with the requirements of our trade customers. Another challenge is to do all of this at a low cost to that we are able to offer our products to the consumer at reasonable prices. Answering these challenges is the aim of our network and, more specifically, of our logistics organisation.

At Reckitt Benckiser we describe ourselves as a 'truly global company with a consumer-orientated vision, with operations in 60 countries, sales in 180 countries and net revenues in excess of £3.5 billion.'

The logistics task in fulfilling our objective, with such a business scope, is immense. We have 44 factories around the world and produce several hundreds of different products from food to home and personal care.

We have grown by over 40% over the last five years, which places further challenges from our logistics systems and people to meet. On the one hand, we need to optimise our systems and minimise costs, on the other hand, we must support the growth of the business and ensure product and process innovation. For us to succeed it is becoming increasingly important to excel in the management of logistics, which becomes a strategic function and a source of differentiation and of competitive advantage. This means that managers in all parts of the business must understand their impact on, and role in, the logistics task.

Logistics Management and Strategy is an excellent text that supports the need to disseminate knowledge and understanding of logistics in an easy-to-read way. While explaining with great clarity the theoretical concepts, it remains very pragmatic and close to business life through the use of concrete examples and well-chosen case studies. It manages to examine logistics knowledge and understanding in depth while at the same time remaining not only very accessible but really pleasant to read.

Finally, its international perspective reflects the nature of logistics today in businesses like Reckitt Benckiser. As another Anglo-Dutch collaboration, Alan and Remko have succeeded in helping to increase our understanding of a rapidly evolving and increasingly crucial area of doing business in the twenty-first century.

Alain Le Goff
Executive Vice President, Global Supply
Member of the Executive Committee
Reckitt Benckiser

Preface

Logistics has been emerging from Peter Drucker's shadowy description as 'the economy's dark continent' for some years. From its largely military origins, logistics has accelerated into becoming one of the key business issues of the day, presenting formidable challenges for managers and occupying some of the best minds. Its relatively slow route to this exalted position can be attributed to two causes. First, logistics is a cross-functional subject. In the past, it has rightly drawn on contributions from marketing, finance, operations and corporate strategy. The late Jim Cooper referred to it as a 'pariah subject' for this reason. Within the organisation, a more appropriate description would be a *business process*, cutting across functional boundaries yet with a contribution from each. Second, logistics extends beyond the boundaries of the organisation into the supply chain. Here, it engages with the complexities of synchronising the movement of materials and information between many business processes. The *systems nature* of logistics has proved a particularly difficult lesson to learn, and individual organisations still often think that they can optimise profit conditions for themselves by exploiting their partners in the supply chain. Often they can – in the short term. But winners in one area are matched by losers in another, and the losers are unable to invest or to develop the capabilities needed to keep the chain healthy in the long term. The emergence of logistics has therefore been dependent on the development of a cross-functional model of the organisation, and on an understanding of the need to integrate business processes across the supply chain.

While its maturity as a discipline in its own right is still far from complete, we believe that the time has come to take a fresh look at logistics management and strategy. Tools and concepts to enable integration of the supply chain are starting to work well, and developments such as e-marketplaces offer far more in the future. Tomorrow's competitive advantage will not come from implementing ERP in itself. It will come from responding to customers at the end of the supply chain better than competition. Logistics plays a vital role in this response, and it is this role that we seek to describe in this book.

Accordingly, we start in Part One with the strategic role of logistics in the supply chain. We continue by developing the marketing perspective by explaining our view of 'putting the end-customer first'. Part One finishes by exploring the concept of value and logistics costs. In Part Two, we review leveraging logistics operations in terms of their global dimensions, and of the lead-time frontier. Part Two continues by examining the impact on logistics of lean thinking and the agile supply chain. Part Three reviews working together, first in terms of integrating the supply chain and second in terms of partnerships. Our book ends with Part Four, in which we outline the logistics future challenge.

This text is intended for MSc students on logistics courses, and as an accompanying text for open learning courses such as the global MSc degrees and virtual

universities. It will also be attractive as a management textbook and as rec-
ommended reading on MBA options in logistics and supply chain management.

In the second edition, we have listened carefully to students and to reviewers
alike and set out to build on the foundation of our initial offering. We have
updated much of the material while keeping the clear structure and presentation
of the first edition. There are lots of new cases and we have updated others. We
have attempted to touch on many of the exciting developments in this rapidly
expanding body of knowledge, such as governance councils, the prospects for
RFID and the future of exchanges

From a teaching perspective we want to highlight the following updates:

- Revised competitive advantages (section 1.3.1).

- Chapter 2 – which has been retitled and largely re-written to reflect our
research into customer-responsive supply chains.

- Chapter 10 – which has been revised to reflect the rapid evolution of the logistics future challenge.

- Fifteen new case studies and two updated case studies.

We hope that our book will offer support to further professional development
in logistics, which is much needed. In particular, we hope that it encourages the
reader to challenge existing thinking, and to break old mindsets by creating a
new and more innovative future.

Acknowledgements

We should like to acknowledge our many friends and colleagues who have contributed to our thinking and to our book. Professor Martin Christopher has provided much stimulating thought. For example, the three of us developed the logistics thinking around the agile supply chain discussed in Chapter 7. Other Cranfield colleagues deserve a special mention: Dr Paul Chapman, Janet Godsell, Dr Andrew White, Simon Templar and Dr Richard Wilding have been particularly helpful. Sri Srikanthan helped us with the financial concepts used in Chapter 3. Members of the Agile Supply Chain Research Club at Cranfield also deserve special mention, especially Chris Poole of Procter & Gamble, Paul Mayhew of Bausch & Lomb and Colin Peacock of Gillette. We have picked the brains of several who have recently retired from the industry, including David Aldridge (formerly of Cussons UK), Philip Matthews (formerly of Boots The Chemists) and Graham Sweet of Xerox. A number of professors from other European universities have contributed ideas and cases to the second edition, including Marie Koulikoff-Souviron (CERAM, Nice), Jacques Colin (CretLog, Aix-en-Provence), and Konstantinos Zographos (Athens University of Economics and Business) Corrado Ceruti (University of Macerata). Many of our MSc graduates, such as Steve Walker and Jane Pavitt, also made important contributions. Professor Yemisi Bolumole (University of North Florida) gave us a lot of help in redrafting earlier versions of the first edition, and we are very grateful to her. Dr Jim Aitken contributed to the Global Lighting case study in Chapter 2, and we have used his work on supplier associations in Chapter 9. We also acknowledge the encouragement of Heather Fyfe and others at Pearson Education in the preparation of this text and the encouragement to write it faster! Also, we thank the reviewers who made many valuable comments on earlier versions of the book and detailed comments on the first edition. We are very grateful to all of these, and to the many others who made smaller contributions to making this book possible. Finally, we thank Lynne Hudston for helping to sort out the rather convoluted manuscript in addition to helping to run our research club at Cranfield!

Publisher's acknowledgements

We are grateful to the following for permission to reproduce copyright material:

Figure 1.2 after *Operations Management*, 2nd edn, reprinted by permission of Pearson Education Ltd (Slack, N. *et al.* 1997); Figure 1.5 after 'Initial conceptual framework for creation and operation of supply networks', *Proceedings of Fourteenth AMP Conference, Turku, 3–5 September*, Vol. 3, reprinted by permission of Professor Christine Harland (Zheng, J. *et al.* 1998); Figure 1.13 after 'What is the right supply chain for your product?', *Harvard Business Review*, March/April 1997, reprinted by permission of Harvard Business School Publishing Corporation (Fisher, M. 1997); Figure 2.3 after Parasuraman, A. and Grewal, D., 'The impact of technology on the quality–value–loyalty chain: a research agenda', *Journal of the Academy of Marketing Science*, Vol. 28, No. 1, pp. 168–74, copyright © 2000, reprinted by permission of Sage Publications, Inc.; Figure 2.4 reprinted from *Relationship Marketing for Competitive Advantage*, Payne, A. *et al.*, Copyright 1995, with permission from Elsevier; Table 2.6 from *Management in Marketing Channels,* 1st edn, reprinted by permission of Pearson Education, Inc. (El-Ansary, A.I. *et al.* 1989); Table 3.2 and Figures 3.1, 3.2, 3.3, 3.4, 3.5, 3.6 and 3.7 courtesy of Sri Srikanthan; Figure 3.8 after 'Costing waste in supply chain processes: a European food and drink industry case study', *Proceedings of the Tenth International EurOMA* Conference, Copenhagen, June, Vol. 1, reprinted by permission of EIASM (Bernon, M. *et al.*, 2003); Table 3.6 from www.supply-chain.org, reprinted by permission of Supply-Chain Council, Inc.; Figure 3.10 after 'Using the balanced scorecard to measure supply chain performance', *Journal of Business Logistics*, Vol. 21, No. 1, reprinted by permission of the Council of Logistics Management (Brewer, P.C. and Speh, T.W. 2000); Figure 3.11 after 'Supply Chain Council and Supply Chain Operations Reference (SCOR) model overview', www.supply-chain.org, reprinted by permission of Supply-Chain Council, Inc.; Figure 4.1 after 'Managers in supply chain management: the critical dimension', *Supply Chain Management: An International Journal*, Vol. 7, Nos. 3 and 4, reprinted by permission of Emerald Group Publishing Ltd, http://www.emeraldinsight. com/scm.htm (van Hoek, R.I. *et al.* 2002); Figure 4.6 after *Europese distributie en waardetoevoeging door buitenlandse bedrijven*, reprinted by permission of Buck Consultants International (Buck Consultants International 1997); Table 7.1 from 'Agile, or leagile: matching your supply chain to the marketplace', *Proceedings of the Fifteenth International Conference on Production Research, Limerick*, reprinted by permission of Professor Denis R. Towill (Mason-Jones, R. *et al.* 1999); Figure 7.2 and Table 7.3 after 'Supply chain migration from lean and functional to agile and customised', *International Journal of Supply Chain Management*, Vol. 5, No. 4, reprinted by permission of Emerald Group Publishing Ltd, http://www. emeraldinsight.com/scm.htm (Christopher, M. and Towill, D.R. 2000); Figure 8.1 after *Journal of Operations Management*, Vol. 19, No. 2, Frohlich, M. and Westbrook, R., 'Arcs of integration: an international study of supply chain strategies', pp. 185–200, Copyright 2001, with permission from Elsevier; Figure 8.2 from Jennifer S. Kuhel (2002) 'Clothes call', *Supply Chain Technology* News, March, pp. 20–1; Figure 8.3 after 'Relationships in the supply chain' in *Logistics and Retail Management: Insights into current practice and trends from leading experts*, edited by J. Fernie and L. Sparks, reprinted by permission of Kogan Page Publishers (Fernie, J. 1998); Figure 8.8 after 'Logistics in the 'three-day-car' age: assessing responsiveness of vehicle distribution logistics in the UK', *International Journal of Physical Distribution and Logistics Management*, Vol. 32, No. 10, reprinted by permission of Emerald Group Publishing Ltd, http://www.emeraldinsight. com/ijpdlm.htm (Holweg, M. and Miemczyck, J. 2002); Figure 8.9 adapted from 'Six supply chain lessons for the new millennium', *Supply Chain Management Review*, Vol. 3, No. 4, reprinted with permission of Supply Chain Management

Review (Derocher, R. and Kilpatrick, J. 2000); Figure 9.1 after 'Building good business relationships – more than just partnering or strategic alliances?', *International Journal of Physical Distribution and Logistics Management*, Vol. 23, No. 6, reprinted by permission of MCB University Press Ltd (Cooper, M. and Gardner, J. 1993); Figure 9.2 after *Improving Purchase Performance*, reprinted by permission of Pearson Education Ltd (Syson, R. 1992); Figure 9.4 after Remko I. van Hoek and Harm A.M. Weken, 'The impact of modular production on the dynamics of supply chains', *The International Journal of Logistics Management*, Vol. 9, No. 2, p. 38, http://www.ijlm.org; Figure 9.6 after 'Integration of the supply chain: The effect of interorganisational interactions between purchasing-sales-logistics', PhD thesis, Cranfield School of Management, reprinted by permission of the author (Aitken, J., 1998); Figure 10.8 after 'RFID in the supply chain, pub ECR Europe', reprinted by permission of the author (Beck, A. 2003).

Case study 1.4 'Talleres Auto', C. Harland; Case study 2.1 'Managing events and promotions in the retail sector', Philip Mathews, formerly Supply Chain Director, BTC; Case study 2.4, 'Tears at teatime at IKEA', based on article by John Arlidge, *Sunday Times*, 26 October 2003; Case study 2.6 'Global Lighting' and Case study 9.2 'Supplier association', Jim Aitken; Case study 3.1 'Bond plc – a marginal costing example', Simon Templar, Cranfield; Case study 4.2 'Time v cost in global supply chains: lessons from the apparel industry', based on *How to Speed up your Supply Chain: Best practice from the apparel industry*, Joris Leeman, forthcoming, 2004; Case study 7.1 'Segmenting the supply chain at Xerox', Graham Sweet; Case study 9.3 'Supply chain internationalization in the Macerata shoe district', Professor Corrado Cerruti, University of Macerata.

In some instances we have been unable to trace the owners of copyright material, and we would appreciate any information that would enable us to do so.

How to use this book

This book is divided into four parts, centred around a model for logistics. The model for logistics is introduced in the first chapter of Part One, which offers an introduction to logistics and its basic contribution to competitiveness, customer service and the creation of value. Part Two of the book focuses on leveraging logistics operations within the context of quality of service and cost performance objectives. Part Three focuses on working together, and Part Four pulls together elements of leading-edge thinking in logistics, homing in on future challenges for the subject.

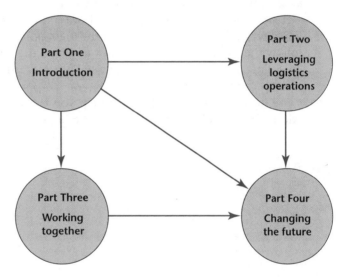

The book has been arranged to take the reader through the subject in logical stages. The limitation of a text presentation is that the subjects are then arranged in sequence, and links between stages have to be made by the reader. We have set out to facilitate cross-linkage task by including:

- *activities* at the end of many of the sections, which are aimed at helping you to think about the issues raised and how they could be applied;
- *discussion questions* at the end of each chapter to help you to assess your understanding of the issues raised, and to give you practice in using them;
- *case studies*, which draw together a number of issues and help you to think about how those issues are linked together in a practical setting. Use the study questions at the end of each case to guide your thinking.

We have sought continually to break up the text with figures, tables, activities and case studies, so you will rarely find two successive pages of continuous text. You should therefore regard the activities and case studies as an integral part of the method used in this book to help you to learn.

Where possible, discuss the activities and case study questions in groups after you have prepared them individually. Discussion helps to broaden the agenda and create confidence in handling the issues! While you are studying this book, think about the logistics issues it raises – in your own organisation or ones that you know well, and in articles in newspapers such as the *Financial Times* and magazines such as *Business Week*. Follow up the website addresses we have included in the text and again link them with the issues raised in the book.

A few words on terminology are appropriate here. We have taken the view that logistics and supply chain management (SCM) are sufficiently different for separate definitions to be needed. We have included these definitions in Chapter 1: logistics is a subset of SCM. 'Supply chain' and 'supply network' are used interchangeably, although we favour 'chain' for a few organisations linked in series and 'network' to describe the more complex interlinkages found in most situations. Again, our position is explained in Chapter 1.

A summary is provided at the end of each chapter to help you to check that you have understood and absorbed the main points in that chapter. If you do not follow the summary points, go back and read the relevant section again. If need be, follow up on references or suggested further reading. Summaries are also there to help you with revision.

We have designed this book to help you to start out on the logistics journey and to feel confident with its issues. We hope that you enjoy it.

Plan of the book

Part One INTRODUCTION	
Chapter 1 Logistics and the supply chain	**Chapter 2** Putting the end customer first

Chapter 3 Value and logistics costs

Part Two LEVERAGING LOGISTICS OPERATIONS	
Chapter 4 Managing logistics internationally	**Chapter 5** Managing the lead-time frontier
Chapter 6 Just-in-time and lean thinking	**Chapter 7** The agile supply chain

Part Three WORKING TOGETHER	
Chapter 8 Integrating the supply chain	**Chapter 9** Partnerships in the supply chain

Part Four CHANGING THE FUTURE

Chapter 10 Logistics future challenge

Part One

INTRODUCTION

Our model of logistics structures the supply network around three main factors: the flow of materials, the flow of information and the time taken to respond to demand from source of supply. The scope of the network extends from the 'focal firm' in darker blue at the centre across supplier and customer interfaces, and therefore typically stretches across functions, organisations and borders. The network is best seen as a system of interdependent processes, where actions in one part affect those of all others. The key 'initiator' of the network is end-customer demand on the right: only the end-customer is free to make up their mind when to place an order. After that, the system takes over.

- *Chapter 1* explains how networks are structured, the different ways in which they may choose to compete, and how their capabilities have to be aligned with the needs of the end-customer.

- Chapter 2 places the end-customer first in logistics thinking, and develops the theme of aligning logistics strategy with marketing strategy.

- Chapter 3 considers how value is created in a supply network, how logistics costs can be managed, and how a balanced measurement portfolio can be designed.

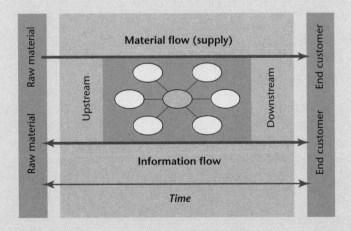

CHAPTER 1

Logistics and the supply chain

Outcomes

The intended outcomes of this chapter are to:

- identify and explain logistics definitions and concepts that are relevant to managing the supply chain;
- identify how supply chains compete in terms of time, cost and quality;
- show how different supply chains may adopt different and distinctive strategies for competing in the marketplace.

By the end of this chapter you should be able to understand:

- how supply chains are structured;
- different ways in which supply chains may choose to compete in the marketplace;
- the need to align supply chain capabilities with the needs of the end-customer.

Introduction

A car takes only 20 hours or so to assemble, and a couple more days are needed to ship it to the customer via the dealers. So why does it take more than a month for a manufacturer to make and deliver the car I want? And why are the products I want to buy so often unavailable on the shelf at the local supermarket? These are questions that go to the heart of logistics management and strategy. Supply chains today are slow, costly and do not deliver particularly good value to the end-customer. But let us start at the beginning, by thinking about logistics and the supply chain in terms of what they are trying to do. It is easy to get bogged down in the complexities of how a supply chain actually works (and very few people actually know how a whole supply chain works!). We shall address many of those details later in this book. First, let us focus on how a supply chain competes, and on what the implications are for logistics management and strategy.

The overall aim of this chapter is to provide an introduction to logistics, and to set the scene for the book as a whole. The need is to look outside the individual organisation and to consider how it aligns with other organisations in a given supply chain. This is both a strategic and a managerial task: strategic, because it brings in long-term decisions about how logistics will be structured and the systems it will use; managerial, because it encompasses decisions about sourcing, making and delivering products and services within an overall 'game plan'.

Key issues   *This chapter addresses four key issues*:

1 **Logistics and the supply chain**: definitions, structure, tiering.

2 **Material flow, information flow and funds flow**: the supply chain and the demand chain.

3 **Competing through logistics**: competitive criteria in the marketplace.

4 **Supply chain strategies**: aligning capabilities across the supply chain.

1.1 Logistics and the supply chain

Key issues: **What is the supply chain, and how is it structured? What is the purpose of a supply chain?**

Logistics is a big word for a big challenge. Let us begin by giving an example of that challenge in practice, because that is where logistics starts and ends.

**CASE STUDY
1.1**

Tesco

Tesco is the UK's largest food retailer, with a sales turnover of more than €50bn. While it has some 450 stores in central Europe, Ireland and the Far East, most are in the United Kingdom, where it has nearly 2,000. This number has increased rapidly as Tesco entered the convenience store market with deals such as the Tesco Express alliance with Esso to run grocery shops at petrol stations. The product range held by the stores has grown rapidly in recent years, and currently stands at 60,000 stock-keeping units (skus) as Tesco broadens its presence in the 'non-food' market for electrical goods, stationery, clothing and the like. This massive range is supported by 2,500 suppliers, who are expected to provide service levels (correct time and quantities) of at least 98.5 per cent by delivering to Tesco within half-hour time 'windows'. Volumes are equally impressive. In a year, some 1.45 billion cases of product are shipped from suppliers to the stores.

Tesco states that its core purpose is 'to create value for customers to earn their lifetime loyalty'. Wide product range and high on-shelf availability across that range are key enablers of that core purpose. So how do you maintain high availability of so many skus in so many stores? This question goes to the heart of logistics management for such a vast organisation. Logistics is about material flow, and about information flow. Let us look at how Tesco deals with each of these in turn.

An early reform for supermarket operation was to have suppliers deliver to a distribution centre rather than to every store. During the 1980s, distribution to retail stores was handled by 26 depots. These operated on a single-temperature basis, and were small and relatively inefficient. Delivery volumes to each store were also relatively low, and it was not economic to deliver to all stores each day. Goods that required temperature-controlled environments had to be carried on separate vehicles. Each product group had different ordering systems. The network of depots simply could not handle the growth in volumes and the increasingly high standards of temperature control. A new distribution strategy was needed.

Under the 'composite' distribution system, many small depots with limited temperature control facilities were replaced by composite distribution centres (called Regional Distribution Centres, RDCs), which can handle many products at several temperature ranges. The opportunity is to provide a cost-effective daily delivery service to all stores. Typically, a composite distribution centre can handle over 30 million cases per year on a 15-acre site. The warehouse building comprises 25,000 square metres divided into three temperature zones: frozen ($-25°C$), $+1°C$ (chilled) and $+12°C$ (semi-ambient). Each distribution centre (DC) serves a group of between 80 and 100 retail stores. Delivery vehicles for composite depots can use insulated trailers divided into chambers by means of movable bulkheads so they can operate at different temperatures. Deliveries are made at agreed, scheduled times. Ambient goods such as cans and clothing are delivered separately. Increasingly, retailers like Tesco are introducing *factory gate pricing*. Instead of suppliers' vehicles delivering goods piecemeal and waiting at DCs to be unloaded, retailer's vehicles can simply drop off a trailer, pick up another, and be back on the road. In this way, retailers can use their scale to negotiate lower transport costs and to make further economies by increased use of two-way loads.

So much for the method of transporting goods from supplier through to the stores, but how much should be sent to each store? With such a huge product range today, it is impossible for the individual store to reorder across the whole range (store-based ordering). Instead, sales of each product line are tracked continuously through the till by means of electronic point of sale (EPOS) systems. As a customer's purchases are scanned through the bar code reader at the till, the sale is automatically recorded for each sku. Cumulative sales are updated every four hours on Tesco Information Exchange (TIE). This is a system based on Internet technology that allows Tesco and its suppliers to communicate trading information. The aim of improved communication is to reduce response times from manufacturer to stores and to ensure product availability on the shelf. Among other things, TIE aims to improve processes for introducing new products and promotions, and to monitor service levels.

Based on the cumulative sales, Tesco places orders with its suppliers by means of electronic data interchange (EDI). As volumes and product ranges increased during the 1990s, food retailers such as Tesco aimed to destock their distribution centres by ordering only what was needed to meet tomorrow's forecast sales. For fast-moving products such as types of cheese and washing powders, the aim is *day 1 for day 2*: that is, to order today what is needed for tomorrow. For fast-moving products, the aim is to *pick to zero* in the distribution centre: no stock is left after store orders have been fulfilled. This means that the same space in the distribution centre can be used several times over. And deliveries to stores are made in three *waves*. Frozen and ambient grocery products for example are distributed to stores at three different times through the day. The first wave is delivered to stores by 8.00am, the second wave in the afternoon, and a third wave in the evening. This helps to improve product availability at stores throughout the day, and thus support increased demand.

Questions

1 Describe the key logistics processes at Tesco.

2 What do you think are the main logistics challenges in running the Tesco operation?

So why is Tesco growing in an intensely competitive market? It describes its core purpose as being 'to create value for customers to earn their lifetime loyalty'. In order to achieve this, Tesco has to understand customer needs and how they can be served. Its products must be recognised by its customers as representing outstanding value for money. To support such goals, it must ensure that the products that its customers want are available on the shelf at each of its stores at all times, day and night. Planning and controlling the purchase and distribution of Tesco's massive product range from suppliers to stores is one of logistics. Logistics is the task of managing two key flows:

- *material flow* of the physical goods from suppliers through the distribution centres to stores;
- *information flow* of demand data from the end-customer back to purchasing and to suppliers, and supply data from suppliers to the retailer, so that material flow can be accurately planned and controlled.

The logistics task of managing material flow and information flow is a key part of the overall task of *supply chain management*. Supply chain management is concerned with managing the entire chain of processes, including raw material supply, manufacture, packaging and distribution to the end-customer. The Tesco UK supply chain structure comprises three main functions:

- *distribution*: the operations and support task of managing Tesco's distribution centres, and the distribution of products from the DCs to the associated stores;
- *network and capacity planning*: the task of planning and implementing sufficient capacity in the supply chain to ensure that the right products can be procured in the right quantities now and in the future;
- *supply chain development*: the task of improving Tesco's supply chain so that its processes are stable and in control, that it is efficient, and that it is correctly structured to meet the logistics needs of material flow and information flow.

Thus logistics can be seen as part of the overall supply chain challenge. While the terms 'logistics' and 'supply chain management' are often used interchangeably, logistics is actually a subset of supply chain management. It is time for some definitions.

1.1.1 Definitions and concepts

A supply chain as a whole ranges from basic commodities (what is in the ground, sea or air) to selling the final product to the end-customer to recycling used product. Material flows from a basic commodity (such as a bauxite mine as a source of aluminium ore) to the finished product (such as a can of cola). The can is recycled after use. The analogy to flow of water in a river is often used to describe organisations near the source as *upstream*, and those near the end-customer as *downstream*. We refer to each firm in a supply chain as a partner, because that is what they are. There is a collective as well as an individual role to play in the conversion of basic commodity into finished product. At each stage of the conversion, there may be *returns* that may be reject material from the preceding firm, or waste that needs to be recycled.

> **A supply chain is a group of partners who collectively convert a basic commodity (upstream) into a finished product (downstream) that is valued by end-customers, and who manage returns at each stage.**

Each partner in a supply chain is responsible directly for a process that *adds value* to a product. A process may be defined as:

> **Transforming inputs in the form of materials and information into outputs in the form of goods and services.**

In the case of the cola can, partners carry out processes such as mining, transportation, refining and hot rolling. The cola can has *greater value* than the bauxite (per kilogram of aluminium).

Supply chain management involves *planning and controlling* all of the processes from raw material production to purchase by the end user to recycling of the used cans. Planning refers to making a plan that defines how much of each product should be bought, made, distributed and sold each day, week or month. Controlling means keeping to plan – in spite of the many problems that may get in the way. The aim is to coordinate planning and control of each process so that the needs of the end-customer are met correctly. The definition of supply chain management used in this book is as follows:

> **Planning and controlling all of the processes that link partners in a supply chain together in order to serve needs of the end-customer.**

'Serving the needs of the end-customer' has different implications in different contexts. In not-for-profit environments such as public health and local government, serving implies 'continuously improving', 'better than other regions/countries' and the like. In the commercial sector, serving implies 'better than competition', 'better value for money' and so on. In either situation, the focus of managing the supply chain as a whole is on *integrating* the processes of supply chain partners, of which the end-customer is the key one. As Gattorna (1998: 2) puts it:

> **Materials and finished products only flow through a supply chain because of customer behaviour at the end of the chain.**

The degree to which the end-customer is satisfied with the finished product depends crucially on the management of material flow and information flow along the supply chain. If delivery is late, or the product has bits missing, the whole supply chain is at risk from competitors who can perform the logistics task better. Logistics is a vital enabler for supply chain management. We use the following definition of logistics in this book:

> **The task of coordinating material flow and information flow across the supply chain.**

Logistics has both *strategic* (long-term planning) and *managerial* (short- and medium-term planning and control) aspects. Tesco has a clear view about the opportunities here. A breakdown of costs in Tesco's part of the UK supply chain is as follows:

- Supplier delivery to Tesco distribution centre (DC)   18%
- Tesco DC operations and deliver to store   28%
- Store replenishment   46%
- Supplier replenishment systems   8%

Nearly half of supply chain costs are incurred in-store. In order to reduce these in-store costs, Tesco realises that the solution is 'to spend more upstream and downstream to secure viable trade-offs for in-store replenishment'. If a product is not available on the shelf, the sale is potentially lost. By integrating external manufacturing and distribution processes with its own, Tesco seeks to serve the needs of its customers better than its competitors.

1.1.2 Supply chain: structure and tiering

The concept of a supply chain suggests a series of processes linked together to form a chain. A typical Tesco supply chain is formed from five such links.

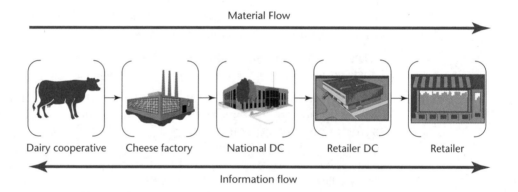

Figure 1.1 From cow to customer

Here, milk is produced by a dairy cooperative and shipped to a cheese factory. Once made, the cheese is shipped to the manufacturer's national distribution centre (NDC), where it is stored and matured for nine months. It can then be shipped in response to an order from the retailer, and is transported first to the retailer's regional distribution centre (RDC). From there, it is shipped to store. Looking at the arrows in Figure 1.1, material flows from left to right. Information is shared across the chain: it is demand from the end-customer that makes the whole chain work.

If we look more closely at what happens in practice, the term 'supply chain' is somewhat misleading in that the 'chain' represents a simple series of links between a basic commodity (milk in this case) and a final product (cheese). Thus the cheese manufacturer will need packaging materials such as film, labels and cases. Cheese requires materials additional to milk in the manufacturing process. So the manufacturer deals with other suppliers than the milk cooperative alone.

Once made, the cheese is dispatched for maturation to the supplier's NDC, and then dispatched to many customers in addition to Tesco. Once at a Tesco RDC, the 'chain' spreads again because up to 100 stores are served by a given RDC. The additional complexity prompts many authors to refer to *supply networks* rather than to supply chains, a point we return to shortly.

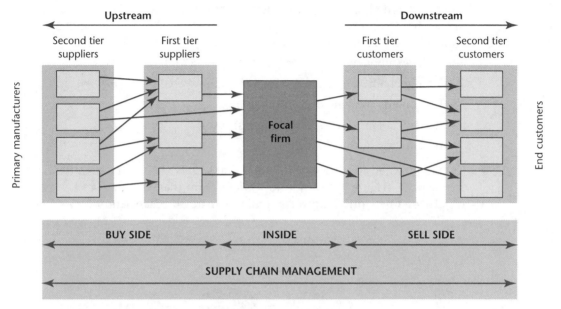

Figure 1.2 Relationships in the supply chain
(Source: After Slack *et al.*, 1997)

A more realistic representation of the supply chain is shown in Figure 1.2, where each link can connect with several others. A *focal firm* is shown at the centre of many possible connections with other supplier and customer companies.

The supply chain can be seen in this diagram as a number of processes that extend across organisational boundaries. The focal firm is embedded within the chain, and its operational processes ('inside') must coordinate with others that are part of the same chain. Materials flow from left (upstream, or 'buy side') to right (downstream, or 'supply side'). If everything is as orderly as it seems, then only the end-customer (to the extreme right of the chain) is free to place orders when he or she likes: after that, the system takes over.

The supply chain is *tiered* in that supply side and demand side can be organised into groups of organisations with which we deal. Thus if we place an assembler such as the Ford plant at Valencia as the focal firm, tier 1 comprises suppliers of major parts and subassemblies who deliver directly to Ford, while tier 2 suppliers deliver to the tier 1s, etc. On the demand side, Ford supplies to the national sales companies as tier 1 customers, who in turn supply to dealers as tier 2, and so on.

Other terms that are used to describe aspects of managing the supply chain are:

● *Purchasing and supply* deals with the focal firm's immediate suppliers.

- *Physical distribution* deals with the task of distributing products to tier 1 customers.
- *Logistics* refers to management of materials and information. Inbound logistics deals with links between the focal firm and its tier 1 suppliers, while outbound logistics refers to the links between the focal firm and its tier 1 customers.

Supply chain management thus appears as the 'end to end' (or 'cow to customer' as we have expressed it in Figure 1.1) management of the network as a whole, and of the relationships between the various links. The essential points were summarised long ago by Oliver and Webber (1982):

- Supply chain management views the supply chain as a *single entity*.
- It demands strategic decision making.
- It views *balancing inventories* as a last resort.
- It demands *system integration*.

A natural extension of this thinking is that supply chains should rather be viewed as *networks*. Figure 1.3 shows how a focal firm (darker blue) can be seen at the centre of a network of upstream and downstream organisations.

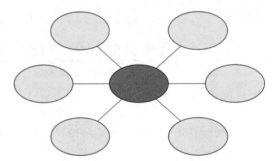

Figure 1.3 A network of organisations

The terms 'supply chain' and 'supply network' both attempt to describe the way in which buyers and suppliers are linked together to serve the end-customer. 'Network' describes a more complex structure, where organisations can be cross-linked and there are two-way exchanges between them; 'chain' describes a simpler, sequential set of links (Harland *et al.*, 2001). We have used the terms interchangeably in this book, preferring 'chain' to describe simpler sequences of a few organisations and 'network' where there are many organisations linked in a more complex way.

Figure 1.3 takes a basic view of the network, with a focal firm linked to three upstream suppliers and three downstream customers. If we then add material flow and information flow to this basic model, and place a boundary around the network, Figure 1.4 shows the network in context. Here we have added arrows showing the logistics contribution of material and information flows, together with the time dimension. Material flows from primary manufacture (for example farming, mining or forestry) through various stages of the network to the end-customer. Material flow represents the *supply* of product through the network in response to demand from the next (succeeding) organisation. Information flow broadcasts *demand* from the end-customer to preceding organisations in the network. The time dimension addresses the question 'How long does it take to get from primary source to the end-customer?' That is, how long does it take to get product through the various stages from one end of the supply chain to the other? Time is important because it measures how quickly a given network can respond to demand from the end-customer. In fact, the concept of flow is based on time:

> **Flow measures the quantity of material (measured in input terms such as numbers of components, tonnes and litres) that passes through a given network per unit of time.**

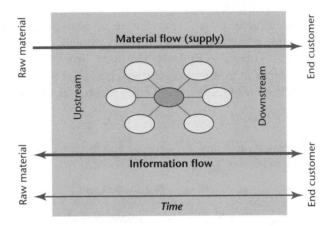

Figure 1.4 The network in context

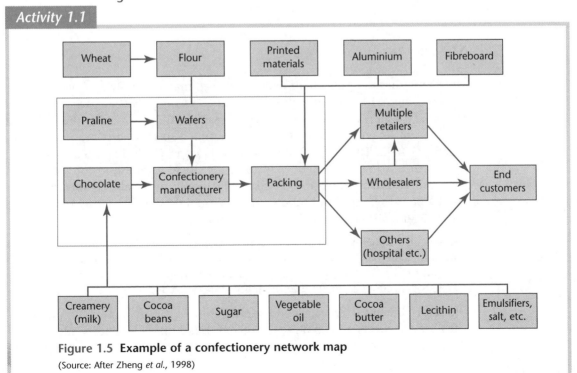

Figure 1.5 Example of a confectionery network map

(Source: After Zheng *et al.*, 1998)

Figure 1.5 shows an example network map of a chocolate bar. Draw a network map showing how your organisation, or one that you know well, links with other organisations. Explain the upstream and downstream processes as far as you can. We expect you to address at least the first tiers of demand and supply. You will derive further benefit from researching additional tiers, and by developing the linkage of relationships that is involved. Explain how these work in practice, and how materials flow between the different tiers.
(Source: After Zheng *et al.*, 1998)

An important point here is that the supply network should be viewed as a *system*. All processes within the network need to be understood in terms of how they interact with other processes. No organisation is an island: its inputs and outputs are affected by the behaviour of other players in the network. One powerful, disruptive player can make life very difficult for everyone else. For example, several auto assemblers optimise their own processes, but disrupt those of upstream suppliers and downstream distributors. The effect is to increase total system costs *and* reduce responsiveness to end-customer demand.

1.2 Material and information flow

Key issue: What is the relationship between material flow and information flow?

As we have already seen, logistics is about managing material flow and information flow. In this section, we examine material flow and information flow in more detail.

1.2.1 Material flow

The aim within a supply chain must be to keep materials flowing from source to end-customer. The time dimension in Figure 1.3 suggests that parts are moved through the supply chain as quickly as possible. And in order to prevent local build-ups of inventory, flow must be orchestrated so that parts move in a coordinated fashion. The term often used is *synchronous*. Caterpillar Inc. makes complex earth-moving equipment, and there are literally thousands of component parts and subassemblies that must come together in the final assembly processes. The vision is that parts and subassemblies should flow continuously through the supply chain, all orchestrated like a ballet (Knill, 1992):

> The goal is continuous, synchronous flow. Continuous means no interruptions, no dropping the ball, no unnecessary accumulations of inventory. And synchronous means that it all runs like a ballet. Parts and components are delivered on time, in the proper sequence, exactly to the point they're needed.

Often it is difficult to see the 'end to end' nature of flow in a given supply chain. The negative effects of such difficulty include build-ups of inventory and sluggish response to end-customer demand. And sheer greed by the most powerful members of a supply chain often means that it is weaker partners (notably small to medium-sized enterprises – SMEs) who end up holding the inventories. So management strategies for the supply chain require a more holistic look at the links, and an understanding that organisational boundaries easily create barriers to flow.

Case study 1.2 describes how one company – Xerox in this case – re-engineered material flow in its distribution system.

CASE STUDY 1.2

Xerox

Once the problems of introducing 'just-in-time' production systems had been solved at the Xerox plant making photocopiers at Venray in Holland, attention shifted towards the finished product inventory. Historically, stocks of finished products had been 'managed' by trying to turn the tap of sales on or off as stocks developed. This was characterised by the familiar 'feast or famine' situations. The objective of the next move for Xerox became clear: making only what you need when you need it, then shipping direct to the customer. But the key question had to be answered: just-in-time for what? The answer is – the customer! And customer surveys showed that three types of delivery were needed:

- Commodity products should be delivered 'off the shelf'.
- Middle-range products were required in five days.
- Larger products that had to be integrated into existing customer processes and systems had to be planned months ahead: but the quoted delivery date had to be met 100 per cent.

It was envisaged that this would lead to a radically different inventory 'profile' in the supply chain. Figure 1.6 shows a traditional inventory profile on the left. Most of the stock was held in local depots waiting for customer orders. If the mix had been incorrectly forecast, too many of the wrong products were in plentiful supply, while needed products were unavailable! Further, a batch of replacement products would take a long time to fight their way through the pipeline. A new 'just-in-time' strategy was conceived to make the supply chain much more responsive. This strategy had a profound effect on the inventory profile, pushing much of the inventory away from the end-customer (where it has maximum added value and is already committed to a given finished product specification). Instead, inventory was mostly held further upstream, where it could be finally assembled to known orders, and where it had lower value. Of course, it has since been possible to remove several of the stages of the distribution process, thereby eliminating some of the sources of inventory altogether!

For commodity products, Xerox coined the term *deliver JIT*: that is, the product had to be delivered out of stock. Where sales forecasts are traditionally poor, the challenge was one of flexibility, simplicity and speed of manufacture. For mid-range products, it was unrealistic to hold 'just in case' inventories of products that are too complex to be assembled quickly. Instead, *finish JIT* was the term coined to describe the new policy of building semi-finished products with the minimum of added value, consistent with being able to complete and deliver the product in the five-day target. Finally, *build JIT* was the term used to describe the new philosophy of building larger products quickly within a defined lead time.

▶

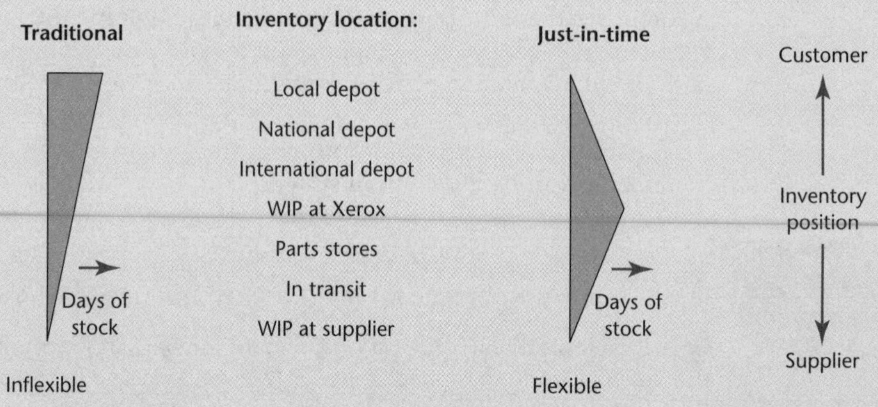

Note: WIP = work in progress, i.e. products being worked on, but not yet ready for sale.
Shaded areas indicate days of stock. The wider the area, the more days of stock in that position.

Figure 1.6 Xerox: the impact on inventories

The impact of the new build philosophies on the downstream supply chain processes can be judged from Figure 1.6. While the traditional inventory profile shows a maximum number of days of stock (shown in the shaded area) at finished product level, this is risky. It always seems that demand is greatest for the very items that are not available! *Postponing* the decision on exact specification until as late as possible in the process, when we are more likely to know precisely what the end-customer wants, helps to create the much flattened inventory profile to the right of the diagram. These are issues to which we return in Chapters 6 and 7 of this textbook. (A development of this case, tracking 'what happened next', is case study 7.1 in chapter 7).
(Source: After Eggleton, 1990)

Questions

1 How did inventory reduction in the supply chain lead to improved competitiveness at Xerox?

1.2.2 Information flow

As asked in the Xerox case study, just-in-time *for what*? It is all well and good to get materials flowing and movements synchronised, but the 'supply orchestra' needs to respond in unison to a specific 'conductor'. The 'conductor' in this analogy is actually the end-customer, and it is the end-customer's demand signals that trigger the supply chain to respond. By sharing the end-customer demand information across the supply chain, we create a *demand chain*, directed at providing enhanced customer value. Information technology enables the rapid sharing of demand and supply data at increasing levels of detail and sophistication. The aim is to *integrate* such demand and supply data so that an increasingly accurate picture is obtained about the nature of business processes, markets and end-customers. Such integration provides increasing competitive advantage.

The greatest opportunities for meeting demand in the marketplace with a maximum of dependability and a minimum of inventory come from implementing such integration across the supply chain. You cannot become 'world class' by yourself!

Figure 1.7 gives a conceptual model of how supply chain processes (supply, source, make, distribute and sell) are integrated together in order to meet end-customer demand (Beech, 1998). Demand signals are shared across the chain rather than being interpreted and massaged by the 'sell' process next to the market. Demand fulfilment is also envisaged as an integrated process, as materials are moved from one process to the next in a seamless flow. Information is the 'glue' that binds the supply chain processes together.

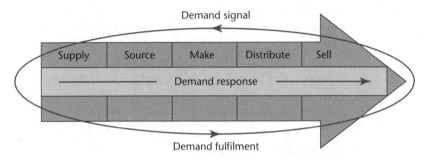

Figure 1.7 Integrating demand and supply chains

(Source: After J. Beech (1998) 'The supply–demand nexus', in J. Gattorna (ed.), *Strategic Supply Chain Alignment*, Aldershot: Gower, pp. 92–103.)

Activity 1.2

Write a brief (200 words) appraisal of material and information flow in the supply network affecting one of the major products in the response you gave in Activity 1.1. Perhaps the current situation is very different from the above ideals?

1.3 Competing through logistics

Key issues: **How do products win orders in the marketplace? How does logistics contribute to competitive advantage?**

There are many potentially conflicting demands on an organisation today. All those unreasonable customers seem to want it yesterday, at no cost, and to be compensated if it goes wrong! Within a given supply chain, it is important that each organisation understands how each group of products competes in the marketplace, and that it aligns its capabilities with those of its partners. It is impossible to be outstanding at everything, and supply chain partners need to give priority to capabilities that give each product group its competitive edge. These are the advantages where supply chain partners 'dig in deep' by giving priority to investment by training and by focusing product development and marketing efforts. They need only match the industry average on other criteria. Let us look at the competitive priorities that can be delivered by logistics in the supply chain.

1.3.1 Competitive advantage

There are various ways in which products compete in the marketplace. Perhaps a given product is something that no one else can match in terms of price. Or maybe you offer a product that is technically superior, such as Gillette razor blades. While new product development has logistics implications, the key advantage provided by logistics – as suggested in the Tesco example in section 1.1 – is *product availability in the marketplace at low cost.* Logistics supports competitiveness of the supply chain as a whole by

> **meeting end-customer demand through supplying what is needed in the form it is needed, when it is needed, at a competitive cost.**

Logistics advantage thus shows up in the form of such competitive factors as better product availability in the marketplace and low product obsolescence. Defining logistics advantage means that we need to set goals that are clear, measurable and quantifiable. Three basic ways of creating logistics advantage are quality, time and cost. There is a fourth, which is controlling variability in logistics processes: the dependability advantage. Let us look at each of these ways of creating advantage in turn.

The quality advantage

The most fundamental objective – in that it is a foundation for the others – is to carry out all processes across the supply chain so that the end product does what it is supposed to do. Quality is the most visible aspect of supply chain performance. Defects and late deliveries are symptoms of quality problems in supply chain processes that are all too apparent to the end-customer. Such problems negatively influence that customer's loyalty. Robust processes are at the heart of supply chain performance. Internally, robust processes help to reduce costs by eliminating errors, and help to increase dependability by making processes more certain.

Part of Nissan UK's continuing concerns is to extend such thinking to all tiers of the inbound supply chain. A basic goal is to reduce defects to 50 parts per million (ppm) for all inbound components. That is a tough target when put in the context of the 2,000 components that are needed to build a vehicle. Externally, superior performance of supply chain processes shows up as unavailability of the product, defects and late deliveries, as stated above. For example, a 'league table' of defects per hundred vehicles is published by J.D. Power Associates (www.jdpower.com). The *Initial Quality Study* is based on responses from more than 47,000 purchasers and lessees of new model-year vehicles, and monitors the number of reported problems that customers experience in the first 90 days of ownership. The study has been the industry standard benchmark of initial vehicle quality since 1987, and is based on problems-per-100 vehicles covering 135 specific problem areas. Consistent top performers are Japanese producers such as Toyota and Nissan, who have established a tough pace for Western competitors to match.

In many logistics situations, quality of service is about selecting the right quantity of the right product in the right sequence in response to customer orders. For example, store orders must be picked from a range of thousands of skus (stock keeping units) at a Tesco RDC. This must be carried out accurately (correct sku, correct quantity) against tight delivery schedules day in day out. *Pick accuracy* (for example, 99.5 per cent correct sku and correct quantity) is widely used to measure the quality of this operation. And increasing requirements for in-store efficiencies mean that categories of product (for example, shampoos and toothpastes) need to be picked in a set sequence to facilitate direct to shelf delivery at the store. Logistics service providers who can implement and maintain the highest standards of service quality place themselves at an advantage over those who cannot.

The time advantage

Time measures how long a customer has to wait in order to receive a given product or service. Volkswagen call this time the *customer to customer* lead time: that is, the time it takes from the moment a customer places an order to the moment that customer receives the car he or she specified. Such lead times can vary from zero (the product is immediately available, such as goods on a supermarket shelf) to months or years (such as the construction of a new building). Competing on time is about survival of the fastest!

Time can be used to win orders by companies who have learned that some customers do not want to wait – and are prepared to pay a premium to get what they want quickly. An example is Vision Express, who offer prescription spectacles 'in about one hour'. Technicians machine lenses from blanks on the premises. Staff are given incentives to maintain a 95 per cent service level against the one-hour target. Vision Express has been successful in the marketplace by re-engineering the supply chain so that parts and information can flow rapidly from one process to the next. Compare this with other opticians in the high street, who must send customer orders to a central factory. Under the 'remote factory' system, orders typically take about 10 days to process. An individual customer order is first dispatched to the factory. It then has to join a queue with orders from all the other high street branches around the country. Once the order has been processed, it must return to the branch that raised the order. While this may be cheaper to do (a central, highly productive factory serves all of the branches), it takes much longer to process an order.

The time advantage is variously described as *speed* or *responsiveness* in practice. Speeding up supply chain processes may help to improve freshness of the end product, or to reduce the risk of obsolete or over-aged stock in the system. Time is an *absolute* measure, that is, it is not open to interpretation like quality and cost. By following a product through a supply chain, we can discover which processes add value and which add time and cost but no value. We explore this further in Chapter 5, which is about managing time for advantage in the supply chain.

The cost advantage

Cost is important for all supply chain processes – that goes without saying. Low costs translate into advantages in the marketplace in terms of low prices or high margins, or a bit of each. Many products compete specifically on the basis of low price. This is supported from a supply chain point of view by low-cost manufacture, distribution, servicing and the like. Examples of products that compete on low price are 'own brand' supermarket goods that reduce the high margins and heavy advertising spend of major brands. They also perhaps cut some of the corners in terms of product specification in the hope that the customer will consider low price as being more important than minor differences in product quality.

The pressure to reduce prices at automotive component suppliers is intense. The assemblers have been setting annual price reduction targets for their inbound supply chains for some years. Unless a supplier can match reduced prices for which products are being sold by means of reduced costs, that supplier will gradually go out of business. As a result, many suppliers are cynical about the 'price down' policies of the assemblers. Reduced prices are the reward of cost cutting, and that is most often a collaborative effort on the part of several partners in the supply chain. As indicated in section 1.1, Tesco can make only limited inroads into its in-store costs without the help of its supply chain partners. On the other hand small dairy farmers continue to be forced out of business because the price of milk paid by supermarkets is 'less than the price of water'. For them, there are few opportunities to cut costs.

Controlling uncertainty: the dependability advantage

Time is not just about speed. It is also about controlling uncertainty in logistics processes. Uncertainty undermines the *dependability* with which a product or service meets target. Although Vision Express offers a one-hour service for prescription glasses, the 95 per cent service level is a measure of the dependability of that service against the one-hour target. Firms who do not offer instantaneous availability need to tell the customer – in other words to 'promise' – *when* the product or service will be delivered. Delivery dependability measures how successful the firm has been in meeting those promises. For example, the UK-based Royal Mail offers a 'first class' service for letters whereby there is a 90 per cent chance that a letter posted today will reach its destination tomorrow. It is important to measure dependability in the same 'end to end' way that speed is measured. Dependability measures are widely used in industries such as train and air travel services to monitor how well published timetables are met. And in manufacturing firms, dependability is used to monitor a supplier's performance in such terms as:

- *on time* (percentage of orders delivered on time, and the variability against target);
- *in full* (percentage of orders delivered complete, and the variability against target).

Logistics operations are concerned not just with the *average percentage of* orders delivered on time but also in the *variability*. A manufacturer has to cope with the day-by-day variability of orders delivered. In practice, this is the more important measure because of the resource implications of 'ups and downs' in the demand being placed on a system. Case study 1.3 explores the impact of variability on a supplier's processes.

CASE STUDY
1.3

Measuring schedule variability

A problem that is all too familiar to suppliers in the automotive industry is that of schedule variability. A vehicle manufacturer issues delivery schedules to specify how many parts of each type are required each day for the following month. And each day a 'call-off' quantity is issued, which specifies how many the vehicle manufacturer actually wants. The two sets of figures are not necessarily the same, although they usually add up to the same cumulative numbers for the month as a whole. In other words, the total scheduled quantities and the total call-off quantities are the same. So what is the problem?

The problem is that the supplier has to cope with ups and downs of call-off quantities that create huge problems for the supplier's process. Let scheduled demand $= S$, and call-off quantities $= A$. Then the difference D between schedule and actual is given by $D = S - A$. If the supplier produces to schedule, then $S > A$, the supplier will over-produce the part and end up with excess stock. Where $S < A$, the effects could either be a reduction in stock held by the supplier, or a shortfall of $(S-A)$ of parts from the supplier. The two conditions ($S > A$ and $S < A$) therefore have different logistics implications.

Figure 1.8 shows that actual demand, totalled across four different parts at a supplier of pressed metal components, may be up to 1,600 units above schedule, or 2,200 below schedule in the case of vehicle assembler W. This range has been divided up into intervals of 100 units. The mode (0–99) indicates that $S = A$ for a frequency of 18 per cent of the observations.

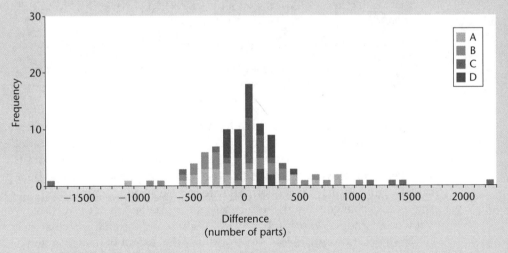

Figure 1.8 **Distribution of differences between scheduled and actual demand for vehicle assembler W**

The standard deviation (SD) for this distribution is 573, which is characteristics of the flat, wide spread of data. Figure 1.9 shows the distribution of S–A for four similar parts from the same supplier but to a different vehicle assembler, X.

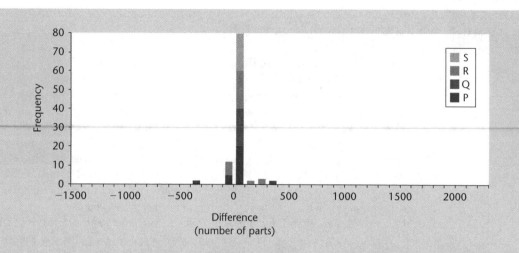

Figure 1.9 Distribution of differences between scheduled and actual demand for vehicle assembler X

This time, the SD for the distribution is 95, representing a much narrower spread of differences than for W.

(Source: Harrison, 1996)

Questions

1 What are the logistics implications for the supplier for delivery reliability to customers X and W?

2 What steps will the supplier need to take in order to satisfy call-off orders from W?

3 If separate parts of the factory were dedicated to customer W and customer X production, which would be the more efficient?

Quality is not just about meeting target pick accuracy, or target defect levels. It is also about controlling variability. The implication of dependability for logistics is that supply chain processes need to be robust and predictable. Toyota UK manages inbound deliveries of parts from suppliers in southern Europe by a process called *chain logistics*. Trailers of parts are moved in four-hour cycles, after which they are exchanged for the returning empty trailer on its way back from the United Kingdom. One hitch in this highly orchestrated process means that incoming parts do not arrive just-in-time at the assembly plant. Toyota demands that its suppliers and logistics partner ALUK plan *countermeasures*. This means that alternative routes for suppliers to deliver to its Burnaston assembly plant in Britain have been planned in advance to deal, for example, with a French channel ferry strike at Calais.

There are other ways in which logistics advantage may be gained, but these are not so readily measurable as the four listed above. They are referred to as 'soft' objectives as distinct from the more easily measurable 'hard' objectives. Examples of soft objectives are:

● *confidence*: queries answered promptly, courteously and efficiently;

- *security*: customer's information and property treated in a confidential and secure manner.

Soft objectives need to be measured in different ways to hard objectives, such as customer attitude surveys.

Logistics is not the only way in which product competitiveness in the marketplace can be enhanced. The performance objectives listed above can be added to (and in some cases eclipsed by) other ways in which products may win orders, such as design and marketing features. No matter how good the logistics system might have been, lack of a 'clam shell' design led to reduction of Nokia's market share for mobile telephone handsets in Europe. Superior product or service design – often supported by brand image – may create advantage in the marketplace. Here, the logistics task is to support the superior design. BMW's supply chain is one of the most efficient there is, mainly because its products are sold (at least in Europe) as soon as they have been made. Finished cars do not accumulate in disused airfields across Europe, like those of the mass producers. Finished product storage adds cost, with no value added from an end-customer perspective.

1.3.2 Order winners and order qualifiers

The relative importance of the above logistics performance objectives is usually different for a given product or service. A helpful distinction is that between order winners and order qualifiers (Hill, 2000):

- *Order winners* are factors that directly and significantly help products to win orders in the marketplace. Customers regard such factors as key reasons for buying that product or service. If a firm raises its performance on those factors, it will increase its chances of getting more business. Thus a product that competes mainly on price would benefit in the marketplace if productivity improvements enabled further price reductions.

- *Order qualifiers* are factors that are regarded by the market as an 'entry ticket'. Unless the product or service meets basic performance standards, it will not be taken seriously. An example is quality accreditation: a possible supplier to major utilities such as PowerGen in Britain and EDF in France would not be considered seriously without ISO 9000 certification. And delivery reliability is a must for newspapers – yesterday's news is worthless! Note that, in both examples, order qualifiers are *order-losing sensitive*: loss of ISO 9000 accreditation would make it impossible to supply to major utilities, and late delivery of newspapers would miss the market.

The different impacts of the two sets of criteria are illustrated in Figure 1.10. Increased performance in an order winner, shown by the solid line, increases competitive benefit for the product in proportion. Order qualifiers, shown by the dotted line, have different characteristics. Attainment of a required performance standard, such as ISO 9000 accreditation, gains entry to the market but no more than that.

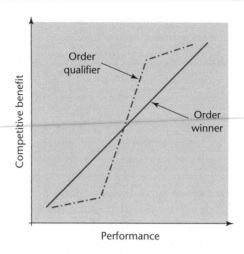

Figure 1.10 Order winners and order qualifiers

Note that order winners and qualifiers are *specific to individual product lines* and the market segments they serve. Table 1.1 provides an example of how two different products made by the same manufacturer and passing through the same distribution channel have different performance objectives. The first product group comprises standard shirts that are sold in a limited range of 'classic' colours and sizes. The second product group comprises fashion blouses that are designed specially for each season in many colours and a choice of styles with associated designer labels.

Analysis of the order winners and qualifiers shows that the two product ranges have very different performance criteria in the marketplace. Of the two, the range of fashion blouses presents more logistics challenges because individual skus are

Table 1.1 Different product ranges have different logistics performance objectives

	Classic shirts	Fashion blouses
Product range	Narrow: few colours, standard sizes	Wide: many colours, choice of styles, designer labels
Design changes	Occasional	Frequent (at least every season)
Price	Everyday low price	Premium prices
Quality	Consistency, conformance to (basic) spec	High grades of material, high standards of workmanship
Sales volumes	Consistent sales over time	Sales peak for given fashion season
Order winners	Price	Product range Brand/label Quality
Order qualifiers	Quality Availability	Price Availability
Logistics priorities	Cost Dependability Quality	Speed Flexibility Quality

much more difficult to forecast. It is not until the season is under way that a picture begins to emerge about which colours are selling most in which region of the market. The logistics challenge is therefore concerned with speed of response and flexibility to changing demand. The logistics challenges between the two ranges are quite distinctive.

Not only can order winners and qualifiers be different for different products and services. They can also *change over time*. Thus, in the early phase of a new product life cycle, such as the launch of a new integrated circuit, the order winners are availability and design performance. Price would often be a qualifier: provided the price is not so exorbitant that no one can afford it, there is a market for innovators who want the best-performing chip that is available. But by the maturity phase of the life cycle, competitors have emerged, the next generation is already on the stocks, and the order winners have changed to price and product reliability. The former order winners (availability and design performance) have changed to become order qualifiers. The logistics challenge is to understand the market dynamics and to adjust capabilities accordingly.

The *actions of competitors* are therefore a further influence on logistics performance objectives. For example, low-price competitors are a feature of most markets, and attempt to differentiate themselves from the perhaps higher-grade but pricier incumbents. Thus competitors like Matalan have sparked fundamental changes in logistics strategy at the long-established UK clothing retailer Marks & Spencer (www.marks&spencer.co.uk). In response to massive loss of sales to cheaper new entrants, Marks & Spencer has ditched many 30-year-old agreements with local UK suppliers in favour of sourcing garments from suppliers in the Far East.

Activity 1.3

Select the top two product lines (in terms of sales) for your firm or one that you know well. Using the headings in Table 1.1, fill in the details for characteristics of both product lines. Aim to use precise details, so identify the actual sales figures instead of putting 'high' or 'low'. Use additional or other headings if they describe the situation better. Go on to identify the principal order winners and qualifiers for each product.

1.4 Logistics strategies

Key issues: What is 'strategy'? How can competitive criteria be aligned within a supply chain? How can logistics strategies be tuned to different product needs?

1.4.1 Defining 'strategy'

Strategy is about planning as distinct from doing. It is about formulating a long-term plan for the supply chain, as distinct from solving the day-to-day issues and problems that inevitably occur. Extending the concept of 'strategy' from Hayes and Wheelwright (1984), the aim for the supply chain as a whole should be

> **the set of guiding principles, driving forces and ingrained attitudes that help to communicate goals, plans and policies to all employees that are reinforced through conscious and subconscious behaviour at all levels of the supply chain.**

Five important characteristics of 'strategy' are as follows:

- *Time horizon*: this is long-term rather than short-term.
- *Pattern of decisions*: decisions are consistent with each other over time.
- *Impact*: changes are significant rather than small-scale.
- *Concentration of effort*: the focus is on selected, defined capabilities rather than 'broad brush'.
- *Comprehensiveness*: all processes in the supply chain are coordinated.

All too often, logistics 'strategy' is set using few such characteristics: decisions are made piecemeal by accident, muddle or inertia. We need, however, to recognise that strategic decisions may indeed be made by such means.

Whittington (1993) proposes four approaches to setting strategy. He starts by proposing different motivations for setting strategy:

- *How deliberate are the processes of strategy setting?* These can range from clearly and carefully planned to a series of *ad hoc* decisions taken on a day-to-day basis.
- *What are the goals of strategy setting?* These can range from a focus on maximising profit to allowing other business priorities such as sales growth to be included.

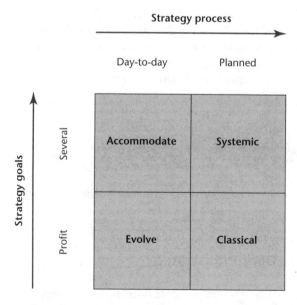

Figure 1.11 Four options for crafting strategy

If we make these two considerations the axes of a matrix, Figure 1.11 suggests four options for crafting strategy.

What are the implications for the way in which supply chain strategy is approached in different organisations? Here is a brief description of the four options:

- *Evolve.* 'Strategy' is not something that is formally undertaken at all. 'Our strategy is not to have a strategy' is a typical viewpoint. Operating decisions are taken in relation to the needs of the moment, with financial goals the main guiding principle.

- *Classical.* While financial goals are again the main guiding principle, these are achieved through a formal planning process. This is called 'classical' because it is the oldest and most influential option.

- *Accommodate.* Here, decisions are back to the day-to-day mode, but financial objectives are no longer the primary concern. Strategy is accommodated instead to the realities of the firm and the markets in which it operates.

- *Systemic.* This option for strategy setting sees no conflict between the ends and means of realising business goals. While goal setting takes place across all major aspects of the business (including human resources, marketing and manufacturing policies), these are linked to the means by which they will be achieved in practice.

1.4.2 Aligning strategies

In section 1.1 we showed the supply chain as a network of operating processes. In section 1.2 we emphasised the need to 'integrate' these processes to maximise flow and focus on the end-customer. And in section 1.3 we saw how supply chains can choose to compete on a range of different competitive priorities. Now is the time to put these ideas together and show how strategies need to be *aligned* across the supply chain.

If different links in the supply chain are directed towards different competitive priorities, then the chain will not be able to serve the end-customer as well as a supply chain in which the links are directed towards the same priorities. That is the basic argument for alignment in the supply chain. Where the links are directed by a common and consistent set of competitive criteria, then that supply chain will compete better in the marketplace than one in which the links have different, conflicting priorities.

And the concept on *focus* says that a given operation should not be subject to too many conflicting priorities. It is difficult to handle high-volume, low-cost products in the same supply chain channel as low-volume, high-variety products, for which flexibility is the name of the game. While the assembly line is the method of choice for assembling cars in volume, development of new models is kept well away from the factory in special facilities until close to launch. This is because the development process demands quite different technical skills and equipment that are better physically separated from the more routine, repetitive assembly line. In the example of the standard shirts and fashion blouses in section 1.3, the associated operations processes would be kept separate ('focused') for similar reasons.

What happens when the processes are not aligned within a supply chain? Let us address that question with case study 1.4 to show the problems that can arise.

CASE STUDY 1.4

Talleres Auto

Talleres Auto (TA) is an SME based in Barcelona. TA attends to broken-down vehicles, providing a roadside repair and recovery service. Two of the parts that TA frequently uses are starters and alternators, which were obtained from a local distributor. In turn, the local distributor ordered parts from a prime distributor. Starters and alternators were obtained from a remanufacturer, who replaced the windings and tested the products using parts bought from a component supplier. A diagram of this part of the supply chain is shown in Figure 1.12.

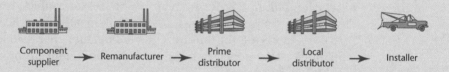

| Component supplier | → | Remanufacturer | → | Prime distributor | → | Local distributor | → | Installer |

- Talleres Auto is the installer
- TA buys starters and alternators from a local distributor
- the local distributor buys from a prime distributor
- the prime distributor buys from a remanufacturer
- the remanufacturer buys components from a component supplier

Figure 1.12 The Talleres Auto supply chain

Most of TA's customers made 'distress purchases' – their car had broken down and they wanted it to be fixed quickly. So TA needed a fast replacement service from the local distributor. While the distributors both recognised the need for fast replacements, the performance of the purchasing department at the remanufacturer was measured on cost savings. Thus the component supplier thought that the name of the game was low cost.

(Source: Harland, 1997)

Questions

1 What were the order winners and order qualifiers at TA?

2 What were the order winners and order qualifiers at the component supplier?

3 What impact on customer service was this mismatch likely to cause?

(Source: C. Harland, 1997)

1.4.3 Differentiating strategies

A supply chain, then, may choose to compete on different criteria. Such criteria need in turn to be recognised and form a part for the business strategies of all of the members of a given network. The choices so made have major implications for the operation of each member. Failure to recognise competitive criteria and their implications for a given product or service *by any member* means that the supply chain will compete less effectively. It is like playing football when the goalkeeper makes an error and lets in a goal that should not have happened – he lets the whole side down.

We complete Chapter 1 with a look at two commonly used supply chain strategies that have very different operational implications. Consider two products with different order winners:

- *Product 1*: a high-volume dishwashing product for which demand is relatively stable throughout the year. While subject to occasional enhancements, these are usually small scale: the life cycle is comparatively long.
- *Product 2*: a fashion ski jacket, which is produced for a given season and which is completely redesigned for the next season. Demand is very difficult to forecast, and the life cycle is short.

Product 1 sells because it is a well-known brand that performs reliably and well, and because it represents good value for money. Order winners are price and brand; qualifiers are quality and delivery reliability. Product 1 demands a supply chain that is focused on low-cost, reliable supply. Efficient operations processes are the name of the game.

Product 2 also sells because it is a well-known brand, but it is also recognised as this season's fashion offering. Price is now a qualifier, while order winners are style and brand. The operations task for the supply chain is flexibility and responsiveness to support the new offering in the marketplace. If it sells well,

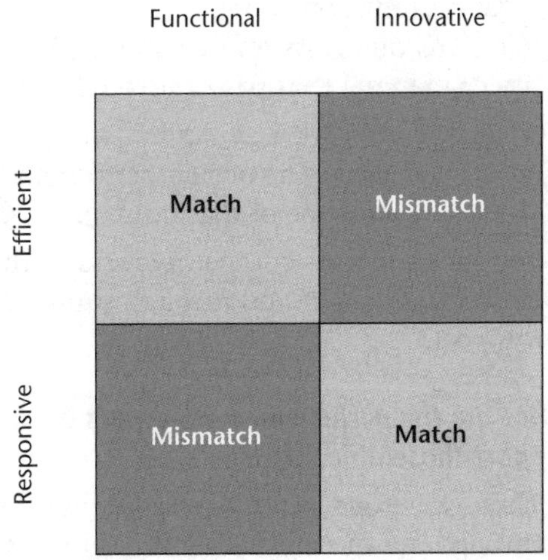

Figure 1.13 Fisher's supply chain matrix

(Source: Reprinted by permission of *Harvard Business Review*. Exhibit on p. 109 from 'What is the right supply chain for your product?', by Marshall Fisher, March/April 1997. Copyright © 1997 by the Harvard Business School Publication Corporation; all rights reserved.)

then the supply chain must be in a position to respond quickly to cash in on the short window of opportunity.

These two different sets of characteristics can be positioned on a matrix to aid the comparison, as shown in Figure 1.13. Product 1 emerges from this analysis as characteristic of a *functional-efficient* supply chain. The product performs a well-known, reliable but scarcely innovative task. Product 2, on the other hand, is a fashion product that is indeed innovative, and which must be supported by a responsive supply chain. Hence its supply chain is described as *innovative-responsive*.

Activity 1.4

1 Using the concepts from this section, analyse the supply chain support for both of the products you analysed in Activity 1.3. What should the supply chain be *(functional-efficient or innovative-responsive)*? What is the reality, and why are the two different?
2 To what extent is there alignment of strategy in the supply chains for these two products?

Summary

How does logistics work within the supply chain?

- Supply chain management is defined as 'aligning the processes of upstream and downstream supply chain partners to deliver superior levels of service to the end-customer while minimising waste'.

- Logistics is defined as 'the task of coordinating material flow, information flow and funds flow across the supply chain'.

- In a supply chain, materials flow from upstream to downstream. Demand information from the end-customer flows in the opposite direction. A given organisation is positioned within a supply 'network', with tier 1 suppliers and tier 1 customers its immediate neighbours. Material flow measures the quantity of material that passes through a given network per unit of time.

- A supply network is a system in which each organisation is linked to the others. Therefore the overall performance of the network results from the combined performance of the individual partners.

- Logistics supports competitiveness of the supply chain as a whole by meeting end-customer demand through supplying what is needed when it is needed at low cost.

What are the performance objectives of the supply chain, and how does logistics support those objectives?

- There are four ways of competing through logistics. The basic ways are through are quality, speed and cost objectives. Briefly, quality is about doing things right, speed is about doing things fast, and cost is about doing things cheaply. A fourth way is through better control of logistics processes, which makes them more dependable.

- Such performance objectives can, and often are, augmented by other objectives that are outside logistics. These include product superiority and brand. Here the logistics task is to support such performance objectives.

- The relative importance of logistics performance objectives varies from one situation to another. It can also vary over time. The concept of order winners and qualifiers helps to prioritise the logistics task. Key influences on relative importance are individual product needs in the marketplace, position in the product life cycle, and competitor activity.

- Logistics strategy is the set of guiding principles, driving forces and ingrained attitudes that help to communicate goals, plans and policies to all employees and which are reinforced through conscious and subconscious behaviour at all levels of the supply chain.

Discussion questions

1 Bill Gates of Microsoft describes the 2000s as 'business @ the speed of thought'. Discuss the importance of speed in the supply chain. How can speed be increased within the supply chain?

2 Suggest logistics performance priorities for the following, explaining why you have come to your conclusions:
    a a low-fare airline such as Ryanair;
    b a fast food chain such as McDonald's;
    c an overnight parcels service such as TNT.

3 What is meant by the term *alignment* in relation to supply chain processes? Why is alignment important in setting a strategy for a given supply chain?

4 What does *flow* mean in a supply chain context? Explain how material flow relates to information flow in a supply network.

References

Beech, J. (1998) 'The *supply–demand nexus*', in Gattorna, J. (ed.), *Strategic Supply Chain Alignment*, pp. 92–103. Aldershot: Gower.

Eggleton, D.J. (1990) 'JIT in a distribution environment', *International Journal of Logistics and Distribution Management*, Vol. 9, No. 1, pp. 32–4.

Fisher, M. (1997) 'What is the right supply chain for your product?', *Harvard Business Review*, March/April, pp. 105–16.

Gattorna, J. (ed.) (1998) *Strategic Supply Chain Alignment: Best practice in supply chain management*. Aldershot: Gower.

Harland, C. (1997) 'Talleres Auto', in Johnston, R., Chambers, S., Harland, C., Harrison, A. and Chambers, S. (eds) (1997) *Cases in Operations Management*, 2nd edn, pp. 420–8. London: Pitman.

Harland, C., Lamming, R., Zheng, J. and Johnsen, T. (2001) 'A Taxonomy of supply networks', *Journal of Supply Management*, Fall, pp. 21–7.

Harrison, B. (1996) 'An investigation of the impact of schedule stability on supplier responsiveness', *International Journal of Logistics Management*, Vol. 7, No. 1, pp. 83–91.

Hayes, R.H. and Wheelwright, S.C. (1984) *Restoring Our Competitive Edge*. New York: John Wiley.

Hill, T. (2000) *Manufacturing Strategy*, 2nd edition, London: Macmillan.

Knill, B. (1992) 'Continuous flow manufacturing', *Material Handling Engineering*, May, pp. 54–7.

Oliver, R.K. and Webber, M.D. (1982) 'Supply chain management: Logistics catches up with strategy', *Outlook*, 6, pp. 42–7.

Whittington, R. (1993) *What is Strategy and Does it Matter?* London: Routledge (repr. 1996 by International Thompson Business Press).

Zheng, J., Harland, C., Johnsen, T. and Lamming, R. (1998) 'Initial conceptual framework for creation and operation of supply networks', *Proceedings of 14th AMP Conference, Turku, 3–5 September*, Vol. 3, pp. 591–613.

Suggested further reading

Christopher, M. (1998) *Logistics and Supply Chain Management: Strategies for reducing cost and improving service*, 2nd edn. London: Financial Times Prentice Hall.

Stock, J.R. and Lambert, M. (2001) *Strategic Logistics Management*, 4th edn. Boston, MA: McGraw-Hill/Irwin.

CHAPTER 2

Putting the end-customer first

Outcomes

The intended outcomes of this chapter are to:
- develop the marketing perspective on supply chain management;
- explain how customer segmentation works, and to emphasise its importance to logistics;
- explain the connection between quality of service and customer loyalty;
- show how segmentation can be used to set logistics priorities.

By the end of this chapter you should be able to understand:
- how supply chains should compete by aligning logistics strategy with marketing strategy;
- how to set priorities for logistics strategy.

Introduction

In Chapter 1 we looked at the logistics task from a perspective of material flow and information flow. We also saw how logistics contributes to competitive strategy and the performance objectives by which we can measure this contribution. But what is it that drives the need for flow in the first place? The essential point to recognise here is that it is the behaviour of the end-customer that should dictate what happens. As quoted in Chapter 1 (Gattorna, 1998),

> materials and finished products only flow through the supply chain because of customer behaviour at the end of the [chain] . . . There is no magic in that insight, and yet many firms and indeed whole channels have long operated without recognising this essential connexion.

Only end-customers should be free to make up their minds about when they want to place an order on the network: after that, the system takes over.

Quality of service addresses the process of handing over products and services into the hands of end-customers. Only after this process has been completed does the product/service reach its full value. And the process offers many opportunities for adding value. Instead of picking up a product from a distributor who is remote from the focal firm, there are opportunities during the sales transaction (for example, help and advice in using the focal firm's products), as well after the sales transaction (for example, after sales service and warranty).

This chapter probes the link between marketing strategy and logistics strategy. It introduces this link, and shows how it is possible to identify logistics priorities – the tasks at which logistics needs to excel.

Key issues   *This chapter addresses four key issues:*

1 **The marketing perspective**: the impact of rising customer expectations and the information revolution.

2 **Segmentation**: and its implications for logistics strategy.

3 **Quality of service**: the link between customer satisfaction and customer loyalty.

4 **Setting logistics priorities**: delivering order winning and qualifying criteria by segment.

2.1 The marketing perspective

Key issue: **What are the marketing implications for logistics strategy?**

'Marketing' is a philosophy that can be applied to the network as a whole. Adapting Doyle's (1994) definition,

> Marketing is the philosophy that integrates the disparate activities and functions that take place within the network. Satisfied [end] customers are seen as the only source of profit, growth and security.

Marketing in practice is a series of plans and decisions that determines how the philosophy will be actioned.

'Satisfied customers' are increasingly hard to find. This has been caused by widespread changes that are affecting the world we live in. Two of the major changes are rising customer expectations and the information revolution (Doyle, 2000). We expand on these below. As Hutter (1998) explains:

> The battleground is the customer's wallet. The protagonists are the world's largest corporations. Their weapons are technologies which increase understanding of individual customers and offer better access to those customers. The victors will be those that can order their entire organisation around the challenges of getting cheaper [access to] more profitable and more loyal customers. The backdrop to this scene is the growing sophistication of consumers themselves. We live in an age of expert buyers. Customers are becoming ever more critical and demanding. They know that they can play the market and are placing higher and higher demands on [suppliers] to give them what they want – and immediately.

Similar statements can be made about not-for-profit areas of developed economies, such as central government, local government and the health service.

In Chapter 1, we referred to 'tier 1 customers' with whom a focal firm deals directly, and to 'end-customers' who are the individuals or businesses that buy the finished 'product' at the end of the supply network. It is therefore usual to refer to two types of customer:

- *Business customers:* who represent the focal firm's immediate trading environment (see Figure 1.2)
- *end-customers:* who represent the ultimate customer for the network as a whole (see Figure 1.4).

We refer to these types of relationships as 'business to business' (B2B) and 'business to customer' (B2C) accordingly. In section 1.2.2 of Chapter 1, we referred to the need to integrate supply chain processes so that they are aligned towards end-customer needs. In this sense, B2B integration should be aligned towards the ultimate B2C process.

We also need to distinguish here between customers and consumers. Webster (2000) defines:

- *consumers* are people who use or consume the product;
- *customers*: are individuals or businesses who buy the product, meaning that they acquire it and pay for it.

It is usual in business today to refer to 'customers' as the next process in a supply chain. This includes 'all types of marketing intermediaries or channel members who buy for resale to their customers'.

2.1.1 Rising customer expectations

Expectations have risen among customers in line with a general increase in wealth among developed countries over the latter half of the twentieth century. This increase in expectations has many causes including:

- better levels of general education;
- better ability to discern between alternative products;
- exposure to more lifestyle issues in the media.

These expectations have led to customers not only aspiring to more desirable products, they are also demanding much better levels of service to be associated with those products.

Businesses are also expecting more from their suppliers. Suppliers need to pay increasing attention to the service aspects of their dealings with industrial customers. This is especially true when the customer has implemented more customer-centric management systems such as just-in-time (Chapter 6).

2.1.2 The information revolution

Of the many technological advances in recent years, the explosion in applications of Internet technology is having the most sweeping effects. Our recent study of the future impact of buyer–supplier Internet-enabled exchanges (Daniel *et al.*, 2003) highlighted three areas:

- *Procurement, supply chain management and new product development.* Exchanges are helping to reduce cycle times and to remove errors and duplication.

Suppliers benefit mostly from reduced transaction costs, enhanced marketing presence and reduced errors. However, buyers are expected to reap greater benefits – particularly in the areas of procurement (reductions in the cost of goods, in transaction costs, and in procurement cycles) and of supply chain management.

- *Buyer–supplier relationships*: Exchanges are expected to increase the level of trust between buyers and suppliers, which is key to good trading relationships. Rather than lead to an increase in the number of suppliers used by buyers, e-hubs will encourage the continued trend of supplier rationalisation and result in longer-term relationships with remaining suppliers. The increased ability to share information between buyers and suppliers made possible by the use of e-hubs will result in increased joint problem solving. This will accelerate the trend of supplier-led innovation and increased outsourcing to suppliers.

- *Impact on industry structure*. Exchanges will contribute to the trend of reducing the number of manufacturers and suppliers in most sectors. Exchanges will encourage the use of open book accounting and will reduce the traditional mark-ups associated with multi-tier supply chains. They support the trend of tier 1 suppliers acting as service providers and directing a network of subsuppliers.

Faced with rising customer expectations and the information revolution, supply chain partners are increasingly asking how they can act together to meet these challenges. The starting point is to analyse needs and wants in order to satisfy a supply chain's end-customers. The marketing perspective has a well-known way to help in this analysis – segmentation.

2.2 Segmentation

Key issue: What is segmentation, and what are its implications to logistics strategy?

Segmentation describes how a given market might be broken up into different groups of customers with similar needs. It means 'describing the market as simply as possible while doing our best to emphasise its variety' (Millier and Palmer, 2000). We start by considering market segmentation from a *customer* perspective in what are usually described as 'fast-moving consumer goods (FMCG)' markets. For example, segmentation of the market for suntan creams and lotions would begin with an understanding of:

- the benefits wanted (e.g. water resistance, oil/non-oil, sun factor);
- the price consumers are prepared to pay;
- the media to which they are exposed (television programmes, magazines, etc.);
- the amount and timing of their purchases.

Profiles of the segments and evaluation of their relative attractiveness to the focal firm can then be developed.

There are many possible ways in which markets can be segmented, including:

- *demographic*: such as age, sex and education;
- *geographic*: such as urban v. country, types of house and region;
- *technical*: the use that customers are going to make of a product;
- *behavioural*: such as spending pattern and frequency of purchase.

Of the various ways to segment markets, we have found that behavioural segmentation, which 'divides buyers into groups based on their knowledge, attitudes, uses or responses to a product' (Kotler *et al.*, 1996) is a powerful way to bridge marketing and logistics. It is vital that the definition of segments is not a marketing-only task, but that logistics is involved. The key point is that there is no value in defining segments that cannot be served because logistics capability does not exist. For example, if most of the spending pattern is around Christmas, then logistics must be capable of supporting the huge surge in demand at that time. Case study 2.1 explains how a retailer views its behavioural segments.

The important characteristics of segments (McGoldrick, 2002) are that they must be:

CASE STUDY 2.1

Managing events and promotions in the retail sector

If consumers only purchased their requirements in line with their use, then it would be relatively easy to reorganise the end-to-end supply chain from shelf to national warehouse using lean principles (see Chapter 6). A simple demand–pull system replenishing tomorrow that which has been sold today, direct to shelf, would streamline store operations and reduce inventories significantly. Retailers like Wal-Mart in the United States and Tesco in Britain have pursued an everyday low price policy in an attempt to maximise this 'steady state' replenishment policy. However, in Europe, most retailers have found that customers enjoy promotions and that promotions boost sales. In any case, events like Christmas and back to school create huge surges in demand.

However, events create surges in demand which retailers must address. Events may be divided in two: seasonal events and promotional events, as shown in Table 2.1:

Table 2.1 Example events and promotions

Events	Promotions
● Valentine's Day	● Three for two
● Mother's Day	● Buy one get one free
● Summer holidays	● 10% off for a week
● Back to school	● Happy hour – 20%
● Christmas	● Triple loyalty card points
	● Gift with purchase

Retailers have no control over the timing of seasonal events and it is usually very difficult to forecast likely demand with normal levels of accuracy. In contrast, promotional events are planned by retailers and their suppliers. Consequently, while demand may be unpredictable, the timing of such events is known in advance. It is surprising, therefore, how often consumers will find that items on promotion are not on the shelf and that display aids and promotional material will be missing. The event which has the greatest effect is Christmas – where sales usually start growing in October, ramp up in November and peak in December. This is the *only* profitable quarter for many retailers. The product is frequently sourced from the Far East and once the order has been delivered there will be no further shipments. Retailers need to plan for this activity months in advance and cross their fingers that they will not miss sales through under-ordering or buy too much with the consequent write-downs in the January sale. The position is further complicated in a national chain where demand patterns will be different store by store and region by region.

Many retailers allocate their Christmas merchandise to individual stores on the basis of previous year's sales for the particular product category and hope for the best. A lean design supply chain is unable to cope with such spiky demand, which will be affected further by marketing efforts and the latest fad. Retailers therefore need to be particularly agile in their approach in order to satisfy unknown demand.

Boots The Chemists (BTC) – the leading UK health and beauty retailer – has approached this problem by outsourcing specific Christmas merchandise deliveries. These deliveries are scheduled at different times of the day from 'normal' deliveries. In this way, while not dealing with the issues created by unpredictable demand, store operations can apply appropriate resources to unload vehicles and put away directly to shelf or indirectly to stockroom. Historically, promotional events in BTC were a fairly hit and miss affair with hundreds of products being promoted within a four-week window. There was a large reliance on good luck for all the elements to come together prior to the start of the promotional period. Inevitably some product, display aids and show material arrived late. Store operations at the end of the supply chain then had to try and mount the promotions with what had been delivered. Consumers were dissatisfied with the result and sales were lost.

The solution was to create a dedicated promotions team within the categories. The team masterminded the overall promotional plan and were made responsible for the delivery of product, display aids and show materials into the national distribution centres (NDCs). A successful trial was then conducted whereby most of the work required to mount the promotion was done by logistics staff in the regional distribution centres (RDCs) for each of their individual stores.

The trial comprised sending allocations of all the promotional requirements to the RDCs from the NDCs. Staff in the RDCs then picked product for a week's anticipated sales (based on historical data for that line by individual store) into totes for direct-to-shelf delivery together with appropriate display aids and show material. The totes were then placed on dollies, rolled on and off vehicles, and wheeled into the shop to the correct gondola end (end of free-standing 'island' shelf in a store). After three days, EPOS data was reviewed, and an accurate prediction of future sales to the end of the promotion was made. This was then used to calculate future replenishment requirements. Finally the merchandising teams were invited to devise clever ways to make shelves look full at the end of the promotion without using a lot of stock. This resulted in fewer 'remainders' from a promotion that had to be written down. BTC is currently implementing its design for a transformed end-to-end supply chain and the work described above is being gradually rolled out.

(Source: Philip Matthews, formerly Supply Chain Director, BTC)

Questions

1 List the logistics challenges of mounting promotions and events at a retailer such as BTC.

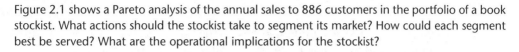

Figure 2.1 shows a Pareto analysis of the annual sales to 886 customers in the portfolio of a book stockist. What actions should the stockist take to segment its market? How could each segment best be served? What are the operational implications for the stockist?

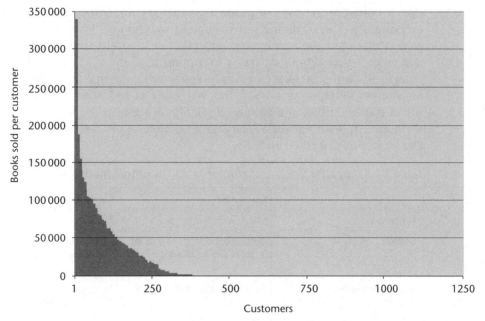

Figure 2.1 Annual sales per customer for a book distributor, shown as a Pareto diagram

- *measurable*: variables that can easily be identified and measured;
- *economically viable*: capable of producing the contribution that justifies the effort and cost of marketing;
- *accessible*: geographically or in terms of media communications;
- *actionable*: can be attracted and served effectively.

The next step is to select target segments and to identify how a focal firm is going to win orders in each. In other words, to define *differential advantage* that distinguishes our offerings from those of our competitors. In logistics terms, the important issues here are the order winning criteria (OWC), and qualifying criteria (QC) for the target segments. These help in turn to define the *marketing mix*.

The marketing mix is the set of marketing decisions that is made to implement positioning strategy (target market segments and differential advantage) and to achieve the associated marketing and financial goals. The marketing mix has been popularly termed the '4 Ps' (McCarthy, 1964):

- *product*: range, sizes, presentation and packaging, design and performance;
- *price*: list price, discounts, geographical pricing, payment terms;

- *promotion*: sales force, advertising, consumer promotion, trade promotion, direct marketing;
- *place*: channel selection, market coverage, distribution systems, dealer support.

Logistics contributes fundamentally to the 'place' decisions, as well as supporting 'product' and 'promotion' decisions. All too often, 'place' activities are viewed as the bit bolted to the back of production that gets inventory away from the factory and into stock-holding points such as warehouses. In order to achieve the goal of 'the right product in the right place at the right time', logistics systems and processes need to be designed to support products in the marketplace.

Segmentation principles can also be applied to industrial marketing. But 'there are distinct differences between the marketing of industrial products and consumer goods' (Millier and Palmer, 2000: 60), as summarised in Table 2.2.

Let us turn to an industrial marketing example to illustrate how new segments can impact on logistics capability.

Table 2.2 Comparison between consumer and industrial marketing

	Consumer	Industrial
Customers	Many, widely dispersed	Few, concentrated
Market	Consumers directly served by retailers and distributors	Derived demand Industrial chain, long and complex
Buying behaviour	Individual and family decision	Group decision Formal procedures High buyer power
Relationships	Low individual buying power	Formal procedures High buyer power
Product	Standard Positioned on emotional and perceptual factors	Technical complexity Specification important Bespoke and customised
Price	Low unit price Take it or leave it No negotiation	High unit price Tender and negotiation Standard items from price list
Promotion	Mass media advertising Role of the brand	Emphasis on personel selling Reputation important
Place	Established retail chain Stock availability Seasonality	Direct Made to order Standard items in stock

CASE STUDY 2.2

Powerdrive Motors

Tom Cross took over as Managing Director at Powerdrive Motors in South Africa three years ago. At the time, the company was an established manufacturer of small electric motors with a strong reputation for product reliability and technical leadership. On the downside, it was also regarded in the trade as having high prices and variable delivery. Tom's first task was to tackle the huge product variety on offer. He saw this as the major problem in addressing the negative views in the marketplace, and also saw opportunities in streamlining design and production. The product range was replaced with a new generation of designs based on a few hundred 'modules', which could be assembled in many different combinations to give variety at low cost. This meant the loss of some customers who had gone to Powerdrive because they could rely on the company's technical leadership to produce designs that suited their particular needs. This was not considered important because the combined sales volume of such customers was under 5 per cent.

Using the new designs, Tom was now able to reorganise the factory into cells that produced major subassemblies such as rotors and stators. The work flow was transformed, and manufacturing throughput time was reduced from six weeks to just four days. Cost improvements mean that average price reductions of between 10 and 15 per cent could be offered.

Powerdrive's customer service policy was redrafted to offer quotations within a maximum of one hour of any enquiry, and for deliveries of finished product to be made within one week 'anywhere in northern Europe'. This new policy was explained to internal sales staff, and to sales representatives and agents employed by the organisation. If 'old' customers wanted special designs that were no longer in the range, the sales staff were instructed to explain Powerdrive's new policy and to politely decline the order.

At first, business soared. Impressed by the lower prices and short delivery times, customers flocked to Powerdrive and sales jumped by 50 per cent. But then things began to go sour. First, the factory could no longer cope with the demands being placed on it. The addition of a large order for lawnmower motors blocked out a lot of production capacity from January to June. Order lead times during this period in particular slid back to former levels. Second, a Brazilian supplier spotted the opportunity to enter the market with prices that undercut Powerdrive by 20 per cent. While only half of the product range was covered by this new entrant, it was the high-volume products that were especially threatened. Further, the new competitor offered three-day lead times from stock that had been established in Europe. Third, some of the former customers who could no longer obtain their bespoke designs from Powerdrive were complaining within the industry that Powerdrive's technical leadership had been sacrificed. Although small in number, such customers were influential at trade fairs and conferences.

Questions

1 Evaluate the changes that took place in the segmentation of Powerdrive's market.

2 Use Fisher's supply chain matrix (Figure 1.13) to suggest what effect the changes to Powerdrive's strategy have had on logistics capability.

Segmentation is often undertaken by adopting the easy way to group customers – by account size. While this is easily measurable, it fails on the fourth of McGoldrick's criteria listed above – it is not actionable in logistics terms. An example from our research in the FMCG sector illustrates the problems of poor alignment between marketing and logistics.

**CASE STUDY
2.3**

Segmentation at CleanCo

CleanCo is a Polish manufacturer of cleaning products that serves the European grocery retailing market. CleanCo currently segments its customers on the value of customer accounts. The primary division is between *national accounts*, for which 10 accounts constitute 70 per cent of sales by value, and *field sales,* which comprise a long 'tail' of more than 200 accounts that together account for only 3 per cent of sales. Due to the size of the field sales structure, a secondary classification groups accounts by channel type: neighbourhood retail, discount and pharmacy. CleanCo recognises the need to reduce the long customer 'tail' and is introducing distributors for orders below a minimum order quantity. CleanCo's current approach to segmentation is summarised in Table 2.3.

Table 2.3 CleanCo – Current approach to market segmentation

National Accounts	Field Sales		
70% sales 10 accounts	30% Sales, 200+ accounts		
	Neighbourhood retail	**Discount sector**	**Pharmacy**

While CleanCo currently segments its retail customers by account size, its sales organisation has identified two significant types of buying behaviour displayed by their customer base, shown in Table 2.4:

- *volume-driven* buying behaviour;
- *margin-driven* buying behaviour.

Volume-driven customers are keen to capitalise on both product and supply chain cost savings in order to pass them on to their customers to drive volume sales. There are two variants of the volume-driven behaviour:

- every-day low price (EDLP);
- discount.

Retailers pursuing an EDLP strategy strive for continuous price reduction from suppliers like CleanCo to drive a fairly consistent, high volume of sales. This should result in a relatively stable pattern of demand in the washing and bathing sector. Discounters on the other hand are looking for bargains so they can 'stack 'em high and sell 'em cheap', a strategy more likely to result in a volatile demand pattern. Margin-driven customers are keen to add value for their customers by offering a wide selection of products and value-adding services. This strategy also results in a relatively stable demand pattern in this sector.

Table 2.4 CleanCo – potential for behavioural segmentation

Volume-driven		Margin-driven
Every-day-low-price (EDLP)	Discount	

A complicating factor when trying to deconstruct the buying behaviour of CleanCo's customers is that several secondary factors are used to support products in the market place. Such factors include product types (e.g. premium, mid, utilitarian), product range (e.g. current products, end of lines, 'b' grade), merchandising requirements (e.g. category captains) and promotions strategy (e.g. roll-back, 12 week, 4 week, Hi-Lo). Promotions are by far the most disruptive of these factors. Although the promotions are generally planned well in advance with the retailers, they cause significant disruption to the supply chain operations due to the peaks and troughs in demand that they create. Furthermore the deeper the promotional activity the greater the volatility created and the greater the disruption to the supply chain. This has the effect of masking what is fundamentally a fairly stable demand pattern with somewhat artificial volatile demand.

Strategic alignment can only be achieved if the supply chain is aligned behind the segmentation strategy that CleanCo has adopted. This is not currently the case with the CleanCo supply chain. Each operation within the supply chain makes decisions or segments its customers based on the functional criteria that affect its part of the supply chain. We have called this lack of alignment 'matrix twist', because the matrix of business processes at each stage of the supply chain has been apparently twisted so that the processes fail to fit with each other. As illustrated in Table 2.5, the decision criteria for CleanCo and its suppliers and customers change at each stage. This not only complicates material flows, but becomes a minefield if one considers it in terms of behavioural segments.

Table 2.5 Supply chain segmentation criteria

Unit of analysis	Supply chain decision	Determined by
Source	Which suppliers?	Raw material commodity type
Make	Which manufacturing site?	Product family type
Deliver	Which manufacturer warehouse?	Historically a function of order size In process of being divided by export paperwork requirements and customer account (arbitrary split)
	Which customer RDC?	Product type and location of store to serve
	Which products to which store?	Demographics of the store's catchment area, which drives layout and range decisions

(Source: Godsell and Harrison, 2002)

Questions

1 What has caused the 'matrix twist' between CleanCo and its retail customers?

2 What actions are needed to straighten out the 'matrix twist'?

2.3   Quality of service

Key issues: **How do customer expectations affect logistics service? How does satisfaction stack up with customer loyalty?**

Most supply chains that involve physical products end with *service* processes such as retailing (grocery or apparel), healthcare (pharmaceutical and other medical goods) and distribution (motor cars). Service processes mean that the end-customer is present in some way, although distribution through web-based shopping, telephone and mail order mean that customers do not have to be physically present. Performance of service processes often differs between employees, between customers and from one hour to the next. If you want good service from the local supermarket, do not go on Saturdays or near to Christmas when the service is under severe capacity pressure. On-shelf availability is at its lowest, and queues at the checkout are at their longest! The key point is that 'service is the combination of outcomes and experiences delivered to and received by the end-customer' (Johnston and Clark, 2001:9).

Quality of service takes place during service delivery, which is the interaction between the customer and the service process. 'Gaps' can emerge between what the service is supposed to be, what the customer expects it to be, and how the customer perceives it when it is delivered (Zeithaml *et al.* 1988, Parasuraman *et al.*, 1991). We can illustrate these gaps as a simplified gap model (Figure 2.2):

- *Gap 1* refers to differences between customer expectations and how these have been developed into a service specification by the supplier.
- *Gap 2* refers to differences between how the specification was drawn up and how it was delivered.
- *Gap 3* refers to differences between what the customer expected and what he perceived was delivered.
- *Gap 4* refers to differences between how supplier and customer perceived the service delivery.

Gaps in quality of service can arise, as seen in the IKEA case study.

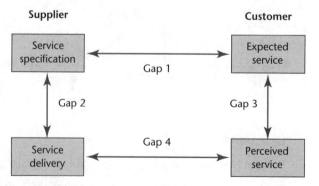

Figure 2.2 Simplified service quality gap model
(Source: after Parasuraman *et al.*, 1991)

Tears at teatime at IKEA

Next week, Jane Fillimore will move into a new flat. You can tell something about the 28-year-old music-industry publicist from Kilburn, northwest London, from the list of furniture she is buying. There is the Pax Brivic wardrobe, the Norden dining table and the Bonde media storage combination. Fillimore wants style – but on a budget. She is part of Generation Ikea.

Not that she wants to be. She hates the Swedish retailer, and only last Sunday had her worst shopping day ever at the firm's superstore in a drab retail park near the new Wembley stadium.

She wanted to pick up the Pax Brevic wardrobe she had ordered the week before. Easy, you might think, but just getting served was an ordeal. When she entered the store, an assistant told her to 'walk the mile of hell' past wannabe-stylish urban living rooms to the giant storage zone.

The store did not have her wardrobe and a salesman sent her back through road works to IKEA's nearby distribution centre. The distribution centre had the wardrobe, but could not give it to her without a receipt. To get one, she had to go back to the main store. But the main store had lost her order, so she had to go to customer service. This department is not called customer service at IKEA, it's called customer returns, and it took her half an hour to find.

By 4.30pm, Fillimore was right back where she started. Exasperated, she put her head in her hands and burst into tears. 'I don't even like the wardrobe', she sobbed. 'I bought it because it's cheap. That's the only reason I come here.' By 5.00pm, the store is closing, and she can only dream of getting her wardrobe by Friday. She could walk back through the little sets that represent the nation's living rooms to try one last time to find her wardrobe, but she can't face it. As she walks out, I ask her if she knows that Argos and Sainsbury are selling furniture. For the first time all day, she breaks into a smile.

'Really?', she grins. 'I'll go there tomorrow. I never want to come back to this place again.'

(Source: Based on an article by John Arlidge, *Sunday Times*, 26 October 2003)

Questions

1 When IKEA was founded 60 years ago by Ingmar Kamprad, he realised that customers did not mind queuing, collecting their purchases and assembling the furniture themselves as long as the price was right. Suggest why gaps in quality of service have opened up.

2.3.1 Customer loyalty

While plugging gaps in service quality helps to improve customer satisfaction, this is a 'qualifier' for long-term customer loyalty. The two concepts are not the same. Piercy (2002) distinguishes them as follows:

● *Customer satisfaction* is what people think of us – quality of service, value for money. It is an *attitude* (how does a customer feel about our product/service?).

- *Customer loyalty* is how long we keep a customer (or what share of their business we take). It is a *behaviour* (do they buy from us more than once?).

Nevertheless, the attitude of customer satisfaction is key to the behaviour of customer loyalty. Parasuraman and Grewal (2000) link the two concepts by proposing the 'key drivers of customer loyalty', shown in Figure 2.3.

The benefits of customer loyalty are potentially huge. The loyal customer should be viewed in terms of life-time spending potential. Thus, a customer of VW Audi Group could be viewed as worth €300k rather than the €30k of today's sales transaction. As Johnston and Clark (2001) put it, loyal customers:

- generate long-term revenue streams (high life-time values);
- tend to buy more than new customers;
- tend to increase spending over time;
- may be willing to pay premium prices;
- provide cost savings compared with attracting new customers.

The logistics challenge is to support the development of customer loyalty by designing and delivering quality of service. Of the three drivers of customer loyalty shown in Figure 2.3, quality of service is 'essential for excellent market performance on an enduring basis' (Berry, 1999: 8–9). The rationale for this is that 'service quality is much more difficult for competitors to copy than are product quality and price'. Supporting product availability through such means as channel selection, market coverage, distribution systems and dealer support all help to nourish customer loyalty. So does logistics support of product characteristics (such as variety or product range) and of marketing initiatives (such as promotions).

2.3.2 Value disciplines

Figure 2.3 refers to 'perceived value'. A development of the service quality – product quality – price model is that of *value disciplines*. Instead of competing on all of these fronts equally, Treacy and Wiersema (1997) argue that companies taking

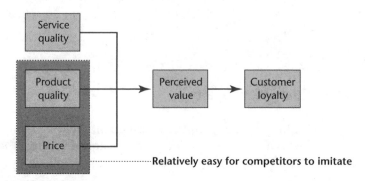

Figure 2.3 Key drivers of customer loyalty
(Source: After Parasuraman and Grewal, 2000)

leadership positions do so by narrowing their competitive focus, not by broadening it. They propose three strategies, or generic value disciplines that can be followed:

- *Operational excellence*. Here, the strategy centres on superb operations and execution, often by providing a reasonable quality at low price. The focus is on efficiency, streamlining operations, supply chain management, every-day low price. Most large international corporations use this discipline.

- *Product leadership*. Here, the leaders are very strong in innovation and brand marketing and operate in dynamic markets. The focus is on development, innovation, design, time-to-market and high margins in a short timeframe.

- *Customer intimacy*. Here, leaders excel in customer attention and customer service. They tailor their products and services towards individual or almost individual customers. The focus is on customer relationship management (see section 2.3.3): they deliver products and services on time and above customer expectations. They also look to life-time value concepts, reliability and being close to the customer.

Source: www.valuebasedmanagement.net/methods_valuedisciplines.html

While most organisations are under pressure to reduce prices, speed up delivery and improve customer service, the best will have a clear focus on their defined competitive strategy. This focus needs to be improved and adapted over time.

Activity 2.2

Using Treacy and Wiersema's value disciplines, revisit case studies 2.2 and 2.3 above. Have the organisations concerned lost focus?

2.3.3 Customer relationship management (CRM)

A development of customer intimacy is customer relationship management (CRM). The principle behind CRM is that marketing strategies are continuously extended in order to strengthen customer loyalty. Eventually, customer and supplier are so closely intertwined that it would be difficult to sever the relationship. In other words, the exit barriers become higher and higher. Figure 2.4 compares CRM thinking with traditional relationships that are limited to buying and selling functions of the organisations concerned (Payne *et al.*, 1995). We explore the issue of partnerships in the supply chain further in Chapter 9.

CRM thinking works particularly well for industrial marketing, or B2B situations. The next case study, Batman, illustrates the evolution of diamond-type relationships.

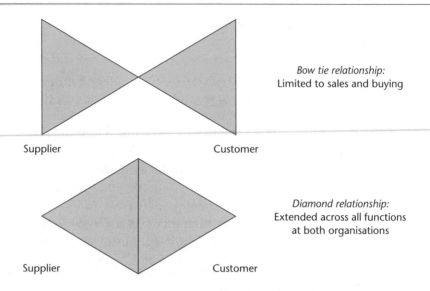

Bow tie relationship:
Limited to sales and buying

Supplier   Customer

Diamond relationship:
Extended across all functions
at both organisations

Supplier   Customer

Figure 2.4 Customer relationship management: bow tie and diamond
(Source: After Payne *et al.*, 1995)

CASE STUDY 2.5

Batman – adding value through quality of service

Everglo Battery, the premier battery manufacturer and service provider in South Africa, looked back on the development of its marketing strategy in four stages. Each had been signalled by advancing the concepts of what is meant by 'quality of service'. Stage 1 had been the basic product: a sealed lead–acid battery for use in mining applications. Batteries were regarded by customers as a mature product and as a 'grudge buy'. Each year, the basic product was under heavy downward price pressure. Stage 2 had been the industry reaction to customer service: the addition of warranty replacement of defective product, of quality assurance (QA) audits of a supplier's design and manufacturing processes, and of parts and service provision.

Stage 3 had recognised the need to go much further in terms of customer service. A whole raft of additional services had been conceived with a view to adding value. Breakdowns were fixed at short notice by means of field service engineers. Everglo products could now be delivered and installed at customer premises. Price lists were simplified by including peripheral equipment, such as contactors, that had to be added to a battery rack in order to make it work. Advice and tips were added to help customers warm to Everglo products. In a proactive move, Everglo introduced charts and advice about the application of battery products in general, and the resulting tables became an industry standard. Parts and service in the field were upgraded to a '24 hour, no-nonsense back-up service'. And customer training built on Everglo's position as an industry leader. Rather than sales seminars, Everglo's were customer training seminars, where the company spoke on behalf of the industry rather than as a supplier.

In spite of having reached a pre-eminent position in mining power supply, Everglo recognised that the centre of Figure 2.5 was in effect a 'black hole'. Each year, com-

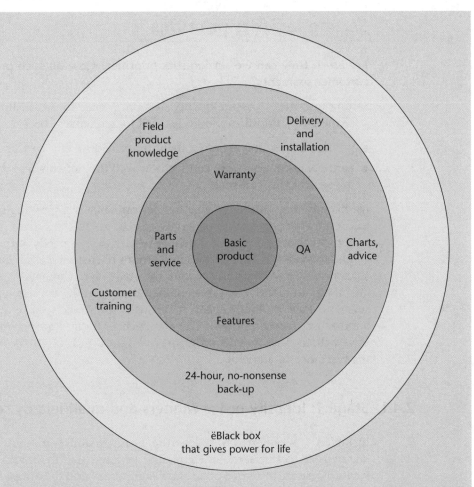

Figure 2.5 Adding value by quality of service

petitors added more services to their basic products too. In effect, the second and to some extent the third circles were being absorbed into the 'commodity' category, and customer expectations increased all the time. A new stage 4 strategy was conceived to take Everglo into a position that competitors would find it even more difficult to follow. The new strategy was coined 'Batman': battery management for life. The aim was nothing less than a total, customer-oriented product management service that provides 'power for life'. The supplier takes over the task of managing the customer's assets, including problem identification, training and managing cash flow. The objective of 'Batman' is to look at the product the way the customer does, performing best at what the customer values most rather than at what the supplier values most.

Questions

1 Has Everglo reached the end of the line in terms of its quality of service strategy?

2 As a competitor to Everglo, what would be your options in response to Everglo's latest moves?

2.4 Setting logistics priorities

Key issues: How can we set logistics priorities? How do such priorities relate to customer segments?

Setting priorities to assure quality of service leads to establishment of performance measures. Priorities should be used to help ensure that:

- partners in a supply network focus on providing end-customer value;
- partners in that network can see how well the network as a whole is performing against this yardstick.

In this way they can judge whether performance is improving or declining, and assess the effect on quality of service of changes to the system.

In order to set priorities for quality of service, the needs of the customer must be understood. It is necessary to find groups of customers that have similar needs that should be serviced in focused, targeted ways. The needs define groups and give them an identity, as we explained in section 2.2 on segmentation. Because segments have different needs, it is usually a mistake to take a 'one size fits all' approach to servicing them. The approach to finding groups in the market follows a three-stage process proposed in Figure 2.6. Each of these stages is examined in more detail below.

2.4.1 Stage 1: Identify order winners and qualifiers by segment

In Table 1.1, we referred to order winners and qualifiers in terms of *product ranges and the markets they serve*. In Figure 2.6, we have used the marketing term of *segments*. These are intended to be equivalent terms, and they must be clearly understood by different parts of the business. Each segment has different needs, and each need must be translated into its logistics equivalent. Thus a bottle of Coke

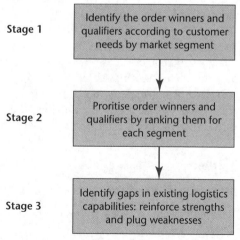

Figure 2.6 Three-stage process for creating logistics advantage

that is 'always within reach' translates into product availability objectives. 'Marketing speak' needs to be translated into logistics implications, the marketing vision into the logistics reality. Order winners and qualifiers thus act as a bridge between marketing and logistics, enabling general statements to be given form and substance. This requires that logistics and marketing explicitly align their roles in delivering value to the customer. Since order winners and qualifiers change over time, this alignment must be regularly updated *and* anticipated future trends included.

2.4.2 Stage 2: Prioritise order winners for each segment

The next stage is to prioritise the order winners for each segment. This is essentially a marketing-led task, and involves allocating points for each order winning criterion for each segment. A convenient way to do this is to allocate 100 percentage points across the order winners that have been identified. In this way, not only can the order of importance be found but also the scale of the difference in importance between criteria can be quantified. A further refinement is to involve sample customers from key market segments in this process, thereby gaining a 'reality check' in this somewhat subjective task.

The relative importance of these measures varies according to the relative priorities of the order winners for each segment. Segment A for example, may place a high priority on delivery speed. Here, response-related measures are the key measures of performance. Segment B on the other hand may place high priority on delivery consistency: speed is less important than dependable order cycle times. Having researched customer needs, the next step is to design a logistics system that delivers competitive service levels and to monitor performance of the system by means of suitably designed controls. We outline performance monitoring principles in sections 3.4 and 3.5 of Chapter 3.

Discussing the data with a cross-functional group in a workshop setting helps to spawn ideas on patterns. It is often easier to make sense of the data if they are used to plot graphs and charts. Venn diagrams such as the one shown in Figure 2.7 are helpful to illustrate patterns that may appear among the analysed data.

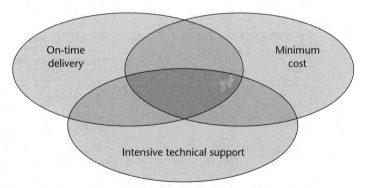

Figure 2.7 Customer segmentation using order winners

2.4.3 Stage 3: Identify gaps, reinforce strengths and plug weaknesses

Having prioritised order winners by segment, the third stage is to compare these priorities with current logistics performance. For example if on-time delivery has been given top priority for a given segment and current logistics performance is rated as poor relative to competitors, the direction of future logistics strategy will be clear. Note that there will be a need for *several different logistics strategies*, because each segment will reveal its own strengths and weaknesses relative to competitors. This point was initiated in section 1.4.3, where we showed how different products could have quite distinctive strategic needs. A common failure of strategy making is to assume a 'one size fits all' approach to logistics capabilities. Products that need more investment – not less – are left to compete internally for resources with products with low-cost needs. Crafting logistics strategy needs to address the differences inherent in different segments. Due attention must also be given to qualifiers that are identified for a given segment. Here, the issue is that logistics capabilities must support performance in the marketplace, so that they do not become *order losing* (see p. 21).

2.4.4 Using market segments to set logistics priorities

Undertaking the above three-stage process helps to create an action plan for creating logistics advantage. In order to ensure that progress is being made in the right directions, performance must be monitored over time against key measures for each segment. Table 2.6 lists examples of service level measures used in retail supply chains (Stern *et al.*, 1989).

Table 2.6 **Selected service level measurements**

Major category	Subcategory
Product availability	Line item availability, Product group availability, Invoice fill, Cases/units
Order cycle time	Order entry, Order processing, Total cycle time
Consistency	In order cycle time, In shipment despatch, In transit time, In arrival time, In warehouse handling
Response time	Order status, Order tracing, Backorder status, Order confirmation, Product substitution, Order shortages, Product information requests
Error rates	Shipment delays, Order errors, Picking and packing errors, Shipping and labelling errors
Product/shipment-related malfunction	Damaged merchandise, Merchandise refusals, Claims, Returned goods, Customer complaints
Special handling	Trans-shipment, Expedited orders, Panic deliveries, Special packaging, Customer backhauls

(Source: El-Ansary, Adel I., Brown, James R., Stern, Louis W., *Management in Marketing Channels*, 1st edn, © 1989. Reprinted by permission of Pearson Education Inc., Upper Saddle River, NJ)

These performance measures are all related to quality, time, cost and dependability advantages (*see* section 1.3.1, p. 16). The different performance priorities will reflect the different logistics strategies that have been identified at stage 3. Measures are used to track performance over time, to set improvement targets, and to benchmark a focal firm's performance against others. The process of setting logistics priorities (stages 1 to 4) is iterative: it needs to be repeated at regular time intervals to cope with the dynamics of the market place and with improving market understanding.

Summary

What is customer service in the context of logistics?

- Business to business (B2B) refers to upstream relationships between members of a network. Business to Customer (B2C) refers to hand-over to the end-customer. B2B relationships therefore need to be aligned towards B2C.

- Marketing is a philosophy that integrates the disparate activities and functions that take place within the network. Loyal customers are seen as the source of profit, growth and security. Marketing in practice starts with analysing segments, evaluating those segments and targeting them. Segments need to be measurable, economically viable, accessible and actionable. Marketing in practice continues by market positioning, which requires differential advantage to be defined, and the marketing mix to be formulated.

- The key logistics contribution to the marketing mix is in the 'fourth P', place. This includes decisions about factors such as channel selection, market coverage, distribution systems and dealer support. Logistics also supports product decisions (for example, product range) and promotion activity.

- Supply networks end with service processes, where the end-customer is present in some way. 'Gaps' can emerge between what the service is supposed to be, what the customer expects it to be, and how the customer perceives it when it is delivered. The size of these gaps has implications for quality of service, a major driver of customer loyalty.

How do we retain customers through logistics?

- The principle here is that loyal customers have many advantages over new ones. The logistics challenge is to reinforce loyalty by exceeding customer expectations via superior quality of service.

- Customer relationship management is based on the principle that marketing strategies should be continuously extended to strengthen customer loyalty. Phases of logistics development are needed, each phase placing increasing demands on the development of logistics capabilities.

- Setting logistics priorities should be carried out with market segments in mind. This is a joint task between marketing and logistics functions. Order winners and qualifiers by segment help develop a common language to assist this task.

Discussion questions

1 suggest ways in which logistics can play a part in the marketing mix for:
   a an airline;
   b a supermarket;
   c an automotive manufacturer;
   d a hospital.

In each case, specify the organisation you have in mind and explain the reasons for your suggestions.

2 The 'Batman' case (case study 2.5) presents what might be described as a 'marketing wish list'. Analyse the likely logistics challenges at each stage of development, and suggest how these might be addressed.

3 Read the case study 'Global Lighting', and answer the study questions at the end.

CASE STUDY 2.6

Global Lighting

This case study contains information on how Global's expectations of quality of service from its suppliers evolved over a number of years. Further changes are affecting these suppliers as Global's own customers continue to demand higher levels of service. If you are unfamiliar with the terms *kanban* and MRP, they are explained in Chapter 6.

Global is one of Britain's largest manufacturers of lighting products. The market for architectural lighting, one of its major product lines, has become increasingly volatile and competitive in recent years. Pressure to supply products more cheaply and more quickly to a higher standard on an international basis has meant that Global has had to work hard on shortening product life cycles and reducing delivery lead times.

During 1996, the new managing director raised the profile of logistics by making an appointment at board level. Following this change in organisational structure, a 'lean' approach to supply chain management and manufacturing was implemented over the next three years. But recently the lean approach to managing the supply chain has been found to have serious shortcomings in terms of meeting increased demand for customised products such as architectural lighting. Consequently, Global's supply chain management strategy has evolved to accommodate the rapid growth in the market for these products. This change resulted in a multifaceted supply chain strategy, which increases Global's ability to meet the mass customisation needs of its customer base. This multiple strategy approach has created many challenges for suppliers.

Prior to 1996

Before 1996 Global's organisation and management of its internal and external supply chains was based on a single, familiar approach. Global managed internal manufacturing operations and material flow on a push principle driven by MRP.

The supply base was managed through an essentially adversarial approach. The supply base was broad, as the strategy of the buying function of the company operated on the principle of lowest price is best. Buyers routinely moved the sourcing of components to a new supplier if the price was lower. New suppliers would be assessed on the basis of price and component quality only, and no obligation of repeat purchase was expected if the supplier did not retain the lowest price. Price, not cost, was the main objective of the buying group.

After 1996

During 1996, the managing director and his changed board of directors developed a new strategy to manage internal and external operations. Manufacturing was restructured to improve customer service and to increase profitability. Following an extensive programme of data collection and analysis, the production facility was segmented into two distinct sections. One section became a low-volume, irregular-demand factory employing operators with broad product knowledge. The other area became the high-volume, regular-demand factory, with focused and repetitive build tasks. These two areas also operated their internal supply chains in distinctly different formats. The low-volume area continued with a push (MRP) strategy, while the high-volume section operated a pull strategy using *kanban*, as shown in Table 2.7.

Table 2.7 **Focused factory structure**

	Low volume	High volume
Material control	MRP	*Kanban*
Product codes	>5,000	<800
Material flow	push	pull
Demand predictability	low	high
Minimum order quantity	1	pallet
Service offer	MTO	MTS

In addition to restructuring the internal supply chain, the historical approach to managing the external chain of suppliers was altered. Because materials constituted more than 80 per cent of the cost of sales, the decision was made to acknowledge vendors as an intrinsic part of the organisation. Improving the performance of the suppliers and the efficiency of the exchange between the firms was recognised as key to Global's success. In order to achieve the necessary improvements a four-phase plan was conceived. Figure 2.8 gives an overview of the four phases.

Phase 1: Supply base reduction
Before Global committed any substantial resource to develop its suppliers, it was necessary to reduce the number of companies that it dealt with. Reducing the number of direct suppliers was essential to maximise the limited time and resources available. In order to reduce the number of suppliers who dealt directly with Global, resourcing and tiering activities were put in place. Suppliers were selected for the ongoing supply base on the following criteria:

- ppm defects (quality performance);
- ability to operate with *kanban* system (delivery performance);
- CAD/CAM facilities (new product development);
- geographical location (new product development and delivery performance);
- price.

►

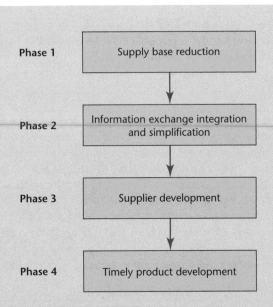

Figure 2.8 The four-phase plan for supplier improvement

If a supplier could not or planned not to operate in accordance with Global's quality, logistical or product development criteria, they were either delisted (and the components switched to another current supplier) or became a tier 2 supplier.

For example, the principal supplier of injection moulding components coordinated purchase and delivery of plastic parts from the other smaller suppliers, which had formerly all been tier 1. The 'before' and 'after' scenarios are shown in Figure 2.9.

The result of these activities was a reduction in direct supplier numbers from 267 to less than 100. This is shown in Table 2.8.

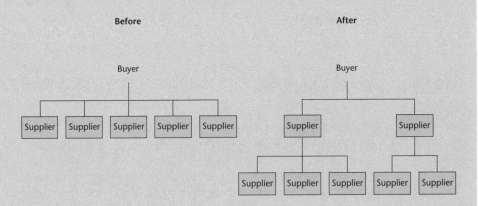

Figure 2.9 Restructuring the supplier base

Phase 2: Information exchange integration and simplification
Following the segmentation of the factory into low- and high-volume sections, and reduction of the supply base, it became possible to simplify communications between

Table 2.8 **Supplier reduction figures**

Year	No. of Suppliers
1995	267
1996	198
1997	132
1998	106
1999	<100

Global and its suppliers. The high-volume factory introduced, with the assistance and agreement of the suppliers, a two-bin, *kanban* material-ordering system. The support of the suppliers in introducing the simple material-ordering system was an early example of greater integration of working practices within the supply base. Only through the agreement of a new way of trading was it possible to stop posting weekly MRP schedules, which were out of step with 'real time' customer demand. Introduction of the *kanban* system reduced waste created by the delay in transmitting demand data. Similarly, waste related to inappropriate processing, unnecessary inventory, unnecessary motion, waiting and transporting was reduced.

Phase 3: Supplier development
Introducing *kanban* proved to be an early and rewarding example of supplier development for Global and its suppliers. However, development was not limited to one-off, functional improvements. Before improvements were attempted in the more complicated arena of new product development, it was planned to introduce cross-functional teams between Global and its supply base through team-building weekends. For example, the managing director of the main die-casting supplier attended a team-building weekend with Global engineers, sales people, manufacturing managers and finance personnel. This weekend experience prompted the die-caster to introduce team building within its own operation, thus helping to reduce new product development times between the two companies.

Phase 4: Timely product development
Lead times for new product development in the lighting industry in 1996 were typically 18–24 months. For an industry that was becoming more and more fashion conscious the time from concept to product delivery was proving costly in terms of competitiveness in the market.

One of the prime driving forces for Global's new management approach towards suppliers was the desire to reduce time and cost to market drastically. Suppliers within this new ethos became involved at the concept stage for new products. Product development activities became concurrent rather than sequential. Designers and engineers of suppliers with CAD and CAM technologies began to interact directly with Global's designers and engineers at each stage of the development process. At the same time, shopfloor operators became involved with designers to bring cohesion between design and build activities. The result of these changes in approach, internally and externally, was a reduction in development lead times for standard production items from 18 months to 14 weeks by early 1999.

▶

Outcomes

Restructuring Global's approach to managing suppliers would have provided limited benefits if it had not occurred in conjunction with changes to Global's internal operations. For example, improvements in the efficiency of the supply chain in terms of introducing a concept such as *kanban* would not have been as effective if a restructuring of manufacturing had not taken place at the same time. Simultaneous internal and external changes propelled Global's performance forward in terms of product development, cost and lead-time reduction, as shown in Table 2.9.

Table 2.9 **Changes between 1995 and 1998**

	1995	1998 MRP	1998 Kanban
Product codes	8000+	>5000	>800
Product development	24 months	6 months	6 months
Delivery lead-times	8–12 weeks	2–4 weeks	0–2 weeks
Costs (1995 index = 100)	100	85	73
Sales volume (1995 index = 100)	100	110	125

The performance improvements shown in Table 2.9 were achieved through the efforts of both supplier and buyer alike. Integration of supply chain activities and information flows accelerated the implementation of lean practices such as *kanban*, which in turn reduced the uncertainty in demand and improved relationships. Operational improvements followed a consistent and deliberate strategy of developing confidence, trust and openness between Global and its suppliers. Those who were prepared to work in partnership to develop improvements gained additional sales volumes, which in turn increased the interdependence of both parties.

Improvements in relational as well as operational performance developed a virtuous circle for both parties. Implementing pull scheduling in the supply base necessitated the simultaneous implementation of a partnering strategy. The demise of the traditional 'arm's length' approach to managing the buyer–supplier exchange helped both parties to improve their business volumes and performance over this period.

(Source: Jim Aitken)

Questions

The next phase of development at Global addresses the continuing growth in demand for customised, non-standard products. Linked to an ever-increasing demand for customisation is the drive for shorter lead times and lower costs. With increasing globalisation of the lighting market, several parts of Global's product portfolio became commodity in nature. Customers in the United Kingdom now have the opportunity to purchase their lighting products from low labour cost countries such as China. But supplying the lowest-price product is not the answer to this problem for UK companies. Instead of competing on price, companies must find alternative ways to retain their customers. One way is through the improvement of customer service.

1 What actions do you think Global could take to respond to the needs of its customers?

2 How will Global's own customer service priorities change as a result of this?

3 What are the opportunities and threats facing suppliers as a result of the likely changes to Global's quality of service priorities?

References

Berry, L.L. (1999) *Discovering the Soul of Service: The nine drivers of sustainable business success*. New York: Free Press.

Daniel, D, White, A., Harrison, A. and Ward, J. (2003) *The Future of e-Hubs: Findings of an International Delphi Study,* Information Systems Research Centre and Centre for Logistics and SCM, Cranfield School of Management.

Doyle, P. (1994) *Marketing Management and Strategy*. New York: Prentice-Hall International.

Doyle, P. (2000) *Value-Based Marketing: Marketing strategies for corporate growth and shareholder value*. Chichester: Wiley.

Gattorna, J. (1998) *Strategic Supply Chain Alignment*: *Best practice in supply chain management*. Gower: Aldershot.

Godsell, J. and Harrison A. (2002) 'Strategy formulation in an FMCG supply chain', *Proceedings of the EurOMA Conference*, Copenhagen.

Hutter, L. (1998) *Focusing on Customers: The role of technology in business*, Introduction. London: Deloitte Consulting/Euromoney Publications.

Johnston, R. and Clark, G. (2001) *Service Operations Management*. London: Financial Times/Prentice Hall.

Kotler, P., Armstrong, G., Saunders, J. and Wang, V. (2004) *Principles of Marketing*, 10th edn. Hemel Hempstead: Prentic Hall Europe.

McCarthy, E. J. (1964) *Basic Marketing: a managerial approach*. Homewood, IL: Irwin.

McGoldrick, P. (2002) *Retail Marketing*, 2nd edn. Maidenhead: McGraw-Hill Education Europe.

Millier P. and Palmer, R. (2000) *Nuts, Bolts and Magnetrons: A practical guide for industrial marketers*. Chichester: Wiley.

Parasuraman, A., Berry, L. and Zeithaml, V. (1991) 'Understanding customer expectations of service', *Sloan Management Review*, Spring, pp. 39–48.

Parasuraman, A. and Grewal, D. (2000) 'The impact of technology on the quality-value-loyalty chain: a research agenda', *Journal of the Academy of Marketing Science*, Vol. 28 No. 1, pp. 168–74.

Payne, A., Christopher, M., Clark, M. and Peck, H. (1995) *Relationship Marketing for Competitive Advantage*. Oxford: Butterworth Heinemann.

Piercy, N. (2002) *Market-led Strategic Change*, 3rd edn. Oxford: Butterworth Heinemann.

Stern, L.W., El-Ansary, A.I. and Brown, J.R. (1989) *Management in Marketing Channels*. Englewood Cliffs, NJ: Prentice-Hall.

Treacy, M. and Wiersema, F. (1994) *The Discipline of Market Leaders*. Reading, MA: Addison-Wesley Publishing Co.

Webster, F. (2000) 'Understanding the relationships among brands, consumers and retailers', *Journal of the Academy of Marketing Science*, Vol. 28, pp. 17–23.

Zeithaml, V., Berry, L. and Parasuraman A. (1988) 'Communication and control processes in the delivery of service quality', *Journal of Marketing*, Vol. 52, pp. 35–48.

Suggested further reading

Christopher, M. and Peck, H. (2003) *Marketing Logistics*, 2nd edn. Oxford: Butterworth-Heinemann.

Doyle, P. (2000) *Value-Based Marketing*. Chichester: Wiley.

McDonald, M. and Dunbar, I. (2001) *Market Segmentation,* 3rd edn. Oxford: Butterworth Heinemann.

CHAPTER 3

Value and logistics costs

The planned outcomes of this chapter are to:

- explain the concept of value and its implications for managing the supply chain;
- explain how total costs can be divided up in different ways, and how they can be applied to managing the supply chain;
- identify how better cost information can be used to create more value.

By the end of this chapter you should be able to understand:

- what is meant by the term 'value creation';
- how logistics costs can be managed for better value creation;
- how activity-based management can be used to identify the cost drivers in your business.

Introduction

In section 1.3 of Chapter 1 we reviewed the way in which different products may have different logistics strategies. While the range of standard shirts compete on price and brand, and demand is relatively stable over the year, fashion blouses compete on style and brand. For a fashion product, the logistics challenge is to be able to support highly uncertain demand in the marketplace. The logistics task for the two supply chains is essentially different, and some companies refer to a 'supply chain for every product' to emphasise this difference.

Here, we develop the information flow aspects of our model in Figure 1.4. We also show how there is another flow in supply chains – *funds flow*. Funds flow in the opposite direction to materials. Funds – in the form of cash – originate from the end-customer, and are used to pay the bills progressively from one supply chain partner to the next upstream. While funds flow has not yet been included in the logistics domain, the fair allocation of funds between supply chain partners will no doubt be an increasingly important aspect of logistics in the twenty-first century.

This chapter probes the cost and performance implications of different logistics strategies. While it may be clear that cost must form a central plank of supply chain strategy for standard shirts, that is not to say that the management team in the fashion blouses company can ignore the cost implications of their actions.

The common theme is the concept of *value*, and the extent to which both management teams are creating value for the end-customer.

While value is based on *cost* from the point of view of the company accountant, the concept of value may have different interpretations outside the company. From the shareholder's point of view, value is determined by the *best alternative use* of a given investment. In other words, value is greatest where the return on investment is highest.

<table>
<tr><td>**Key issues**</td><td>*This chapter addresses five key issues:*</td></tr>
</table>

1 **Where does value come from:** different views of value, and how it can be measured using return on investment.

2 **How can logistics costs be represented:** three different ways to divide up total costs.

3 **Activity-based costing:** a process-based alternative to allocating overheads.

4 **A balanced measurement portfolio:** balancing the needs of all stakeholders.

5 **Supply chain operations reference model (SCOR):** a further process-based approach to measuring supply chain costs and performance.

The chapter assumes a basic knowledge of a profit/loss account and balance sheet. If finance is not your long suit, then a helpful accompanying financial text is *Management Accounting for Non-Specialists* (Atrill and McLaney, 2004). We acknowledge the assistance from our colleague at Cranfield, Sri Srikanathan, for his help with this chapter. Figures 3.1 to 3.7 and Table 3.2 are from his lectures.

3.1 Where does value come from?

Key issue: **How can shareholder value be defined? What is economic value added, and how does it help in this definition?**

Creating shareholder value is widely used today to describe the main objective of a business. In its simplest form, shareholder value is created when the shareholder gets a better return by investing in your business than from a comparable investment. A *comparable investment* is one that has a similar level of risk. You might make the same return on €100 000 from playing roulette as you do from buying a house, but the risk profiles are very different! In order for a business to create superior shareholder value, it must have a competitive advantage. Return on investment (ROI) is an important measure that is widely used to assess shareholder value.

3.1.1 Return on investment (ROI)

One way of looking at the creation of shareholder value is to end the year with a lot more money than at the start. If this extra money results from profitable trading, then management has been successful in *improving the productivity of cap-*

ital. Return on investment (ROI) is measured as profit (in €) before interest and tax as a percentage of capital employed (also in €):

% ROI = 100 × € Profit / € Capital employed

The term 'investment' is used because capital employed is equivalent to the money invested in the business. ROI can also be seen as the outcome of profitability and asset utilisation:

$$\text{ROI} = \frac{\text{Profit}}{\text{Sales}} \times \frac{\text{Sales}}{\text{Capital employed}}$$

Let us look at the detail behind each of these ratios, and the way they fit in with each other. Figure 3.1 gives a family tree of the way return on investment is made up. Let us look at the potential for improving each from a point of view of managing the supply chain better.

Sales

Superior customer service improves sales, and makes our company more valued to the customer in the long term.

● Improving customer responsiveness is a key goal for managing the supply chain.

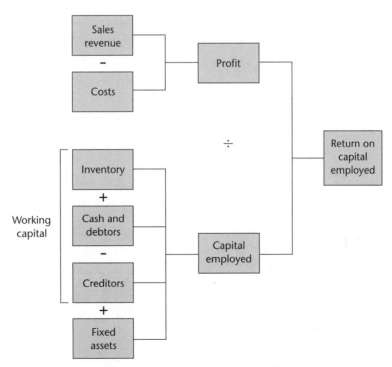

Figure 3.1 The make-up of return on capital employed (investment)
(Source: Courtesy of Sri Srikanthan)

Costs

The supply chain is a potential gold mine for making bottom line improvements to business performance. But directors of many businesses are impatient for cost improvement, and consider that cutting stocks and headcount is all that is needed. This may achieve short-term margin improvement, but strategic supply chain management is about improving the way things are done and hence improving long-term performance.

- Supply chain modelling shows that manufacturing and distribution costs together with inventories can be optimised while customer service is maximised.
- Studies in efficient consumer response (ECR) have shown that cutting out non-value-added products and inefficient promotional activity can reduce overall costs by 6 per cent. (ECR is discussed in Chapter 8.)

Working capital

Note that the combination of inventory, cash and debtors *less* creditors is called working capital. Each of the elements of working capital is considered in turn.

Inventory

This is a major asset in many businesses. It is there to buffer uncertainty of supply and demand, and to permit immediate availability when replenishment times are too lengthy. However, inventory is often regarded as a hindrance rather than a help: it ties up cash, it needs resources to be stored and it becomes obsolete!

- A primary goal for supply chain management is to replace inventory with information. Try to minimise the use of forecasts and to increase the use of real demand.
- Question any means for automatically replenishing inventory.

Cash and debtors

The key task here is to make the time between receipt of customer order and receipt of the cash as short as possible. Progress against this ideal not only makes the company more competitive by reducing lead times, but also improves its cash position. This means that business processes from sales order processing to distribution should be integrated and free from waste.

- Debtors (customers who owe us money) can be minimised by basic controls such as regular review and problem resolution. Sending out incomplete invoices is an invitation for non-payment!

Creditors

Creditors are people we owe money to. In supply chain terms, this term applies mainly to our suppliers. Many organisations think that lengthy payment terms to suppliers maximise credit and therefore improve the balance sheet. The downside of this thinking is that suppliers factor in the credit terms to their prices, and their own balance sheets become saddled with debt.

- Plan material requirements and distribution requirements to maximise flow of parts through the supply chain as needed.
- Discipline goods inwards to check delivery date, quality and correct prices. There is no point in starting the credit cycle early!
- If the supplier is a smaller company, it may be that the cost of capital is higher than it is for your company. It may be worthwhile to consider negotiating with the supplier to pay early, and therefore getting a share of the money that the supplier is paying in interest to the bank.

Fixed assets

The value-generating assets of a business that form the focus of supply chain management are a heavy drain on capital. They include manufacturing facilities, transport and distribution. They contribute to high *fixed costs* for an operation: that is, costs that do not change much with throughput. Such costs are therefore highly volume sensitive, as we shall see.

- Many organisations respond by a 'maximum variable, minimum fixed' policy. This is helped by *outsourcing* all but the core capabilities, which are retained in-house. Thus transport and warehousing are today often outsourced to specialist 'third-party logistics providers' such as Exel and UPS.

Activity 3.1

1 Review the categories in Figure 3.1 and compile your own list of the way in which these categories can be influenced (made better or worse) in an organisation.
2 What are the implications for supply chain strategy?

3.1.2 Financial ratios and ROI drivers

ROI is an important measure for assessing shareholder value and is underpinned by two main drivers:

- increased profitability;
- increased asset utilisation.

As discussed section 3.1.1, these two supporting drivers are the key determinants for increasing ROI and hence shareholder value. An understanding of the financial ratios that affect these two drivers is essential when formulating an organisation's supply chain strategy. While financial ratios are based on historical information, and therefore have limitations, they have a number of advantages for an organisation. They can be:

- a benchmark for comparing one organisation with another ;
- used as a comparator for a particular industrial sector;
- used to track past performance;
- a motivator for setting performance targets;
- an early warning indicator if the organisation's performance starts to decline.

Table 3.1 provides a guide to linking ROI and its drivers with the financial ratios for a manufacturing company (CIMA, 1989).

This form of analysis can be applied to benchmark an existing operation with a competitor, or it can be used to assess the implications on ROI against potential trade-offs, such as comparing an in-house operation with a third party outsourcing opportunity.

The use of financial ratios in relation to time are key to monitoring working capital and the 'cash to cash' cycle. Key time-related ratios include:

- *Average inventory turnover*: the number of times inventory is turned over in relation to the cost of good sold.
- *Average settlement period for debtors*: the time taken for customers to pay their invoices.
- *Average settlement period for creditors:* the time taken for an organisation to pay its creditors.

Reductions in working capital will have a beneficial effect on an organisation's ROI. For example, inventory reductions increase on both profitability (reduced costs) and capital (increased asset utilisation). Supply chain decisions have an impact on costs *and* assets, so they affect both the drivers of ROI. Understanding the trade-offs involved is key to increasing value.

Table 3.1 ROI and its key drivers

Level 1	Level 2	Level 3	Level 4
Return on investment	Net profit / Sales	Production costs as a % of sales	Pay costs as a % of sales Materials as a % of sales
		Selling costs as a % of sales	Pay costs as a % of sales
		Administration costs as a % of sales	Pay costs as a % of sales
	Sales / Total assets	Fixed assets as a % of sales	Property as a % of sales Plant as a % of sales Vehicles as a % of sales
		Current assets as a % of sales	Inventory as a % of sales Debtors as a % of sales Cash as a % of sales

Section 3.2 of this chapter tackles the issues concerning the visibility of costing information.

3.2 How can logistics costs be represented?

Key issues: What are the various ways of cutting up the total cost 'cake', and what are the relative merits of each?

We all have a pretty good idea of what the total costs of a business are in practice. The costs of such items as materials used, power and wages all lead to bills that have to be paid. What is not so clear is how these costs should be allocated to supply chain processes – or even to products for that matter. Christopher (1998) states that problems with traditional cost accounting as related to logistics include:

● the true costs of servicing different customer types, channels and market segments are poorly understood;

● costs are captured at too high a level of aggregation;

● costing is functionally oriented at the expense of output;

● the emphasis on full cost allocation to products ignores customer costs.

This section reviews commonly used ways of representing costs (fixed and variable, direct and indirect), and one less commonly used way (engineered and discretionary). If you are already familiar with the concepts of variable and fixed costs and break-even charts, then start at section 3.3. Bear in mind that the total cost picture is always the same; the different ways of representing them are simply different ways of 'cutting the cake'. Let us look at the total cost as a cube instead of a cake. Then the three different ways of representing costs can be shown as different ways of cutting up the cube (Figure 3.2).

The important point here is that the total cost is constant: it is the ways we *analyse* that cost that are different. Why analyse it in different ways? To gain better information about our cost basis so that we can manage the business better. Let us look in turn at each of these ways to cut the total cost cube.

3.2.1 Fixed/variable

One popular way of analysing costs is to consider the effect of *volume of activity* on them. Costs tend to respond differently as the volume changes:

● *fixed costs* tend to stay the same as volume of activity changes, or at least, within a given volume range;

● *variable costs* change as the volume of activity changes.

Fixed costs include things such as warehouse rental, which is charged on a time basis (€/month). As volume of activity increases, additional warehouses may be

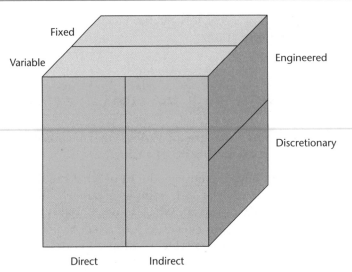

Figure 3.2 Three ways to cut the 'total cost cube'
(Source: Courtesy of Sri Srikanthan)

added round Europe, and we get the familiar *stepped fixed costs*, as shown in Figure 3.3. The same relationship would apply if volumes were reduced and a warehouse closed.

Variable costs include things such as direct materials, which are ordered in line with demand. If demand increases, we buy more. Starting with zero cost at zero activity, variable costs increase roughly in line with volume, as shown in Figure 3.4.

If we add the variable costs to the fixed costs against a given range of volume (so that the fixed costs remain completely fixed), and add in the sales revenue (which also increases in line with volume), we arrive at the break-even chart shown in Figure 3.5. The sloping line that starts at O is the sales revenue. The total cost line starts at F, and represents the sum of fixed and variable costs. The point at which the sales revenue line crosses the total cost line is the break-even point. Below this point, a loss will be incurred; above it a profit will be made.

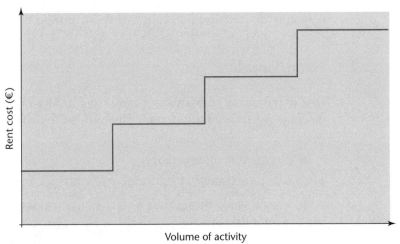

Figure 3.3 Rent cost against volume of activity
(Source: Courtesy of Sri Srikanthan)

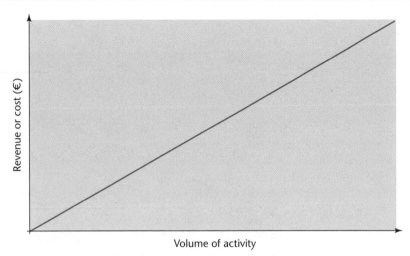

Figure 3.4 Direct material costs against volume of activity
(Source: Courtesy of Sri Srikanthan)

A helpful concept in evaluating break-even charts is that of contribution:

Contribution = Sales less variable costs

Therefore contribution is the fixed costs plus the profit. Contribution is useful in decision making. High contribution per unit indicates a more volatile business: that is, one that is more risky. Therefore we should expect a business with high contribution/unit to provide a higher return on investment in the longer term. Look at the two break-even charts in Figures 3.6 and 3.7. What are the differences between the two situations? What has happened to the break-even point, and why?

Chart A shows a situation with high variable costs and low fixed costs. In chart B, the situation is reversed. The break-even point has moved well to the right: that is, chart B requires a higher volume to break even than A. This is because a much higher volume of sales is needed to cover the high level of fixed costs.

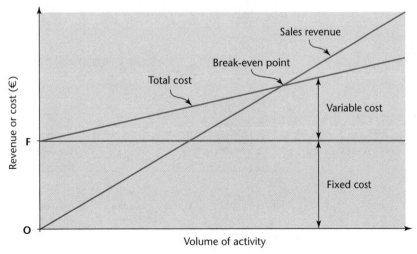

Figure 3.5 Break-even chart
(Source: Courtesy of Sri Srikanthan)

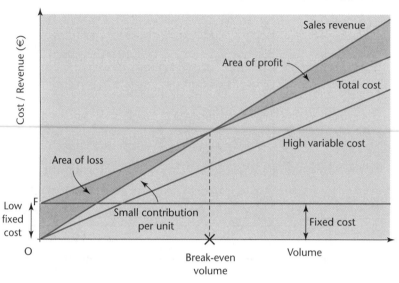

Figure 3.6 Break-even chart A
(Source: Courtesy of Sri Srikanthan)

Furthermore, additional volume has a small impact on chart A, whereas it has a much higher impact on chart B. So high fixed costs and low variable costs lead to greater volume sensitivity. Accordingly, profitability (the area above the break-even point) is affected much more by volume changes in chart B. In terms of contribution, chart A represents a situation with low contribution/unit, and therefore low risk in comparison with chart B.

The supply chain implications of such considerations are that we are most often faced with chart B situations. For example, core resources such as warehousing and distribution systems create little opportunity to reduce investments

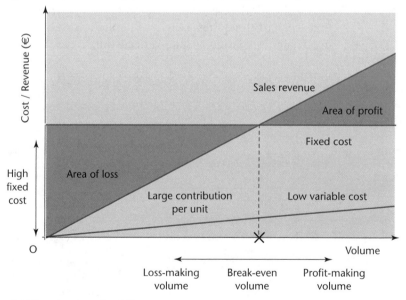

Figure 3.7 Break-even chart B
(Source: Courtesy of Sri Srikanthan)

in line with reducing sales volumes other than the step changes shown in Figure 3.3. We are back to the advice for increasing ROI given in section 3.1.1 above: to increase sales and reduce costs. The reassuring point is that every 1 per cent increase in sales or 1 per cent reduction in costs has a leveraged effect on profits.

CASE STUDY 3.1

Bond plc – a marginal costing example

Bond plc is planning to manufacture a new product with an initial sales forecast of 3,600 units in the first year at a selling price of €800 each. The finance department has calculated that the variable cost for each truck will be €300. The fixed costs for the manufacturing facility for the year are €1,500,000. Using the information provided by the sales forecast and the finance department it is now possible to calculate the planned profit, the contribution and the break-even point for this venture by leveraging the nature of fixed and variable costs.

Planned profit	€	Planned break-even point	€
Sales revenue	2,880,000	Fixed costs	1,500,000
Less variable costs	1,080,000	Contribution per unit	
Contribution	**1,800,000**	Sales value – variable cost	500
Less fixed costs	1,500,000	Break-even point (units)	
Profit	**300,000**	Fixed costs/Contribution per unit	3,000

If Bond plc achieves its sales forecast of 3,600 units then the company will make a planned profit before tax of €300,000. Crucially the company's break-even point is 3,000 units at which point Bond plc makes no profit but also no loss, because sales revenue (€2,400,000) equals all the variable costs (€900,000) and all the total fixed costs associated with production process (€1,500,000). Any additional unit sold after this point will provide Bond with profitable sales revenue. The difference between the planned profit and the break-even point is called the margin of safety. In the case of Bond plc this equates to 600 units.

(Source: Simon Templar, Cranfield)

Questions

What happens to the break-even point if:

1 Fixed costs increase by 10 per cent?

2 The sales price reduces by 5 per cent?

3.2.2 Direct/indirect

Another way to cut up the total cost 'cube' is to analyse costs in terms of whether or not they can be directly allocated to a given product. Two further categories emerge:

- *Direct costs* can be tied to specific products. The most obvious examples are direct labour and direct materials. Thus we can allocate exactly the cost of bought-in parts to the products into which they are built.

- *Indirect costs* are whatever is left over after direct costs have been allocated. Indirect costs are also called 'overheads', and include everything from the managing director's salary to the rent rates paid for the distribution centre – anything that cannot be allocated directly to a given product.

Directness of costs is concerned with the extent to which costs can be allocated directly to given products. This is a completely different concept from that of fixed/variable costs. While there is a tendency to associate fixed costs with indirect and variable with direct, there is no necessary relationship at all. Thus direct labour costs tend to be fixed, at least in the short term.

As stated above, the reason for analysing costs differently is *to gain better information about our cost basis so that we can manage the business better*. Direct and indirect costs help us to decide the full cost of a product or service when more than one are offered. If there were just a single product, life would be easy, because all of the costs could be allocated to that one product. Most businesses are much more complex than that, and are faced with the issue of how indirect costs should be apportioned to products. The most popular way to spread indirect costs is on the basis of direct labour. This is not the 'correct way', nor is it the only way.

One way in which to get a closer view of how fixed costs behave by product is to use a method called *direct product profitability* (DPP). This method has been widely used in the retail industry to understand the way in which logistics costs behave for each product. The understanding is achieved by allocating fixed costs by making assumptions about how these are incurred by a product as it moves through the logistics system.

A good DPP system should take account of all the significant differences in the ways products are developed, sourced, produced, sold and distributed. In order to make this analysis practical, products will normally need to be grouped together. Product groups need to recognise shared technologies, processes, fixed assets, raw material inputs and packaging methods. The key objective of product groupings is to remove the need for apportioning costs, and thereby not to apportion profit across the products.

An example DPP is shown for a manufacturing company in Table 3.2. Note that not all of the fixed costs have been assigned. DPP assumes that only those costs that can rationally be allocated may be deducted. Thus DPP may be viewed as a development of direct/indirect costing in that it attempts to convert into direct costs logistics costs that would otherwise have been regarded as fixed. In this way, DPP seeks to provide more accurate information about which products are contributing most to profitability – and which are contributing least.

The principle at stake here is that good accounting and financial analysis force us to ask more questions about what is going on in our business. DPP can have a role to play here: it attempts to allocate logistics costs more specifically to products (and, in this case, orders as well) than is possible by spreading 'fixed' costs on the basis of an assumption such as direct labour. The assumption would otherwise be that direct labour actually 'drives' the overheads, which is highly doubtful.

Table 3.2 Direct product profitability (DPP)

	€	€
Gross sales for product group		X
● Less product-specific discounts and rebates		X
Net sales by product		X
● Less direct costs of product		X
Gross product contribution		X
● Less product-based marketing expenses	X	
Product-specific direct sales support costs	X	
● Less product-specific direct transportation costs:		
Sourcing costs	X	
Operations support	X	
Fixed-assets financing	X	
Warehousing and distribution	X	
Inventory financing	X	
Order, invoice and collection processing	X	X
● Less product-attributable overheads		X
Direct product profitability		X

(Source: Courtesy of Sri Srikanthan)

CASE STUDY 3.2

Direct product profitability

Filmco makes two thin film (gauge = 12μm) products for packaging applications in the food industry. Product A is coated so that it can subsequently be printed on; product B is uncoated. There is no changeover time on the production line, because all that needs to happen is that the coating drum is switched on or off. Once produced on the film-making lines, the film is slit to width and to length to customer order. Roughly 40 per cent of Filmco's output is A, and 60 per cent B, and film-making takes place 360 days/year on a continuous basis because of the high capital cost of the process.

A DPP study was carried out at Filmco to determine the relative profitability of the two products A and B by major customer. The method was adapted from that shown in Table 3.1 because Filmco is a manufacturing environment. Here is how it was done:

a Invoice price: this was the total sales value invoiced to the customer.

b Cost of placing orders: the total cost of the sales office (salaries, etc.) was divided by the number of orders dispatched that month. This cost per order (€150) was allocated to each order placed by each customer.

c Manufacturing cost: a variable cost for each product was found by collecting raw material, labour, power, packaging and waste costs. Manufacturing overheads (fixed costs) were allocated on the basis of direct labour. Because of the small difference in manufacturing methods, the manufacturing costs for the two products were similar. They were €2,107 for A and €2,032 for B.

d Storage costs: the total cost of the warehousing operation is €800k/year. There are 8,300 pallet locations, and the cost/day for a pallet was calculated as €0.30 assuming 360 working days. The storage cost for a given order was calculated as the number of pallets × the number of days × €.30.

▶

e Opportunity costs: orders must wait in the warehouse until the last reel has been produced. An order with a value of €3,000 that stays for seven days in the warehouse
   with an interest rate of 14 per cent is said to have an opportunity cost of €8.20.
f Transport cost: this was based on a price per tonne delivered to a given customer.
g Total cost: this was the sum of b to f for a given order.
h DPP: this was sales price less total cost g.

Table 3.3 gives a sample of the DPPs for four orders for customer P. The average DPP
for customer P over all orders shipped over a given month was 19.6 per cent, while that
for customer Q was 23.1 per cent and customer R was 33.0 per cent.

Table 3.3 DPP for customer P for a sample of four orders in a given month

Order no.	Film	Weight (t)	a	b	c	d	e	f	g	h
186232	A	482	1,210	150	876	1.08	1.88	79	1,108	8.4%
185525	A	2,418	5,997	150	4,344	7.83	9.33	190	4,702	21.6%
185187	B	4,538	13,000	150	8,402	20.80	30.33	343	8,946	31.2%
185351	B	2,615	7,576	150	4,897	14.58	17.68	198	5,277	30.3%

Question

1 What can we tell from the above analysis in Table 3.3 and the average DPPs per customer? (Consider in particular the differences in DPP between the four orders shown,
  and between the three customers P, Q and R.)

3.2.3 Engineered/discretionary

A third way of analysing costs is to consider *the ease of allocating* them. Some
things are easy to cost; others may require considerable thought and analysis
because they are difficult to cost under current methods. This line of thinking
creates a third way of cutting the total cost cube:

- *Engineered costs* have a clear input–output relationship. In other words, the
  benefit of a given cost is measurable. For example, if it takes 10 hours to produce 10 boxes of product A in the factory, then we have a clear output benefit
  (1 box) for the cost of each hour of input.

- *Discretionary costs* do not have a clear input–output relationship. Here, the
  input cost is clear but the output benefit is unclear. For example, the cost of
  the contract cleaners who clean the factory is clear, but the benefit they produce is not easily quantifiable.

The challenge is to convert discretionary costs into engineered costs, so that we
can quantify better the competitive impact of a given course of action. A classic
example of converting discretionary costs into engineered costs has been the
conversion of 'quality' as a discretionary concept into engineered 'quality costs'
(Dale and Plunkett, 1995). This was achieved by breaking down the concept of
quality into three cost drivers:

- *Prevention.* This comprises the costs of measures to prevent defects from taking place, such as training and process capability studies.
- *Appraisal.* This comprises the costs incurred in detecting defects, which would include testing and inspection.
- *Internal and external failure.* Internal costs are scrap, rework and the associated costs of not getting it right the first time. External failure costs are rectification after products have reached the final customer, such as warranty claims, returns and repairs.

In this case, it was argued, greater investment in prevention would result in the overall cost of quality being reduced over time.

The principle is to convert discretionary costs into engineered costs where possible. As indicated in the above examples, it is usually possible to make an estimate of what the engineered costs are, perhaps accompanied by a sensitivity or risk analysis. Without such guidelines, decisions would have to be taken on 'gut feel' – or, as usually happens, not taken at all! In other words, the logistics team may have an excellent project for increased flexibility in the distribution centre, but because they have not quantified the savings (outputs) the application for funding is rejected.

CASE STUDY 3.3

Glup SA

Glup SA supplies a range of household soaps to supermarkets in northern Europe. There are 12 stock-keeping units (skus) in the range. The logistics manager has determined that an investment of €0.5 million on improved material handling equipment would convert the main distribution centre into a more flexible facility. A number of benefits in improved product availability have been identified – but current information is largely in the form of discretionary costs. Glup's assessment of the benefits and its plans to convert the justification into engineered costs are outlined below.

Improved in-store availability

This is the percentage time for which a product is available on the shelf. If the product is not available on the shelf, then it will lose sales to competitive products that are available, such as supermarket own brands. (Availability is a classic 'order losing sensitive' qualifying criterion as described in section 1.3, Chapter 1.) Current available data at Glup are scant, but suggest that average in-store availability is as low as 85 per cent for a given stock-keeping unit (sku). In order to convert this discretionary benefit into an engineered cost, Glup intends to measure the time for which each of the 12 product lines is unavailable each week. One way to do this is to use a market research agency to conduct sample studies of product availability in selected stores at random times across the working week. This will yield an availability guide, such as the 85 per cent figure referred to. The new system will, it is believed, reduce this unavailable time. Glup then plans to model the new material-handling equipment methods using simulation, and to calculate the new in-store availability. The reduced non-availability time could then be converted into additional contribution for each sku to give an engineered cost saving.

▶

Reduced transportation costs

The new equipment would also allow lower transportation costs, because trays of different skus could be mixed together on the same pallet. Glup again intends to use simulation modelling to identify the opportunities for savings using this method. It is considered that this will offer the opportunity to reduce overall transport costs by more flexible loading of the trailers used to distribute the products to Glup's customers.

Promotions and new product launches

It is considered that the new equipment will enable promotions and new product launches to be delivered to selected stores more accurately and more quickly. Demand uncertainty in such situations is very high: for example, a recent 'three for the price of two' promotion created a fivefold increase in sales. In order to launch a new product it is first necessary to drain the pipeline of old product, or to 'write it off' as obsolete stock. If the more flexible warehouse system can reduce the length of the pipeline from factory to supermarket, it is argued, then a real saving in time or obsolete stock is possible. Glup again intends to measure this by simulation. It will then be necessary to determine by how much sales will increase as a result of the new product advantages. This will be estimated by Glup marketing people, who will use experience of previous promotions and new product launches. The engineered cost will be the additional time for which the new product is available multiplied by the additional estimated sales volume multiplied by the contribution per unit. Alternatively, it will be the reduction in obsolete stocks multiplied by the total cost per product plus any costs of double handling and scrapping.

Question

1 Comment on Glup's plans to create engineered costs from the perceived benefits of the new material-handling equipment.

3.3 Activity-based costing (ABC)

Key issues: **What are the shortcomings of traditional cost accounting from a logistics point of view? How can costs be allocated to processes so that better decisions can be made?**

The driving force behind activity-based costing (ABC) is that the traditional way of allocating indirect costs by spreading them to products on the basis of direct labour is becoming difficult to manage. While direct labour used to constitute a substantial portion of product costs, today that rarely applies. Therefore overhead rates of 500 per cent on direct labour are not uncommon. Just a small change in direct labour content would lead to a massive change in product cost.

Cooper and Kaplan (1988) explain the problem by referring to two factories: Simple and Complex. Both factories produce 1 million ballpoint pens each year; they are the same size and have the same capital equipment. But while Simple produces only blue pens, Complex produces hundreds of colour and style variations in volumes that range from 500 (lavender) to 100,000 (blue) units per year. A visitor would notice many differences between the factories. Complex has far more production support staff to handle the numerous production loading and scheduling challenges, changeovers between colours and styles, and so on. Complex would also have more design change issues, supplier scheduling problems, and outbound warehousing, picking and distribution challenges. There would be much higher levels of idle time, overtime, inventory, rework and scrap because of the difficulty of balancing production and demand across a much bigger product range. Because overheads are allocated on the basis of direct labour, blue pens are clobbered with 10 per cent of the much higher Complex overheads. The market price of blue pens is determined by focused factories such as Simple, so the blue pens from Complex appear to be unprofitable. As a result, the management of Complex considers that specialist products such as lavender – which sell at a premium – are the future of the business, and that blue pens are low priority. This strategy further increases overheads and costs, and perpetuates the myth that the unit cost of each pen is the same. Traditional cost systems often understate profits on high-volume products and overstate profits on low-volume, high-variety products. ABC principles would help the management of Complex to make more informed product decisions. The management of Simple has no need for another costing system; the current one works well for them.

ABC recognises that overhead costs do not just happen, but are caused by activities, such as holding products in store. ABC therefore seeks to break the business down into major processes – such as manufacture, storage and distribution – and then break each process into activities. For example, the distribution process would include such activities as picking, loading, transport and delivery. For each of these activities, there must be one cost driver: what is it that drives cost for that activity? For example, the cost driver for the storage activity may be the volume of a case, whereas the transport activity may be driven by weight. Once we know the cost driver, we need to know how many units of that cost driver are incurred for that activity, and the cost per unit for the cost driver. For example, the cost driver for the transportation activity may be the number of kilometres driven, and the cost per kilometre would be the cost per unit of the cost driver. This yields the cost of the activity and, when summed across all of the activities in a process, the total cost of that process.

ABC is difficult to implement because we need first to understand what the discrete processes are in a business where the existing links between functions are not well understood. There is then the issue of identifying the cost driver, which requires a fresh way of looking at each activity. For example, the cost driver for a warehouse fork-lift operator would be the number of pallets moved. The cost driver for stocking shelves would be the number of pieces that must be stacked in a given time period. A further problem occurs if there is more than one cost driver for a given activity. You are then faced with the same problem as with overhead allocation: on what basis should the cost drivers be weighted? Usually, this problem shows that activities have not been broken down into sufficient detail, and that more analysis is needed. ABC can therefore become complex to implement.

In spite of the implementation challenges, logistics and ABC go hand in hand (van Damme and van der Zon, 1999). It is a very rational way to analyse costs, and logistics practitioners recognise that providing a service is about managing a sequence of activities. Logistics or supply chain managers are particularly well placed to understand, analyse and apply ABC. They understand business processes and the activities that go with them. Theirs is a cross-functional task. The value chain stares them in the face!

The procedure of determining cost drivers is often considered to be more valuable than the ABC system itself. Activity-based management enables the cost structure of a business to be examined in a new light, allowing anomalies to be resolved and sources of waste highlighted. It may also help in better targeting investment decisions.

3.3.1 ABC example

Complex Ltd has four production lines, which each operates for 8,000 hours a year. Each line makes a number of products, which are based on size and colour. Many changeovers are therefore required, each incurring set-up and maintenance costs. Traditionally the maintenance costs have been allocated on the basis of machine hours, so each production line is charged equally. This year, the maintenance budget of €1 million has been divided into four, so each line is charged with €250,000.

Sales and marketing are concerned that certain products are losing market share, and this is due to price relative to the competition. All departments have been instructed to investigate costs and to suggest improvements. How can activity-based costing (ABC) improve this situation? By identifying the cost driver for maintenance, in this case the number of changeovers, costs can be allocated to each production line on this basis. Costs are then matched to the activity that generates them, so avoiding cross-subsidies.

The results are illustrated in Table 3.4. Maintenance costs have now been transferred to the production lines that incur the activity. For example, costs on line A have doubled to €500,000, while costs on line D have reduced to €50,000. ABC in this example has not taken cost out of the process, but has reallocated the costs to give a better understanding of the cost base. Complex is now in a better position to make decisions that affect the cost competitiveness of the product range.

Table 3.4 **Different ways of allocating maintenance costs**

Production lines	A	B	C	D	Total
Machine hours	8,000	8,000	8,000	8,000	32,000
No. of changeovers	50	30	15	5	100
Equal allocation	250,000	250,000	250,000	250,000	1,000,000
Allocation by activity	500,000	300,000	150,000	50,000	1,000,000
Difference	250,000	50,000	−100,000	−200,000	0

3.3.2 Cost time profile (CTP)

A key benefit of being able to cost logistics processes is that cost information can be used in conjunction with time information. The synergies of the two can then provide opportunities for identifying activities which either create value or which create waste.

The cost time profile (CTP) (Bicheno, 2000) is a graph, which plots cumulative time against cumulative cost for a set of discrete activities that together form a process or a supply chain. The CTP utilises outputs from two sources:

- *activity times*: from time-based process mapping (TBPM) process time recording system (see Chapter 5);
- *activity costs*: from a process costing system that is underpinned by activity-based costing.

As discussed earlier, ABC strives to achieve an equitable distribution of overhead costs to activities. Table 3.5 illustrates cumulative time and cost for a process comprising six activities.

Such data can be used to construct a *cost time profile*. Bernon *et al.* (2003) record the process in terms of time and cost for a poultry product from receipt of live bird to delivery of finished product to the retailer. Overall, the process takes an average of 175 hours to complete. The profile shows areas that consume time and cost within the supply chain, highlighting areas for future investigation that could yield savings. For example, distribution accounts for 35 per cent of process time, but only 3 per cent of total cost. Slicing and packaging are more in line, since they account for 25 per cent of total cost and are responsible for 28 per cent of the total process time. Figure 3.8 shows the time cost profile for this process.

Bicheno (2000) stresses the importance of interpreting both the horizontal and vertical lines of the CTP:

- *Long, horizontal lines* tend to occur when there is a relatively small increase in total cost as a result of an activity that runs over a relatively long period of time. An example is storage of raw materials in an inbound distribution centre prior to production, as illustrated by activity B.
- *Steep, vertical lines* tend to occur when costs are consumed over a relatively short period of processing time. An example is direct costs in a manufacturing process, as illustrated by activity C.

Thus a focus on the long, horizontal sections of the CTP graph may have the highly desirable effect of reducing cost and time while simultaneously improving quality. The application of time compression tools and techniques (see Chapter 5) facilitates these process improvements.

Table 3.5 Cumulative time and cost data by activity

Activity	A	B	C	D	E	F
Cumulative time %	14	64	65	67	97	100
Cumulative cost %	25	45	83	85	95	100

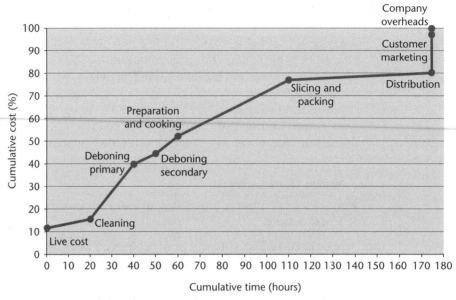

Figure 3.8 Cost time profile for poultry product

(Source: After 'Costing waste in supply chain processes. A European food and drink industry case study' *Proceedings of the Tenth International EurOMA Conference*, Copenhagen, June, Vol. 1, reprinted by permission of EIASM (Bernon, M. *et al.*, 2003)

Focusing on the vertical sections of the CTP curve highlights the major cost areas of the process, and provides a starting point to investigate which activities are creating the highest costs in a given process. The application of process re-engineering (Davenport, 1993) in association with target costing techniques will be beneficial in identifying cost-saving opportunities.

3.4 A balanced measurement portfolio

Key issues: Who are the key stakeholders in a business, and what needs to be achieved in order to satisfy them? How can a balanced set of measures of performance be developed in order to address stakeholder satisfaction and stakeholder contribution?

Many organisations have suffered from undue emphasis on particular measures of performance within the firm. For example, a preoccupation with labour productivity may lead to excessive stocks of inbound parts ('Do not run out of raw materials otherwise bonuses will suffer.') Such a preoccupation may also lead to excessive stocks of outbound products, because the most important priority is to keep workers busy, whether the product can be sold or not! While this priority may be good for productivity, it may well disrupt flow in the supply network: inbound parts are ordered too early, and outbound products are made too early. What is good for one measure (productivity in this case) is bad for others (inventories and material flow).

In reality, management today is faced with the challenge of performing across a whole range of objectives. Different groups of stakeholders in a firm include shareholders, employees, customers, suppliers, the local community and government. This is not a comprehensive list, and industries such as pharmaceuticals have other important stakeholders, including regulators such as the Drug Enforcement Agency. The challenge for the directors of a firm is to *balance* the diverse interests of these groups of stakeholders. We review the interests of each group in turn:

- *Shareholders* typically have a passing interest in a firm in which they invest. They will keep their shareholding as long as it provides a return that is competitive with other investments. Shareholders are impressed by high dividends and share appreciation resulting from profitability and growth of the business. Failure to deliver adequate returns often turns shareholders against the management of the day!

- *Employees* often have a long-term commitment to a firm, and are concerned with employment stability, competitive wages and job satisfaction. Failure to deliver on such goals may create negative reactions such as loss of motivation and loyalty, difficulty in recruitment, and various forms of industrial action.

- *Customers* are in theory the most important stakeholder in a free market economy. It is their demand that draws material through the supply network. Failure to keep customers satisfied creates the risk of loss of business.

- *Suppliers* are interested in such benefits as long-term business, involvement in new product development, and of course payment on time. Failure to meet such benefits leads to sanctions such as disruption of supply and higher prices.

- *Local community*. Here, the interests are in the firm as a local employer, with a reputation for civic responsibility and long-term commitment to the region as an employer and as a ratepayer. Failure to deliver against such interests may lead to environmental disputes and difficulty in obtaining planning permission.

- *Government* is interested in the firm as a contributor to employment and value creation in the economy, and as a source of revenues. Failure to meet government laws, on the other hand, may lead to prosecution or even closure of the business.

Thus the directors of a business are faced with the need to manage the potentially conflicting interests of the stakeholders, keeping each within what Doyle (1994) refers to as a *tolerance zone*. Each stakeholder has a limit beyond which the risk of disruption to the business increases rapidly. An upper limit exists as well. For example, a preoccupation with profits may please shareholders for the time being, but may result in negatives from labour exploitation and low levels of investment. While bumper profits appear in year 1, these are rapidly eroded as the negatives cut in during later years. In the end, the whole business suffers. The challenge for the directors is to keep all stakeholders just satisfied, keeping each within the tolerance zone.

3.4.1 Balanced measures

While balance between stakeholders is one issue, another is the balance between financial and operational measures of performance, and between history and the future. Kaplan and Norton (1996) point to the shortcomings of traditional cost accounting systems. Traditional systems are geared to the needs of the stock market, and are essentially historical and financial in emphasis. Modern systems, they argue, need to be balanced between financial and operations, and between history and the future. A way of showing the relative emphasis between traditional measures and balanced measures is to show relative priorities by means of circles, where larger circles imply a greater priority and number of measures in use, as shown in Figure 3. 9.

In developing a modern performance measurement system it is necessary to take all of these factors into account, and to create a balanced performance measurement system. That is the objective of the 'balanced scorecard'.

In practice, Kaplan and Norton propose that the balanced scorecard should balance the financial perspective (goals for future performance and measures of past performance) with similar goals and measures for the underlying drivers of long-term profitability. These drivers are identified as the business process perspective, the innovation and learning perspective and the customer perspective.

3.4.2 Supply chain management and the balanced scorecard

Extending the balanced scorecard into the context of the supply chain, Brewer and Speh (2000) consider that performance measurement systems must be aligned to supply chain practices:

> If firms talk about the importance of supply chain concepts, but continue to evaluate employees using performance measures that are . . . unaffected by supply chain improvements, then they will fail in their supply chain endeavours.

They have developed a supply chain framework that links the four perspectives of the balance scorecard to corresponding supply chain management goals, as illustrated in Figure 3.10.

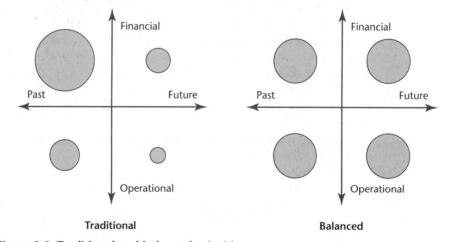

Figure 3.9 Traditional and balanced priorities

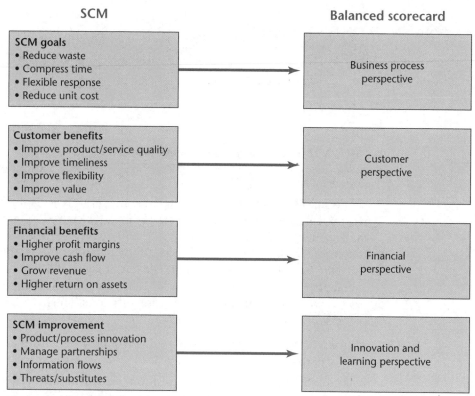

Figure 3.10 Linking supply chain management to the balanced scoreboard
(Source: After Brewer and Speh, 2000)

Consistent with our view that different supply strategies are needed to support different product needs in the marketplace, the aim should be to identify consistent groups of measures that support particular supply strategies.

3.5 Supply chain operations reference model (SCOR)

Key issues: **How can process thinking be applied to measures across the supply chain? What is the supply chain operations reference model, and how is it constructed?**

The previous two sections looked at process-based performance measures within an organisation. This section reviews a model that places a focal firm in the context of the supply chain. In order to help companies to understand their supply chain performance and opportunities for improvement, a cross-industry framework has been developed by the Supply Chain Council. You can visit the council website at *www.supply-chain.org*

This section gives an introduction to SCOR based on publicly available material; in order to obtain detailed benchmarking data from the model, your organisation would need to become a member. In common with ABC, the SCOR model uses a process-based approach to the supply chain.

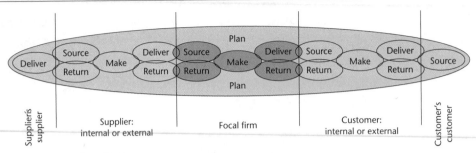

Figure 3.11 Five distinct management processes

(Source: After Supply Chain Council and Supply Chain Operations Reference (SCOR) model overview. www.supply-chain.org)

The supply chain operations reference model (SCOR) is founded on four distinct management processes. The supply chain is viewed in terms of overlapping management processes – source, make and deliver – within an integrated planning framework that encompasses all of the organisations in the chain, as shown in Figure 3.11. It is a process-based version of Figure 1.1 in Chapter 1. The management processes of the 'focal firm' is seen as linked with corresponding processes within supplier and customer organisations. The five distinct management processes can be described as follows:

- *Plan*: the tasks of planning demand and supply set within an overall planning system that covers activities such as long-term capacity and resource planning.
- *Source*: the task of material acquisition, set within an overall sourcing system that includes activities such as vendor certification and vendor contracting.
- *Make*: the task of production execution, set within an overall production system that includes activities such as shop scheduling.
- *Deliver*: the day-to-day tasks of managing demand, orders, warehouse and transportation, and installation and commissioning. These tasks are set within an overall delivery management system that includes order rules and management of delivery quantities.
- *Return*: the return of non-conforming goods for replacement or rectification, and the recycling of materials no longer needed by the customer.

There are four levels to the SCOR model:

- *Level 1*: a broad definition of the plan, source, make and deliver management processes, which is used to set competitive objectives.
- *Level 2*: defines core process categories that are possible components of a supply chain.
- *Level 3*: provides the information needed to plan and set goals for each element that comprises the level 2 categories.
- *Level 4*: the implementation plan needed to put improvements into play.

Table 3.6 shows 13 metrics at level 1 in the SCOR model, and is taken from the SCOR website (*www.supply-chain.org*). The intention is that an individual company should not attempt to be 'best in class' in all areas. Rather, a given company should target its strength in four to six selected areas to create differ-

Table 3.6 **Supply chain performance is tied to measurements that can be benchmarked**

SCOR Level 1 Supply chain management	Customer-facing		Internal-facing	
	Supply chain reliability	Flexibility and responsiveness	Cost	Assets
Delivery performance	◅			
Order fulfilment performance	◅			
Fill rate				
Order fulfilment lead time				
Perfect order fulfilment	◅			
Supply-chain response time		◅		
Production flexibility		◅		
Total logistics management cost			◅	
Value-added productivity			◅	
Warranty cost or returns processing cost			◅	
Cash-to-cash cycle time				◅
Inventory days of supply				◅
Asset turns				◅

(Source: www.supply-chain.org)

entiation in the marketplace. The company will also need to ensure that it stays competitive in the other areas. Note that the customer-facing measures are what we referred to in section 3.2 as 'discretionary costs', while the internal-facing measures are 'engineered costs'. By drilling down into levels 2 and 3 of the SCOR model, the aim is to identify the cost drivers and so convert discretionary costs into engineered costs: that is, to convert supply chain performance directly into revenue, cost and margin. Also note that the internal-facing metrics encourage improvement of ROI (section 3.1) by reducing costs and maximising asset turns. Participating companies in the Supply Chain Council may obtain benchmarking information on how their organisation's performance compares with others: see the website given above.

In order to illustrate how such concepts could be applied in practice, Table 3.7 shows actual performance against the SCOR level 1 metrics for a given company. It also shows how those metrics compared with the SCOR database in terms of what was needed to achieve parity with the 'competitive population', what was needed to gain advantage, and what was needed to show superior performance. Where is this supply chain positioned in terms of its competitive performance? Not very well, it seems! *All* of the level 1 metrics are below parity with the exception of order fulfilment lead times. External metrics such as delivery performance and perfect order fulfilment are seriously adrift. Production flexibility is way behind the competitive population, suggesting that the master schedule is 'fixed' for too long a period – and there will no doubt be underlying causes of that. Internal measures are not in good shape either, with a poor cost performance and a seriously uncompetitive asset utilisation record

Table 3.7 Supply chain performance evaluated within the context of the competitive environment

Supply chain scorecard v. 3.0				Performance versus competitive population		
	Overview metrics	SCOR level 1 metrics	Actual	Parity	Advantage	Superior
		Delivery performance to commit date	50%	85%	90%	95%
EXTERNAL	Supply chain reliability	Fill rates	63%	94%	96%	98%
		Perfect order fulfilment (on time in full)	0%	80%	85%	90%
		Order fulfilment lead times (customer to customer)	7 days	7 days	5 days	3 days
	Flexibility and responsiveness	Production flexibility (days master schedule fixed)	45 days	30 days	25 days	20 days
INTERNAL	Cost	Total logistics management costs	19%	13%	8%	3%
		Warranty cost, returns and allowances	NA	NA	NA	NA
		Value-added per-employee productivity	$122K	$156K	$306K	$460K
	Assets	Inventory days of supply	119 days	55 days	38 days	22 days
		Cash-to-cash cycle time	196 days	80 days	46 days	28 days
		Net asset turns (working capital)	2.2 turns	8 turns	12 turns	19 turns

Summary

What is 'value' in the context of the supply chain?

- Return on investment (ROI) is a widely used method for measuring shareholder value. ROI focuses logistics management on controlling costs, working capital and fixed assets.

- Logistics is concerned with material flow, information flow and funds flow (Chapter 1). It is therefore a cross-functional concept that addresses management processes of plan, source, make, deliver and return. These processes are repeated across the supply chain.

- Traditional cost accounting is unhelpful in making logistics-related decisions because it is insensitive to processes and to cost drivers. Traditional cost accounting tends to understate profits on high-volume products and to overstate profits on low-volume/high-variety products.

How can logistics costs be better represented?

- Logistics costs can be better described by using a variety of methods of allocating costs to products. The purpose of such a variety of allocations is to gain better information about the cost base of logistics operations, and hence to take better decisions. For example, direct product profitability (DPP) attempts to allocate logistics costs more specifically to products by considering how they use fixed resources. Another principle is to convert discretionary costs such as product availability into engineering costs such as profit contribution from increased sales.

- Activity-based costing (ABC) seeks to understand what factors drive costs, and how costs are incurred by logistics processes that span the organisation and the supply chain in general. It is essentially a process-based view of costing, and again seeks to enhance the quality of logistics decision making.

- Financial measures that are rooted in the past are insufficient for taking rational logistics decisions. A balanced measurement portfolio is called for, one that takes into account the needs of different stakeholders in a business. The balanced measurement portfolio is extended into the supply chain by means of the supply chain operations reference model (SCOR).

Discussion questions

1 Explain what is meant by the term *value* in a supply chain. How can value best be measured in a supply chain context?

2 Why are processes important in terms of managing logistics? Suggest how the processes of plan, source, make, deliver and return might differ in the case of the two factories Simple and Complex described in section 3.3.

3 What are the advantages of cutting the 'total cost cube' in different ways? Summarise the different perspectives on logistics costs provided by fixed/variable, direct/indirect and engineered/discretionary costs, and by activity-based costing.

4 Suggest balanced measurement portfolios for the two factories Simple and Complex described in section 3.3. In particular, suggest key performance measures in the areas of strategy, process and capability.

References

Atrill, P. and McLaney, E. (2004) *Management Accounting for Non-Specialists*, 4th edn. London: Prentice Hall.

Bernon, M., Mena, C., Templar, S. and Whicker L, (2003) 'Costing waste in supply chain processes: A European food drink industry case study', *Proceedings of the 10th International EurOMA Conference, Copenhagen, June 2003*, Vol. 1, pp. 345–54.

Bicheno, J. (2000) *The Lean Toolbox*, 2nd edn. Buckingham: Picsie Books.

Brewer P.C. and Speh, T.W. (2000) 'Using the balanced scorecard to measure supply chain performance', *Journal of Business Logistics*, Vol. 21, No.1, pp. 75–93.

Christopher, M. (1998) *Logistics and Supply Chain Management: Strategies for reducing cost and improving service*, 2nd edn, p. 8. London: Financial Times Pitman.

CIMA (1989) *Management Accounting, Official Terminology*. London: CIMA.

Cooper, R. and Kaplan, R.S. (1988) 'Measure costs right: make the right decisions', *Harvard Business Review*, September/October, pp. 96–105.

Dale, B.G. and Plunkett, J.J. (1995) *Quality Costing*, 2nd edn. London: Chapman & Hall.

Davenport, T.H. (1993): *Process Innovation: Re-engineering work through information technology*, Boston, MA: Harvard Business School Press.

Doyle, P. (1994) *Marketing Management and Strategy*. New York: Prentice-Hall.

Kaplan, R. and Norton, D. (1996) *The Balanced Scorecard*. Boston, MA: Harvard Business School Press.

van Damme, D.A. and van der Zon, F.L. (1999) 'Activity based costing and decision support', *International Journal of Logistics Management*, Vol. 10, No. 1, 71–82.

Suggested further reading

Atrill, P. and McLaney, E. (2004) *Management Accounting for Non-Specialists,* 4th edn. Harlow: Financial Times Prentice Hall.

Part Two

LEVERAGING LOGISTICS OPERATIONS

Part Two uses the basic understanding of logistics strategy and management developed in Part One to focus in on critical roles for logistics operations. This covers the centre panel of our model of logistics: the flow of materials, lead times and the network in a global context.

Despite its role in corporate success, the logistics task ultimately boils down to orchestrating the flow of materials and information in the supply chain. The aim is to support products and services in the marketplace better than competitors are able to do. You could say that the logistics task is about making strategic objectives a reality by executing against demand and making value propositions to customers a reality.

Chapters 4 and 5 look at the basic dimensions of logistics operations: their international reach and their contribution to a timely response to demand. Chapters 6 and 7 then take that thinking a level higher by introducing key managerial concepts that play a role in logistics operations. Just-in-time and 'lean thinking', explained in Chapter 6, have been pillars of management thinking for some time, and have proved to be an important way of coordinating the manufacturing and upstream part of the supply chain in an efficient manner. The agile supply chain (Chapter 7) is a more recent concept that focuses on leveraging responsiveness to customer demand. Here, logistics plays a crucial role in aligning material flow across the supply network with customer demand, and in ensuring execution in a flexible and customised manner.

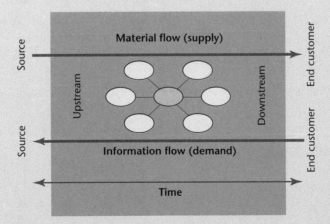

CHAPTER 4

Managing logistics internationally

Outcomes

The intended outcomes of this chapter are to:

- identify challenges that internationalisation presents to logistics management;
- consider the structure and management of a global logistics network.

By the end of this chapter you should be able to:

- understand tendencies towards international logistics;
- understand challenges of international logistics networks;
- understand how to begin to balance these in organising for international logistics.

Introduction

The early roots of logistics are in international transport, which was a central element of many fundamental models in economic theory. In traditional location theory, for example, transport costs were optimised in relation to distance to market and production locations. The origins of internationalisation can be traced back to the expanding trade routes of early civilisations. Discoveries made in excavations from Europe, Asia, Africa and the Americas reveal artefacts made hundreds or even thousands of miles away from the site, at the edges of their respective known worlds. Developments in transport, navigation and communication have progressively expanded horizons. Measured in transport time and costs the world has shrunk to the dimensions of a 'global village'. Many take for granted the availability of products from around the world and safe, fast inter-continental travel on container carriers and aircraft. It is in this context that a clear link exists between logistics and economic development. The connectivity of all regions of the world is essential for international trade. As a result, many projects aimed at supporting regional economic development focus on the infrastructure needed to support integration into the global economy. Much of the infrastructure to support international trade and business is founded on logistics operations.

The logistics dimension of internationalisation conjures up a vision of parts flowing seamlessly from suppliers to customers located anywhere in the world, and a supply network that truly spans the entire globe. Often basic products such as deep-freeze pizzas combine a multitude of locations from which ingredients are sourced, and an international transport network that links production locations to warehouses and multiple stores. The enormous geographical span of this logistics system cannot be recognised in the price of the product. This can be explained by transport having become just a commodity in the global village. At the micro-level of the individual company, however, the reality is that there are few examples of truly global supply chains. There are many barriers to such a vision.

For example, local autonomy, local standards and local operating procedures make the integration of information flow and material flow an uphill task. Local languages and brand names increase product complexity. Global supply chains are made more complicated by uncertainty and difficulty of control. Uncertainty arises from longer lead times and lack of knowledge over risks and local market conditions. Coordination becomes more complex because of additional language and currency transactions, more stages in the distribution process, and local government intervention through customs and trade barriers. Additionally, there are many instances in which a truly globalised logistics system is not necessary, and where 'internationalisation' is a more accurate description. Internationalisation certainly is an increasing feature of the majority of supply chains. International sourcing of component parts and international markets for finished goods are extending as world trade increases.

As part of that process location factors used in positioning logistical operations around the globe are changing. Figure 4.1 ranks international location factors from a survey among 300 companies in Europe (van Hoek *et al.*, 2002). Interestingly, important as physical distribution still is, the traditional domain of logistics is no longer the most important factor. In today's digital world, information infrastructure is more important – as is the availability of qualified personnel. Information and communication technology, if used properly, can enable global, instant connectivity and coordination of transport flows. The inclusion of qualified personnel reflects the changing roles and responsibilities of logistics personnel. They have become far more focused on brains than on boxes! In addition to that, most recent years have also reinforced that internationalisation is not free, easy or risk free. Based upon wars, terror threats and transportation breakdowns companies have been forced to structurally alter their risk approaches, in particular in international logistics.

Within the context of this changing global landscape for logistics the overall aim of this chapter is to analyse the internationalisation of logistics, and to explore how to begin to organise international supply chains. Figure 4.2 shows the frame for this chapter; drivers and enablers need to be balanced out with risk factors in organising logistics internationally. Essentially, this means developing and designing an international logistics network, managing risks and developing international governance structures.

Key issues	*This chapter addresses five key issues:*

1 **Drivers and logistics implications of internationalisation**: the trade-off facing internationally operating businesses.

2 **The trend towards internationalisation**: three strategies for improving the transition to global supply chains.

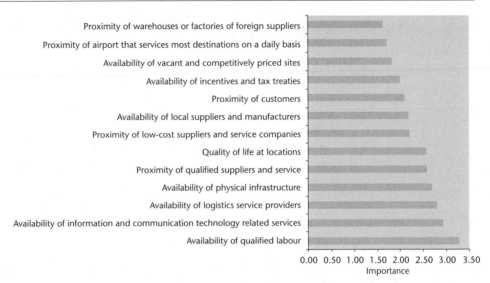

Figure 4.1 **Ranking of international location factors**
(Source: After van Hoek *et al.*, 2002)

3 **The challenge of international logistics and location**: barriers to international logistics.

4 **Risk management approaches in international logistics**: two levels of risk readiness and several specific steps to take.

5 **Organising for international logistics**: proposes principles by which international logistics networks should be organised.

6 **Governance of international logistics for effective local execution**: the need to manage globally without limiting local responsiveness.

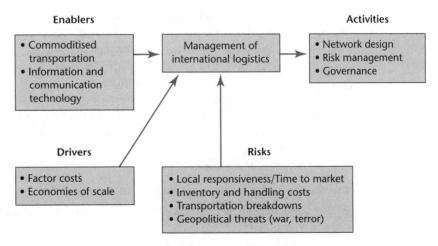

Figure 4.2 **Decision framework for international logistics**

4.1 Drivers and logistics implications of internationalisation

Key issue: **What are the trade-offs between responsiveness to local markets and economies of scale?**

Despite the general trend towards internationalisation, the business approach is not taking place by means of any universal patterns. In assessing the nature of cross-border interfaces in logistics, three questions can be asked:

- Does internationalisation imply a universal global approach for the supply chain?
- Does internationalisation require a 'global' presence in every market?
- Does internationalisation distinguish between the companies that globally transfer knowledge and those that do not?

The arguments presented in this section suggest that the answer to each of these questions is 'no'.

The 'single business' concept of structuring the supply chain in the form of uniform approaches in each country is losing ground. 'McColonisation' has recently been abolished, when McDonald's announced localisation of its business in such areas as marketing and local relations. In response to local crises in quality, and suffering from local competition, the corporate headquarters were downsized to help empower the local organisation. The same applies to the Coca-Cola Company, which has abandoned 'CocaColonisation' – based on a universal product, marketing and production and distribution model – for the same reasons. In favour of local brands and product varieties, Procter & Gamble is doing the same. In supply chains we find regional variations in the application of international principles.

This does not mean to say that localisation is the new mainstay. Unilever, a traditionally localised competitor of Procter & Gamble, has announced a decrease in the number of brands, and has rationalised operations away from strict localisation over the past decade, and probably will continue to do so for a while. Somewhere between local and global extremes, Procter & Gamble and Unilever will meet each other in a new competitive area.

Looking at the different drivers of internationalisation, three basic global shifts in international investment and trade have been identified, with a possible fourth coming to the forefront in modern markets, as listed in Table 4.1. Such shifts of course have an impact on international trade and the flow of goods. In particular, destinations change as well as logistics requirements. The 'fourth generation' recognises the logistics trade-off between responsiveness to local markets and internationalisation.

At a company level, generic drivers of internationalisation include:

- a search for low-factor and supply costs (land, labour, materials);
- the need to follow customers internationally in order to be able to supply locally and fast;
- a search for new geographical market areas;

● a search for new learning opportunities and exposure to knowledge (such as by locating in California's Silicon Valley – a 'hot spot' in development of international electronics, software and Internet industries).

The importance of these drivers varies by company and with time. Considering the sequence of global shifts, proximity to production factors such as labour and low material costs can be considered more basic than market- or even knowledge-related drivers. Furthermore, the importance of the respective drivers is dependent upon the internationalisation strategy of the company involved. Table 4.2 provides examples of strategic contexts, and – in the bottom row – the logistics implications of those strategies. The multi-domestic and global strategies represent two extremes, while the integrated network strategy represents a balance between them. The consequences of this 'balancing act' for logistics are analysed below.

4.1.1 Logistical implications of internationalisation

Internationalising logistics networks holds consequences for inventory, handling and transport policies.

Table 4.1 The fourth-generation global shift in Europe

Generation	First	Second	Third	Fourth
Period	1950s–60s	From 1960	From 1980	Emerging now
Primary drivers	Labour shortage	Labour costs and flexibility	Market entrance	Responsiveness to customer orders
Shift of labour and investment towards	European countries without labour shortage	Newly Industrialised Countries, low labour cost countries	Eastern Europe, China, Latin America	Western Europe
Transport routes	Still significantly continental	Increasingly intercontinental	Adding additional destination regions	Beginning to refocus on continental
Nature of international flow of goods	Physical distribution of finished products from new production locations	Shipping parts to production locations and exporting finished products	Physical distribution towards new market regions	Shipping semi-finished products to Europe, where they are finalised in response to customer orders, while within the logistics system

Table 4.2 Dimensions of different internationalisation strategies

Dimension	Setting in a pure multi-domestic strategy	Setting in a pure global strategy	Setting in an integrated network strategy
Competitive moves	Stand-alone by country	Integrated across countries	Moves based on local autonomy and contribution of lead subsidiaries, globally coordinated
Product offering	Fully customised in each country	Fully standardised worldwide	Partly customised, partly standardised
Location of value-adding activities	All activities in each country	Concentration: one activity in each (different) country	Dispersal, specialisation, and interdependence
Market participation	No particular pattern; each country on its own	Uniform worldwide	Local responsiveness and worldwide sharing of experience
Marketing approach	Local	Integrated across countries	Variation in coordination levels per function and activity
Logistical network	Mainly national; sourcing, storage and shipping on a national level and duplicated by country	Limited number of production locations that ship to markets around the globe through a highly internationalised network with limited localised warehouse and resources	Balanced local sourcing and shipping (e.g. for customised products and local specialties) and global sourcing and shipping (for example for commodities)

(Source: Based on Yip (1989) and Bartlett and Ghoshal (1989))

Inventory

Centralising inventories across multiple countries can hold advantages in terms of inventory-holding costs and inventory levels that are especially relevant for high-value products. On the other hand, internationalisation may lead to product proliferation due to the need for localisation of products and the need to respond to specific local product/market opportunities.

Handling

Logistics service practices may differ across countries as well as regulation on storage and transport. Adjusting handling practices accordingly is a prerequisite for internationalisation. Furthermore, the opportunity to implement best practice across various facilities may also be possible. Both of these practices assist the process of internationalisation.

Transport

Owing to internationalisation logistics pipelines are extended and have to cope with differences in infrastructure across countries, while needing to realise delivery within the time to market. This may drive localisation. On the other hand, the opportunity for global consolidation may drive international centralisation.

Within this final, central, consideration in the globalise–localise dimension of logistics, global businesses face a challenge that can be summarised in terms of a simple trade-off between the benefits of being able to consolidate operations globally on the one hand, and the need to compete in a timely manner on the other.

4.1.2 Time-to-market

Time-to-market has particular significance for the management of the global logistics pipeline. This subject is considered in depth in Chapter 6, although we shall touch on the following issues here:

- product obsolescence;
- inventory-holding costs.

Product obsolescence

The extended lead time inherent in international logistics pipelines means that products run the risk of becoming obsolete during their time in transit. This is especially true for products in industries with rapid technological development, such as personal computing and consumer electronics, and for fashion goods such as clothing and footwear.

Inventory-holding costs

Lead time spent in the logistics pipeline increases the holding cost of inventory. In addition to the time spent in physical transit, goods travelling internationally will incur other delays. These occur at consolidation points in the process, such as in warehouses where goods are stored until they can be consolidated into a full load, such as a container. Delay frequently occurs at the point of entry into a country while customs and excise procedures are followed.

4.1.3 Global consolidation

Global consolidation occurs as managers seek to make the best use of their assets and to secure the lowest-cost resources. This approach leads to assets such as facilities and capital equipment being used to the fullness of their capacity and economies of scale being maximised. Resources are sourced on a global scale to minimise cost by maximising purchasing leverage and again to pursue economies of scale. The types of resource acquired in this way include all inputs to the end product, such as raw materials and components, and also labour and knowledge. Familiar features of global consolidation include:

- sourcing of commodity items from low-wage economies;
- concentration at specific sites;
- bulk transportation.

Sourcing of commodity items from low-wage economies

Two sourcing issues are used by organisations operating internationally:

- consolidation of purchasing of all company divisions and companies;
- sourcing in low-wage economies.

Such organisations seek to consolidate the purchasing made by all their separate divisions and operating companies. This allows them to place large orders for the whole group, which enables them to minimise costs by using their bargaining power and seeking economies of scale. At its extreme, a company may source all of its requirements from its range of a given commodity, such as a raw material or component, from a single source.

Internationally operating companies are on a constant quest to find new, cheaper sources of labour and materials. This trend led to the move of manufacturing from developed industrial regions to lower-cost economies. Examples of this are:

- western Europe to eastern Europe;
- United States to Mexico;
- Japan to the 'Asian Tigers' of South Korea, Taiwan, Hong Kong and Singapore.

These developing economies have seen impressive growth over recent years. This has led to increased prosperity for their people and rising standards of living. However, these advances in social standards raise the cost of labour and other resources. Therefore, the relentless search for the lowest production cost has led to some companies resourcing commodity items to lower-wage countries in Asia, North Africa and South America.

In some cases this movement of facilities around the globe has come full circle, with Asian companies setting up plants in the United Kingdom not only to gain access to the EU market but also to take advantage of low wages.

Concentration at specific sites

Consolidation of purchasing applies not only to commodity goods but also to high-value or scarce resources. Research and development skills are both high-value and scarce. Therefore there is an incentive to locate at certain sites to tap into specific pools of such skills. Examples of this are 'Silicon Valley' in California and 'Silicon Fen' near Cambridge as centres of excellence in IT. Companies originally located in these areas benefit from research undertaken in the nearby universities.

Companies become more influential in directing such research and benefiting from it if they have a significant presence in these locations. This is helped if global research is consolidated on a single site. While this may mean missing out on other sources of talent, consolidated R&D gives a company a presence that helps to attract the bright young minds who will make their mark in these industries in the future, and it allows synergies to develop between research teams.

Activity 4.1

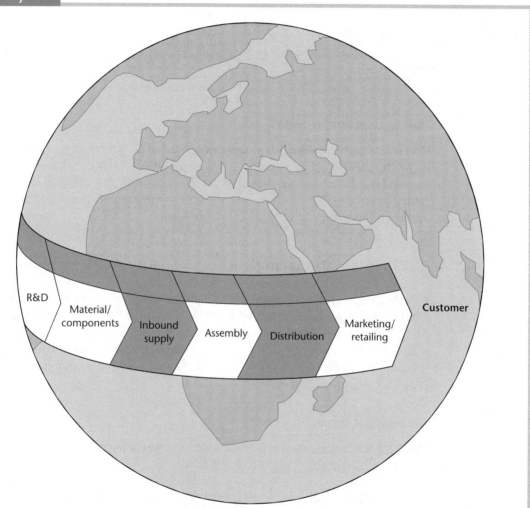

Figure 4.3 The international logistics pipeline

The international logistics pipeline is made up of the same basic elements as any other pipeline. However, this pipeline has a number of special characteristics. Use Table 4.3 to make a list of the characteristics that you believe make a global logistics pipeline different from one that operates only nationally.

Table 4.3 Characteristics of the international pipeline

Elements of the pipeline	Special characteristics of the international pipeline
Research and development	
Material/component sourcing	
Inbound supply	
Assembly	
Distribution	
Marketing/retailing	

Bulk transportation

One of the more obvious advantages of operating a company in a global manner is the cost advantage of consolidated transportation. Taking Procter & Gamble as an example, 350 ship containers, 9,000 rail car and 97,000 truck loads are transported every day. The opportunity for cost saving by coordinating these movements and maximising utilisation is significant.

4.1.4 Risk in international logistics

In addition to time to market and inventory risks, events of recent years have forced companies to adapt to the new supply chain reality of expecting the unexpected. Companies are not only responding to current volatility and geopolitical risks, they are also developing new risk management approaches based upon the realisation that decades of globalising supply chains has come at a price: a heightened and different risk profile.

Geopolitical threats

The 2003 SARS crisis and the second Gulf War were major events in and of themselves; they were also consecutive and made huge impacts on supply chain continuity and execution feasibility. Trade routes had to be altered and global travel was limited. In addition to that, structurally heightened government security measures and screening are indicators of risks involved in international logistics. Logistics making the global economy a reality can never be a given and a non-issue that deserves no second thought.

Transportation breakdowns

Transportation may be a commodity, that does not mean that it is a given and that nothing can go wrong. A several-week strike in the US west coast ports in 2002 lasted long enough to almost cripple the US economy. With hundreds of cargo ships floating outside the ports shipments were not arriving at US destinations. This meant that factories were shut down and stores were emptying. It also had a ripple effect on global trade overall. For example: return shipments were not happening because no ships were leaving the ports either. With so many ships and containers tied up other routes could not be served either. And in fact a resulting global shortage of containers caused a slowdown of shipments in many other port regions. So shipments on other routes, in different harbours and even shipments using different modalities were affected.

Risk and security concerns are not a one-time issue but require a continuous risk management process. Helferich and Cook (2003) found that this is much needed because for example:

- only about 61 per cent of US firms have disaster recovery plans;
- those that do typically cover data centres, only about 12 per cent cover total organisational recovery;
- few plans include steps to keep a supply chain operational;
- only about 28 per cent of companies have formed crisis management teams, and even fewer have supply chain security teams;
- an estimated 43 per cent of businesses that suffer a fire or other serious damage never reopen for business after the event.

According to Helferich and Cook (2003) this can partially be explained by the fact that there are competing business issues, managers might not recognise their vulnerability and might assume that the government will bail them out. Peck (2003) has published a self-assessment for supply chain risk and an operational-level tool kit.

4.2 The tendency towards internationalisation

Key issue: How can we picture the trade-offs between costs, inventories and lead times in international logistics?

In order to remain competitive in the international business environment, companies seek to lower their costs while enhancing the service they provide to customers. Two commonly used approaches to improve the efficiency and effectiveness of supply chains are focused factories and centralised inventories.

4.2.1 Focused factories: from geographical to product segmentation

Many international companies, particularly in Europe, would have originally organised their production nationally. In this situation, factories in each country would have produced the full product range for supply to that country. Over time, factories in each country might have been consolidated at a single site, which was able to make all the products for the whole country. This situation, in which there is a focus on a limited segment of the geographical market, is shown in Figure 4.4(a).

The focused factory strategy involves a company's consolidating production of products into specific factories. Each 'focused factory' supplies its products internationally to a wide market and focuses on a limited segment of the product assortment. This situation is shown in Figure 4.4(b).

Traditional thinking is that this organisation strategy will deliver cost advantages to a global company. While this is true for production costs, the same is not necessarily true for inventory-holding costs and transport costs.

Activity 4.2

Focused factories have an impact on the important trade-off between cost and delivery lead time. Make a list of the advantages and disadvantages of focused factories. One example of each has been entered in the table below to start you going.

	Cost	Lead time
Advantages	Lower production costs through economies of scale	Specialised equipment may be able to manufacture quicker
Disadvantages	Higher transport cost	Longer distance from market will increase lead time

---

4.2.2 Centralised inventories

In the same way that the consolidation of production can deliver cost benefits, so can the consolidation of inventory. Rather than have a large number of local distribution centres, bringing these together at a small number of locations can

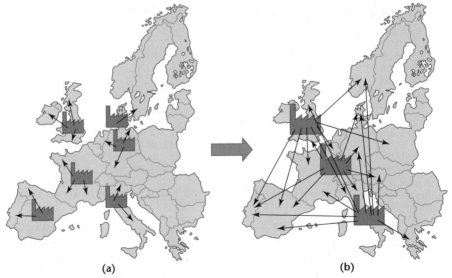

(a)   (b)

Figure 4.4a Focused markets: full-range manufacture for local markets
Figure 4.4b Focused factories: limited-range manufacturing for all markets

save cost. Saving can be achieved in this way by coordinating inventory management across the supply pipeline. This allows duplication to be eliminated and safety stocks to be minimised, thereby lowering logistics costs and overall distribution cycle times. Both may sound contrary to the fact that the transport pipeline will extend, owing to the longer distribution legs to customers from the central warehouse, in comparison with a local warehouse. Nevertheless, through centralising inventory major savings can be achieved by lowering overall speculative inventories, very often coupled with the ability to balance peaks in demand across regional markets from one central inventory. Figure 4.5 characterises the different operating environments where centralised inventory may be a more relevant or a less relevant consideration, based upon logistics characteristics.

In product environments where inventory costs are more important than the distribution costs, centralised inventories are a relevant concern. This is typically the case for products of high value (measured in costs per volume unit). Microchips are an extreme example: these products are of such high cost per volume unit that distributing from the moon could still be profitable! Distribution costs have a marginal impact on logistics costs per product, assuming of course that transport costs are mainly a function of volume and weight. Products that require special transport, such as antiques, art, confidential documents or dangerous chemicals, may represent a different operating environment.

A second dimension that needs to be taken into consideration is that of distribution lead times. Here, we focus on physical distribution from warehouse to customer, and not on the inbound pipeline. Centralising inventory may lead to

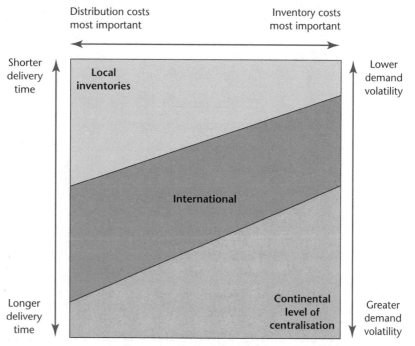

Figure 4.5 Inventory centralisation against logistics costs and service dimensions

lower factory-to-warehouse distribution costs because shipments can be consolidated into full container loads. Where service windows to customers are very compressed there may not be sufficient time to ship products from a central warehouse and allow for the required transit time within the service window. This is why, for example, hospitals and pharmacies retain in-house stocks of products, almost irrespective of their inventory costs. Critical medicines and surgical appliances need to be available instantly and locally, regardless of inventory costs.

In general transport costs have continued to decline over time as a relative cost item because of innovations in transport technology, the commoditisation of transport (such as container ships), and the oversupply of transport capacity for basic transport. These factors in themselves contribute to the increasing internationalisation of logistics: physical distance becomes less important, even for bulky products. However, the lead time dimension loses some of its relevance, from a transport point of view. Customer demand can be very volatile and unpredictable. *Accuracy* of delivery (the right quantity) can therefore be a more demanding challenge than *speed* (the right time). Speed is available through different transport modes (container ship, air cargo, express, courier, for example) at reasonable prices. In very volatile markets, control over international inventories by means of centralised inventories can be crucial. Overall delivery reliability ('on time in full') tends to increase significantly, much to the benefit of an organisation's performance in terms of service requirements. The ability to balance peaks across market regions from a central inventory is among the additional advantages. Different levels of inventory centralisation can be applied according to different dimensions. Taking the European market as an example, the range is from local inventories (by country or even by location) through international (a selection of countries) to the complete continent. Many companies now include the Middle East and Africa as a trading bloc (Europe, Middle East and Africa – EMEA).

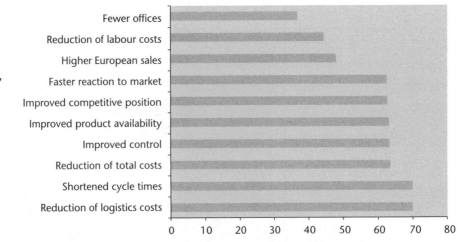

Figure 4.6 Realised benefits of centralised inventories in Europe
(Source: After Buck Consultants International, 1997)

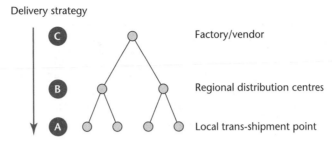

Figure 4.7 **Delivery strategies in a global network**

Figure 4.6 lists commonly stated advantages of centralised inventories as reported in a late-1990s study by companies that had experienced benefits in this area. So the research population here is companies that fall in the bottom-right quadrant of the Figure 4.5.

Centralised inventory management and focused factories enable different delivery strategies to be combined. Figure 4.7 depicts a simple distribution network that enables three different delivery strategies (listed in Table 4.4) to be applied as appropriate. For example, an opportunity to think globally arises where the main product relies more on the designer label and its promotion and marketing and less on its manufacturing origins. The key to success in clothing is often about fashionable design and labelling. Low labour costs (rather than material costs) of production can then be achieved by outsourcing to low-wage economies, often in the Far East.

CASE STUDY 4.1

Nike's central warehouse operation

Nike consolidated its European warehousing in the early 1990s by reducing the number of its warehouses in Europe from 22 to just one, based at Laakdal in Belgium. Laakdal receives Nike products – such as sports footwear and clothing – from all over the world, and serves retail stores across Europe.

In Europe, Nike initially worked through distributors, selecting local partners in each country. By the 1980s the market had grown to the point where the company decided to buy up its distributors gradually. Nike then converted them into wholly owned subsidiaries. To a large extent, however, each distributor operated autonomously. Each local warehouse had its own logistics infrastructure and its own salesforce. They ordered products individually and controlled their own stock. As a result, a range of service levels evolved, which differed from country to country. There was virtually no coordination of inventory allocation. Thus unused stock stored in one country was often needed in another country, and vice versa. Continued growth in the early 1990s soon created a shortage of warehouse capacity. In response to these bottlenecks, the distribution centres focused most of their efforts on solving distribution problems; but their real priority should have been sales and marketing.

In the light of a strategic evaluation conducted in 1991, Nike decided to centralise its European activities. The first step was to set up a European headquarters in the Netherlands. The second step was to centralise all of its European distribution operations. The main reasons for centralising distribution were as follows:

▶

- There were major problems in getting apparel to the retailer by the due date. Long lead times on advance orders and unreliable suppliers were blamed for this.
- Local management was not adequately informed about the arrival date of shipments. This led to a corresponding failure to keep customers informed of when they might expect to receive their orders.
- It was difficult to keep collections together. When retailers wanted to put together a special collection, it often proved impossible to have that order sent as a single delivery.
- It was difficult to ensure consistent value-added services. It was recognised that labelling, adding price tags, repacking and other services were potentially an important part of the package. However, not all countries were equipped to provide these services.
- Computer systems had been developed autonomously in each country. Most of these systems had serious deficiencies. As a result, communication within the distribution network was very difficult.

In 1992, Nike decided to build a European Distribution Centre (EDC) in Laakdal, Belgium. The first high bay for apparel was opened in September 1994, and the first high bay for footwear was opened a year later. The centralised operation works as follows. When the apparel arrives in Laakdal, it goes through seven steps:

1 *Receiving and palletising.* The containers are taken off the river barges and opened, and the boxes, which are taken out of the containers, are given a bar code. With this barcode, the computer assigns a storage location to the boxes. Next, the boxes are placed on a pallet. All the handling cranes are manually controlled. They can handle both boxes and pallets. Each crane has an on-board computer, which informs the driver where to stock the pallets or boxes. This procedure is more efficient and flexible than a fully automatic system.

2 *Quality control.* After receiving the products, they are taken to quality control (QC), a unit with 12 people. Colours and sizes are checked. Also, the employees look for defects and conduct washing trials. QC is an important activity. Without it, Nike cannot guarantee the quality of its products to its customers. This goes back to Nike's policy of switching among various suppliers to get cost benefits. Because there is no long-term relationship between Nike and the supplier, Nike has to control the quality of products received in Europe. Another reason for QC is that Nike's quality standards may differ from those of its suppliers.

3 *Storage.* As soon as the goods pass QC, the products are stored. The storage bays form an immense warehouse. For example, a high bay for apparel is 28m high, 125m long, and 42m wide.

4 *Picking (apparel) and sorting (shoes).* At the unit for picking and sorting, the products are sorted by order. A computer terminal, using radio frequency, lets the pickers know exactly which product is needed and where it is stored. Most of the footwear is sorted on an automatic conveyor system by a machine that can handle orders for up to 160 customers at a time. The automated process makes this a paperless warehouse. The products are transported to a pick pool when the date of delivery approaches.

5 *Value-added services.* From the picking and sorting unit, most of the products are transported to the processing division. Here, the products are finished in accordance

with client-specific orders. For example, this is where labelling and special packing are done. Offering value-added services and high quality was one of the major goals of the Customer Service Group. These activities are very labour-intensive, and liable to human error. For that reason, value-adding activities are performed for only one order and type of product at a time.

6 *Packing (apparel) and checking and sealing (shoes).* After a computer-controlled check, the apparel is packed in boxes. This is done at a packing station. But prior to packing the goods, operators check the apparel, which was delivered at their station by the conveyor belt against the order specifications. For footwear, a scanner checks whether the boxes contain the correct shoes. After a confirmation, the boxes are sealed automatically.

7 *Shipment.* Boxes are consolidated automatically by order and country of destination. Then they are ready to go.

The steps of (1) receiving and palletising, (2) quality control, (5) value-added services, and (6) packing, checking and sealing are done in a low-bay area; for the others high-bay areas are also used.

Questions

1 How does the seven-step logistics process at Laakdal provide competitive advantage for Nike?

2 Can you identify any logistics issues that are not adequately covered in the above description?

Table 4.4 **Three different delivery strategies**

Delivery strategy	Description	Pros	Cons
A	Direct shipment of fast-moving, predictable lines. Held locally, probably pre-configured	Short lead time to customer	Multiple inventory points leading to duplication of stocks
B	Inventory of medium velocity, less predictable demand lines held at generic level awaiting final configuration	Lower overall levels of inventory, consolidated shipments to distribution centres and concentrated handling	Longer lead time to customers
C	Slowest-moving lines, least predictable. Perhaps one shared global inventory or make to order	Low overall inventory levels	Long lead time to customers

4.3 The challenge of international logistics and location

Key issues: What are the risks in international logistics in terms of time and inventories, and how can they be addressed?

International logistics is complex, and different from localised logistics pipelines. The main differences that need to be taken into consideration are:

- extended lead time of supply;
- extended and unreliable transit times;
- multiple consolidation and break points;
- multiple freight modes and cost options.

Information technologies can help to circumvent these challenges in general, and the proper location of international operations in particular can help to resolve some of these challenges.

4.3.1 Extended lead time of supply

In an internationally organised business most products produced in a particular factory will be sold in a number of different countries. In order to manage the interface between the production and sales teams in each territory, long lead times may be quoted. This buffers the factory, allowing them to respond to the local variations required in the different markets.

4.3.2 Extended and unreliable transit times

Owing to the length and increased uncertainty of international logistics pipelines, both planned and unplanned inventories may be higher than optimal. A comparison of the length of domestic and international product pipelines and their associated inventories is shown in Figure 4.8. Variation in the time taken to undertake international transport will inevitably lead to increased holding of inventory with the aim of providing safety cover.

4.3.3 Multiple consolidation and break points

Consolidation is one of the key ways in which costs in pipelines can be lowered. Economies of scale are achieved when goods produced in a number of different facilities are batched together for transport to a common market.

The location of consolidation points depends on many factors that are not really appropriate to consider in a simple assignment such as this. That said, here is one solution. Products manufactured in India should be consolidated at the site on the east coast (near Madras) for shipping to Singapore. Here they are consolidated with the output from the Thai and Singapore factories and shipped to Hong Kong.

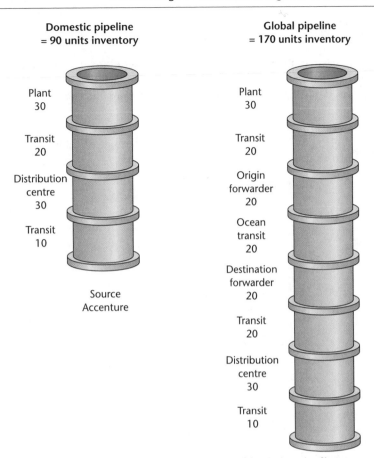

**Domestic pipeline
= 90 units inventory**

Plant
30

Transit
20

Distribution
centre
30

Transit
10

Source
Accenture

**Global pipeline
= 170 units inventory**

Plant
30

Transit
20

Origin
forwarder
20

Ocean
transit
20

Destination
forwarder
20

Transit
20

Distribution
centre
30

Transit
10

Figure 4.8 Comparison of domestic and international logistics pipelines
(Source: After van Hoek (1998) 'Reconfiguring the supply chain to implement postponed manufacturing',
International Journal of Logistics Management, Vol. 9, No. 1, pp. 95–110)

Products are consolidated at a Chinese port, possibly Shanghai, and transported by rail or sea to Hong Kong. All the other manufacturing sites deliver direct to Hong Kong, where products from all the various facilities are consolidated and shipped to Los Angeles.

It is worth noting that, after arrival in Los Angeles, this process runs in reverse. The consignment will be broken down at various 'break points' throughout North America and the goods distributed to market via hubs.

4.3.4 Multiple freight modes and cost options

Each leg of a journey between manufacture and the market will have a number of freight mode options. These can be broken down in simplistic terms into air, sea, rail and road. Within each of these categories lies a further range of alternative options. Each of them can be assessed for its advantages and disadvantages in terms of cost, availability and speed. When the journey along the supply chain involves multiple modes, the interface between them provides further complication.

A footwear company has a number of manufacturing facilities around Asia, as shown in Figure 4.9. There are six manufacturing sites in China, including Hong Kong, three in India, and one each in Thailand, Singapore and Taiwan. Singapore and Hong Kong also have the facility to act as regional consolidation sites.

Draw arrows on the map showing where the flow of exports to the North American market could be consolidated. Write a brief description that explains your reasons for choosing these consolidation points and the flows between them.

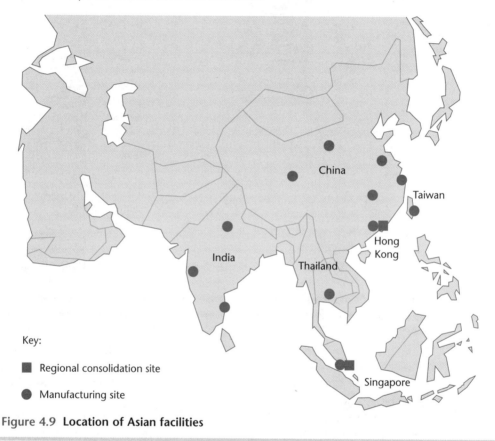

Key:

■ Regional consolidation site

● Manufacturing site

Figure 4.9 Location of Asian facilities

4.3.5 Location analysis

A structural component of international logistics pipeline design is the location design. As demonstrated, for example, in the Nike case example, selecting an operating format for the pipeline and locations for the operations represents longer-term commitments to underlying operating formats. As Figure 4.10 shows, there is a sequence to the decision making process involved that incorporates the business (left-hand side) and geographical decision making (right-hand side). The business decision making evolves from a strategic commitment through a decision support analysis project to implementation of the resulting

Activity 4.4

Consider each of the four freight modes in terms of their cost, speed and availability, and write in the respective box in the table 'high', 'medium' or 'low'. Explain your answers in the 'Rationale' box on the right.

Freight mode	Cost	Speed	Availability	Rationale
Air				
Sea				
Rail				
Road				

Note that these comparisons are fairly subjective, and your answers will reflect your experience of the different freight modes in your industry, product type and geographic location.

plan as a selected location. In parallel the location analysis starts at the level of relevant continent (Europe in the case of Nike), through relevant countries and regions to consider in the plan, to the selection of a location (Laakdal, Belgium, in the case of Nike).

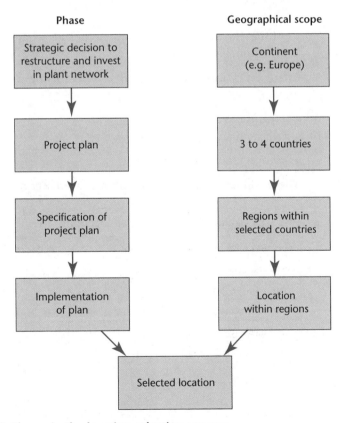

Figure 4.10 **Phases in the location selection process**

In the location decision making process location factors such as those listed in Figure 4.1 play a crucial role. The typical four-phase decision making process can be structured using the following steps:

1 Deciding upon the appropriate level of centralisation–decentralisation using for example Figures 4.6 and 4.10. In the case of Nike it was decided that a threshold had been reached that made centralisation of inventories in Europe relevant.

2 Selecting relevant location criteria: in Nike's case these included factors such as the availability of physical infrastructure including sea, road and rail connections, the availability of warehouse sites, and a central position in the European market where relevant.

3 Selecting criteria weightings. In Nike's case, infrastructure and proximity to market were key, keeping short delivery timetables in mind.

4 An economic trade-off analysis of structures and relevant locations.

Table 4.5 displays a representative trade-off table for two locations by relevant weighted criteria.

4.4 Organising for international logistics

Key issue: How can supply chains be better organised to meet the challenges of international logistics?

There are at least three elements in organising for international logistics. These are:

● layering and tiering;

● the evolving role of plants;

● reconfiguration processes.

These will be outlined in the following subsections.

Table 4.5 **Trade-offs between two locations**

Location criteria	Weight	Score region A	Score region B
Railways	1	4	1
Water connections	1	4	1
Road connections	2	2	4
Site availability	2	2	3
Central location	3	1	2
...	...		
Total		19	22

Key: Score on a five-point scale ranging from poor to excellent

4.4.1 Layering and tiering

Internationalisation is often looked at from the point of view of asset centralisation and localisation. However, the wider organisational setting needs to be taken into account as well.

A commonly used maxim is *global coordination and local operation*, which relates to laying out the flow of information and coordination differently from the map of the physical operations. For example, Hewlett Packard operates a globally consistent and coordinated structure of product finalisation and distribution in contrast to its continental operations. The company runs a final manufacturing and central distribution operation in Europe, the United States and Asia for each continent. The operations are structured and run exactly the same, with the only difference being the regions and customers. Furthermore, including tiers of players in the supply chain, these operations are largely outsourced. Facilities are often owned and operated on a dedicated basis by a contract manufacturer and third parties. Hewlett Packard only brings in some management to assure global coordination. Thus, although the company operates in a globalised way, its products are tuned to local markets by means of local logistics operations. Therefore developments in information and communication technology (ICT) do not eliminate the need for such local operations.

Another example can be found in the automotive industry. In this industry, major original equipment manufacturers (OEMs) structure their plant networks globally, while making suppliers build their plants in the immediate vicinity of the OEM plant. The distance or broadcasting horizon between the two plants is defined by the time between the electronic ordering of a specifically finalised single module on the on-line system and the expected time of delivery in sequence along the assembly line. Time horizons for order preparation, finalisation, shipment and delivery tend to be in the area of an hour and a half or less. This causes localisation of the supplier or co-location, while the OEM plant services a continental or even global market.

4.4.2 The evolving role of individual plants

Ferdows (1989) projects the theories of Bartlett and Ghoshal (1989) on the role of individual plants/factories in achieving the targeted international capabilities of global efficiency, local responsiveness and worldwide learning, or a combination of the three. Using the same type of approach, with location considerations on the horizontal axis and performed activities on the vertical axis, van Hoek (1998) adjusted the model for distribution centres. The model indicates the way in which the growth of performed activities changes the demands placed on the capabilities of the plant and changes the location requirements. Location is concerned with the response of governments to globalisation: adjusting local taxes, incentives and infrastructure to favour selection of their territory.

In Figure 4.11 a traditional warehouse is projected to possibly develop into a semi-manufacturing operation with product finalisation among its responsibilities and added value. This also contributes to the creation of a flexible facility for responding to local markets. The model also indicates a possible downgrading of the plant, with its two-way arrows showing development paths. These developments could be driven by poor location conditions, an inability to reach supply chain objectives, or the ability to reach the supply chain objectives more easily at other plants in the company's network. This suggests that the role of individual plants could be seen as an internal competitive issue for plant management. Most relevant, the evolutionary roles and functions of individual plants within the evolving supply chain are specific issues of concern for the realisation of global objectives.

4.4.3 Reconfiguration processes

Related to this last point, the achievement of the required changes in international logistics pipelines is a central issue. In the research presented in Figure 4.11 (van Hoek, 1998), it was found that, across companies, large differences can

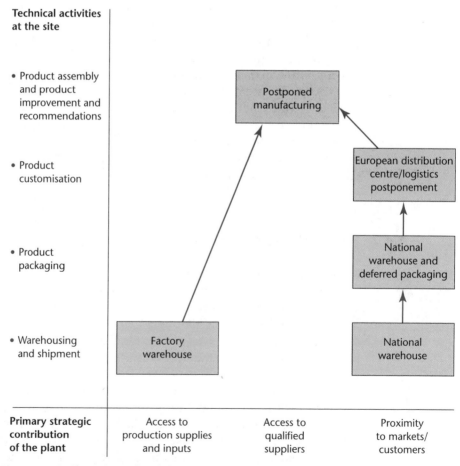

Figure 4.11 Changing role of distribution centres

be found in reconfiguration paths. This was found even in cases where the same supply chain structure (a traditional factory warehouse, as displayed in Figure 4.11) was targeted. Differences included:

- *Supply chain scope/activities involved.* Was only final manufacturing relocated, or did sourcing undergo the same treatment?
- *Focus.* Were activities moved into the market, e.g. localised or centralised within the market? Did the move have a single or multiple focus?
- *Tendency.* Were activities moved out of the (European) market or vice versa, with single or multiple tendencies?
- *Timetable.* Was it a single-step process or did it involve various steps spanning out the process over a longer period of time?
- *Pace.* Was it an overnight change or the result of a gradually changing process?
- *Authority.* Was it directed from a global base (top down) or built up region by region (bottom up)?

The differences can be explained through differences in the supply chain characteristics of companies, among which are:

- *Starting point.* Is the base structure localised or globalised?
- *Tradition.* Does the company have a long history with the baseline in the market, or can it build from scratch (brownfield or greenfield)?

Table 4.6 summarises the differences found in companies implementing postponed manufacturing as an example of a reconfiguration process. The same argument could be applied to the difference between a central European warehouse and a country-based, localised distribution network.

Figures 4.12 and 4.13 represent the reconfiguration process from local distribution through logistics centralisation to postponed manufacturing (final manufacturing in the warehouse). The differences in the implementation path are based upon the different starting points. The path with a localised starting point goes through centralisation within Europe starting from autonomous, duplicated local structures. The path with a global starting point builds a small European presence and then migrates through the increase of European presence centrally (representing a further location into Europe, rather than a further centralisation from within Europe).

Case study 4.2 explores issues and trade-offs found in developing competitive solutions when organising for international logistics.

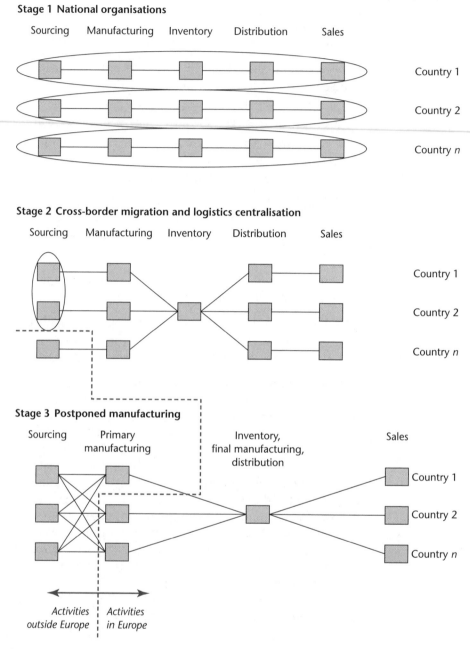

Figure 4.12 **Stages in the implementation of postponed manufacturing: local starting point**

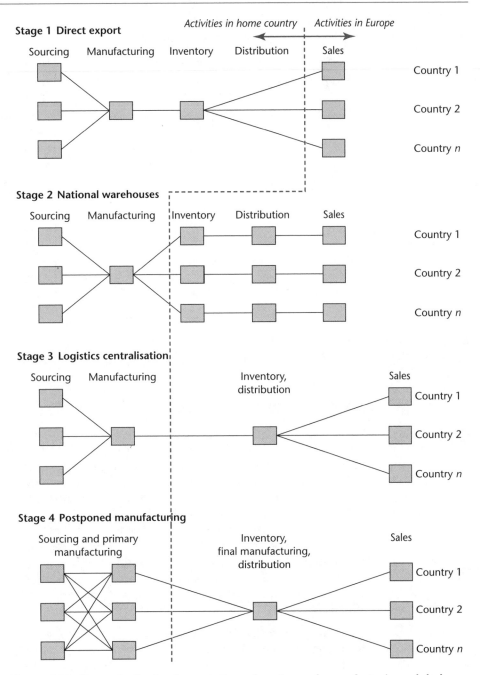

Figure 4.13 **Stages in the implementation of postponed manufacturing: global starting point**

Table 4.6 Differences in reconfiguration processes for companies depending upon starting point (global or local)

Starting point	Global structure	Localised structure
Heritage in market	Little, greenfield approach	Extensive, brownfield approach
Supply chain scope	Narrow, involving inventory and final manufacturing	Broad, involving inventory, manufacturing and sourcing
Focus	Decentralising final manufacturing and inventory into market	Centralising inventory and final manufacturing at continental level and globalising manufacturing and sourcing
Tendency	Single, placing activities into market	Multiple, relocating within market and moving outside market
Timetable	Short (1–10 months)	Long (number of years)
Authority	Global, top-down directions	Local, bottom-up iterative process

CASE STUDY 4.2

Time v cost in global supply chains: lessons from the apparel industry

Vertical integration v. outsourcing

The success of vertical retailers like H&M, Zara, Gap and Next in the last 10 years has forced manufacturers of brand labels like Esprit and Levi, and department stores like El Corte Ingles and Marks & Spencer, to speed up their supply chains. Partly, this has been achieved by integrating their processes and systems upstream (towards their suppliers) and downstream (towards their wholesale customers) in the supply chain.

The competitive environment in the apparel industry is increasingly tough. Retail prices are under pressure; competition is extending from products that were traditionally limited to upper, middle or lower segments of the market – and increasingly from the sports industry; gross margins are shrinking; retail store costs and personnel costs are going up. Those who do not manage their assortment planning and inventories well are continuously under pressure to mark down their merchandise. Vertical retailers have responded by:

- increasing the probability of designing a bestselling product by dramatically shortening its time-to-market (see Chapter 5);
- piloting products in the stores and then replenishing the bestsellers within 14 days by new types of make-to-order processes;
- driving the inventory sales productivity (as measured by stock turn, sales per square metre and mark down percentage) by keen assortment and delivery planning;
- integrating the IT systems from point of sale back into garment production factories and from there towards fabric suppliers;
- focusing on quality of workmanship through fitting and process quality.

Brand label manufacturers traditionally do not own their retail stores, and department stores do not own their factories. This easily leads to competitive disadvantage in comparison with the vertical retailers, who have their own retail stores and have tight control over their manufacturers. To survive in today's marketplace against the vertical retailers, brand labels and department stores need to integrate their processes and systems from point of sale back into the factory. How can this be done?

Core competencies and time-to-market

Companies like Esprit and Nike have initiated strategies to become vertical retailers themselves. Elements of this strategy are to focus on core competencies and to offload all non-core activities to specialists who can manage such activities better and at a lower price. Another element of the strategy is to increase the number of collections from 4 to between 6 and 12 per year. This enables them to be closer to market and thus to forecast and fulfil product demand more accurately. Of course, closeness to market increases the pressure on faster, timely product development and product delivery. The product life cycles of the individual collections are shorter, which leads to enhanced requirements for responsiveness on all supply chain partners. There can be no buffers, and deliveries have to be on time and in full. As a result of this each partner in the chain has increased needs for information, flexibility and transparency. Therefore, vertical retailers must have an excellent supply chain that is fast, flexible, reliable and which provides full transparency at low cost. That is in addition to having good products and closeness to market!

Developing a global SCM network

Re-engineering supply chain processes as part of the verticalisation strategy forces apparel and sports companies to focus on outsourcing all non-core activities and development of a global supply network. Outsourcing of non-core activities, like managing warehousing and distribution centres, frees up management time which can be utilised for managing the supply chain end-to-end. The development of a global supply network consists basically of four components:

- enforcing end-to-end supply chain thinking within the focal firm, its suppliers and its logistics service providers;
- setting up a physical infrastructure with selected lead logistics providers (LLPs) who manage logistics hubs at sourcing origin and market destination (see Figure 4.14);
- using central databases on the Internet (SCM portal and supplier portal) where all logistics partners, suppliers and buyers can view order status and product development in real time;
- empowering LLPs to manage selected service level agreements on behalf of the focal firm in terms of cost and time.

Besides development of the above components of the supply chain, it is important to consider *trade-offs*. These are decisions that have to be made for each step in the supply chain. Figure 4.15 provides an overview of the steps and trade-offs in the supply chain from sourcing areas in Asia, eastern Europe and South America towards a European market destination.

▶

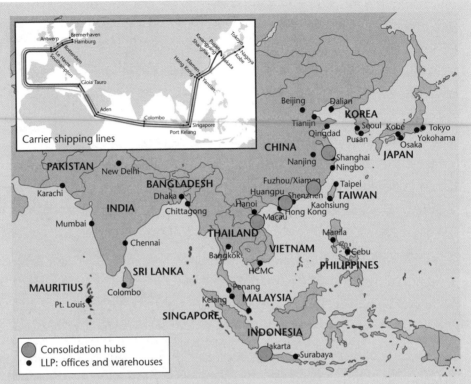

Figure 4.14 Example of physical infrastructure set-up with LLP origin in Asia

Source	ASIA	E. EUROPE	S. AMERICA
Shipper	Direct shipment, consolidation	Direct shipment, consolidation	Direct shipment, consolidation
Shipping mode	Sea/air/land	Land/air/sea	Sea/air
European DC	Pick/pack, cross dock	Pick/pack, cross dock	Pick/pack, cross dock
Transport (DC to store)	Trailers, express	Trailers, express	Trailers, express

Figure 4.15 SCM tools and trade-offs in the supply chain

Cost v. time

Which trade-offs are to be made? For example when sourcing in China while selling in Germany, what process set-ups are possible? When focusing on *cost* the focal firm needs to make sure that shipments are in full container loads, shipped by sea, packed as cross-dock shipments that are then transported to retail stores via a cross-dock warehouse as consolidated shipments once a week. However, this slows down the process time substantially to about 20 days. When focusing on *time* the focal firm needs to ensure that shipments are packed by retailer store at the factory, shipped by air and transported directly to stores without going through a cross-dock warehouse. This process is fast (2–5 days) but it is also very costly, and can only be justified with exclusive branded products with high gross margins. Therefore, companies like Esprit and Nike have a *range* of logistics strategies. Some of these set delivery windows which focus on time, while others minimise cost.

(Source: Based on *How to Speed up your Supply Chain: Best practice from the apparel industry*, Joris Leeman, forthcoming, 2004.)

Questions

1 What are the strategic drivers that are forcing focal firms in the apparel industry to change their supply strategy?

2 Why is time-to-market so important in the apparel industry? How does it impact supply chain processes?

3 Which trade-offs must be made when setting up a global SCM network for the apparel industry? Discuss the trade-offs regarding sourcing countries versus quality.

4.5 Managing for risk readiness

Key issue: **developing appropriate responses to risk in both the short and long term.**

Supply chain disruptions such as transportation breakdowns and geopolitical risks can have many impacts: empty distribution channels, stores and goods stuck upstream leading to lost sales, revenue and customers. And they can be the result of plant shut downs due to supplier discontinuity or collapse, bottlenecks in the transportation system or many other events in the supply chain. There are at least two levels at which companies are responding to risk in international logistics: preparing for immediate response to risks and structurally preparing for risk in international supply chains.

4.5.1 Immediate risk readiness

Recent events have shown that immediate responses to risks can include four things:

- raised inventory levels to assure a cushion for supply disruptions of key parts and supplies;
- redrawing transportation scenarios in the light of the possible logistics melt-down of global trade-routes;
- supplier hedges are put into place and;
- global sourcing and supplier rationalisation efforts are being reconsidered actively.

Inventory policies to reflect volatility levels

Shortly before the second Gulf War, General Motors and Toyota asked their just-in-time suppliers to raise inventory levels in order to avoid early and extensive plant shut downs. It added short-term costs but as a hedge against supply dis-ruptions it can be a real money saver down the line while assuring service to the customer competitors might not be able to offer. LaCrosse Footwear raised its safety stock six-fold for certain products in order to ensure the ability to ship to customers on short notice.

Redo transportation network redesign

Based upon possible risks or an actual situation, scenarios for transportation routes at risk can be developed together with contingency plans on a route-by-route and plant-to-plant basis. Airlines altered services to the Middle East before the Gulf War for example. Here are three other examples:

- Hewlett Packard maintains the ability to shift production between assembly facilities in Europe, North America, South America and Asia as part of a formal continuity plan to be implemented in a crisis;
- Chrysler quickly shifted component shipment from air to express truck serv-ice in response to transportation bottlenecks after the terrorist attacks of 11 September 2001 in the US;
- Continental Tyres' crisis team put together a list of all customers, parts and suppliers outstanding, identified critical shipments by the afternoon of the attacks, and expedited those critical parts by land transport and through con-tingency relationships with transport firms.

Reconsider sole and global sourcing arrangements

Despite the benefits of supplier rationalisation and focused factories, risk man-agement does imply there is real rationale for lining up alternative suppliers in different locations and for manufacturers to develop a thorough understanding of their suppliers' capabilities and vulnerabilities. Companies are responding in two ways: considering alternative and back-up sources and proactively auditing the supply base for financial and operational sustainability in these tough times. Hewlett Packard for example, has secondary suppliers for all critical components as part of its continuity plan.

4.5.2 Structural risk readiness

Because risk needs to be a continuing focus, companies are increasingly devoting dedicated teams to risk management in the supply chain. These teams can do several things:

- develop contingency plans and risk protocols;
- audit preparedness;
- train plant management and staff;
- report to senior management on risk profiles and preparedness.

Most important, however, is not to have risk management in the supply chain solely the responsibility of a team, but to use the team to create an organisation-wide focus and effort. Most often teams *help* plant management and various functions in the organisation, instead of telling them what to do. Henkel, the German consumer goods company for example, has appointed risk teams to work with various departments in assessing risk. It raises fundamental awareness across the organisation, and is the basis for developing contingency plans pro-actively.

Summary

Why international logistics?

- A major driver of the internationalisation of business has been labour shortages and costs in established markets, and the availability of low-cost production in newly industrialised regions. A further driver has been the need to follow customers into new local markets, and to create new learning opportunities.
- This has created phases in internationalisation of operations, and hence of the logistics pipelines that are associated with them. Logistics pipelines differ from market to market and from company to company over time.
- Global sourcing can create economies of scale for transportation through multiple consolidation as organisations orchestrate their global networks, and focus key areas such as manufacturing and R&D.

What are the logistics implications of internationalisation?

- The localisation of products and services to meet specific market needs creates implications for inventory, handling and transport.
- Time-to-market can be extended by the additional distances and complexity of the network. Product obsolescence and inventory holding costs need to be managed in different ways.
- Manufacturing focus needs to be re-thought to cover new markets, along with new delivery strategies.

How do we organise for international logistics?

● New solutions for layering and tiering the supply network are being tried out, such as co-location of suppliers with OEM plants in the automotive industry. Meanwhile, the role of individual plants may be modified to allow more flexible response to local markets, for example by carrying out final assembly in local distribution centres.

● The key to success of internationalisation strategies is the rationalisation of sourcing, production and distribution. At the same time, the organisation needs to be sensitive to local markets and preferences. Crucial also is to ensure risk preparedness in international supply chains.

Discussion questions

1 What are the benefits and limitations of international logistics? Illustrate your response by referring to the sourcing of standard shirts and fashion blouses (shown in Table 1.1 in Chapter 1) from manufacture in the Far East.

2 Tiering of the supply network is referred to in section 4.4.1 above, and also in Chapter 1, section 1.1, and in the Global Lighting case study at the end of Chapter 2. Describe the advantages of tiering in terms of globalisation, touching on areas such as outsourcing and the focused factory.

3 Identify six potential sources and causes of risk in global supply chains. Use the references to Peck (2003) below to propose countermeasures.

References

Bartlett, C.A. and Ghoshal, S. (1989) *Managing Across Borders*. Boston, MA: Harvard Business School Press.

Buck Consultants International (1997) *Europese distributie en waardetoevoeging door buitenlandse bedrijven*. Nijmegen: BCI.

Ferdows, K. (1989) 'Mapping international factory networks', in Ferdows, K. (ed.), *Managing International Manufacturing*, pp. 3–22. Amsterdam: Elsevier Science.

Helferich, O.K. and Cook, R.L. (2003) *Securing the Supply Chain*. Oak Brook, IL: Council of Logistics Management.

Peck (2003): *Creating Resilient Supply Chains: a practical guide*, and *Understanding Supply Chain Risk: a self-assessment work book*. Available for free download, courtesy of the UK Department for Transport, at www.som.cranfield.ac.uk/som/scr

van Hoek, R.I. (1998) 'Reconfiguring the supply chain to implement postponed manufacturing', *International Journal of Logistics Management*, Vol. 9, No. 1, pp. 95–110.

van Hoek, R.I. Chatman, R. and Wilding, R. (2002) 'Managers in supply chain management: the critical dimension', *Supply Chain Management: An international journal*, Vol. 7, Nos. 3 and 4, pp. 119–25.

Yip, G.S. (1989) 'Global strategy . . . in a world of nations?', *Sloan Management Review*, Fall, pp. 29–41.

Suggested further reading

Dicken, P. (2003) *Global Shift: Reshaping the global economic map in the 21st century*. London: Sage Publications.

Gourdin K. (2001) *Global Logistics Management: A competitive advantage for the new millennium*. Oxford: Blackwell.

CHAPTER 5

Managing the lead-time frontier

Outcomes

The intended outcomes of this chapter are to:

- introduce time-based competition definitions and concepts;
- show how the lead time needs to be managed to serve customer expectations;
- explain how organisations compete through responsiveness.

By the end of this chapter you should be able to understand:

- how organisations compete through managing lead time;
- how time can be used as a performance measure;
- P-times and D-times and the consequence when they do not match;
- different solutions to reduce P-times;
- how to apply a methodology for implementing these solutions.

Introduction

This chapter takes a strategic view of time and the impact of time on logistics performance. It provides an introduction to the nature of time-based competition and how time can provide competitive advantage in logistics. As we saw in section 1.3, logistics supports the competitiveness of the supply chain as a whole by meeting end-customer demand through supplying what is needed, when needed and at low cost. Because logistics supports time and place commitments in the supply chain, it can be argued that the lead time frontier accounts for at least half of logistics success.

Competing on time is the principle of taking timely completion of supply chain tasks to a higher level: that of compressing cycle times for supply chain operations for internal and external benefits. External benefits include:

- lowering overall cycle time and providing services faster;
- outrunning competition.

These benefits are especially important in the context of improving responsiveness to customers and volatile markets. Chapter 7 will return to these points.

Internal benefits include:

- shorter cash-to-cash cycles, thereby releasing working capital and reducing asset intensity of the supply chain;
- lowering inventories in the pipeline and storage by speeding up turnover times for work in progress and inventory.

These benefits are especially important within lean or waste elimination approaches, as will be developed in Chapter 6. This chapter focuses on how time-based solutions link with competitive strategy.

Key issues   *This chapter addresses five key issues as follows:*

1 **Introduction to the role of time in competitive advantage**: using time in logistics management and strategy.
2 **P:D ratios and the lead-time gap**: the gap between the time it takes to get the product to the customer (P-time) and the time the customer is prepared to wait (D-time).
3 **Time-based mapping**: how to create visibility of time across the network.
4 **Managing timeliness in the logistics pipeline**: strategies and practices for coping when P-time is greater than D-time.
5 **A method for implementing time-based practices**: implementing time-based practices across the network.

5.1 The role of time in competitive advantage

Key issue: **What is time-based competition, how does it link to other initiatives, and what is the purpose of it?**

5.1.1 Time-based competition: definition and concepts

Many attempts at business improvement focus on cost reduction and quality improvement. While a great deal of benefit has been achieved by many organisations through these efforts, most of the obvious opportunities for improvement have now been taken. This has led to time emerging as a fresh battleground in the search for competitive advantage. A working definition of competing on time is:

The timely response to customer needs

The emphasis in this definition is on 'timely'. This means responding to customers' needs on time – neither early nor late. The implication of this definition is that the organisation must focus its capabilities on being responsive to the customer.

Traditionally, people often have the opinion that you cannot have low cost *and* high quality, or low cost *and* fast delivery, or fast delivery *and* high quality. The belief is that some kind of trade-off is necessary, meaning that more of one advantage means less of another. For example, better quality means putting in more inspectors, which increases costs. Such thinking was shown to be flawed when the quality movement of the 1980s showed that good quality actually *reduces* costs (Crosby, 1979). The trade-off between cost and quality can be altered by preventing defects from happening in the first place by investing in the *prevention* of defects through such measures as:

- designing the process so that defects cannot occur (error proofing);
- designing products so that they are easy to make and distribute;
- training personnel so that they understand the process and its limitations.

This investment leads to savings in *detecting* defects, by removing the need for inspection, and in avoiding the *failures* that lead to scrap and the cost of resolving customer complaints. The result is that overall quality costs (prevention + detection + failure) can be reduced by spending more on prevention.

Understanding trade-off relationships lies at the heart of an organisation's ability to achieve competitive advantage. Relationships that need to be understood and harnessed include recognising that:

- costs do not have to increase in order to improve quality, they can reduce;
- costs do not have to increase when lead times are reduced, they can also reduce;
- costs do not have to go up as product variety increases and times reduce, they can also reduce.

Each of these trade-offs has important links with strategy. Not least, when it comes to harnessing lead time reduction it is clear that organisations that put responsiveness to the customer first need to change the way they go about their business. This involves redesigning systems and processes to allow these goals to be achieved.

5.1.2 Time-based initiatives

When a company attacks time directly, the first benefits to show up are usually shorter cycle times and faster inventory turns. Lower overhead costs usually follow, as the costs of dealing with breakdowns and delays begin to disappear from the system. So by seeking time reduction, *both* time reduction and cost reduction are often the rewards.

Attacking the sources and causes of delays helps reduce quality defects in product and service. Thus by focusing on time, customers' needs are met more quickly and a quality benefit will often accompany the time benefit.

5.1.3 Time-based opportunities to add value

There are several ways in which a company can use time to help meet customer needs better and therefore add more value. The most common examples of this are:

- increased responsiveness to customer needs;
- managing increased variety;
- increased product innovation;
- improved return on new products;
- reducing risk by relying less on forecasts.

We deal with each of these opportunities in turn.

Increased responsiveness to customer needs

Increased responsiveness to customer needs is the most common reason for organisations to invest in time-based approaches to performance enhancement. Many elements of customer service are dependent upon time. These include how long it takes to deliver a product or service, achieving on-time delivery and how long it takes to deal with customer queries, estimates and complaints.

High levels of responsiveness to customers tend to correlate to greater loyalty from them and therefore more business over time. Such responsiveness is also addictive to the customer, creating customer lock-in. Once they get used to short lead times they often reorganise their own products and services to customers to make use of responsiveness from their suppliers, such as by holding less inventory and promising their own customers shorter lead times. Once they start to do this they find it hard to accept longer times again.

Customers of time-based organisations do not have to carry as much raw material or component stock and therefore benefit from a cost saving. In order to profit from the service they provide, a time-based organisation needs to demonstrate to customers that the total cost of doing business is lower and to recover some of this value. This can be achieved by winning more business and/or by charging more.

Managing increased variety

Shortened lead times in product development, the supply chain and manufacturing help factories deliver a variety of products without the traditional cost penalty. The same is also true of service organisations that can design and supply a range of new offerings in line with changes in market needs. By reducing overall lead time, product complexity and process set-up times, the production of a particular product can be scheduled more frequently with smaller production batches. This improves the variety of products available to a customer over a given time.

Increased product innovation

Time-based organisations are more likely to meet customer needs accurately by using short product development times to produce new products that meet customer needs. The shortening of product development lead time means that innovations can be capitalised on to maximum effect. If a company innovates through product design faster than its competitors it will become increasingly competitive. Conversely, if your competitors are innovative then reducing the time to develop imitations will underpin a 'fast follower' strategy to keep up.

Improved return on new products

Reducing product development lead time means that a product can get to market earlier. This has a number of important advantages:

- the sales life of the product is extended;
- a higher price can be charged;
- new customers can be won;
- a high market share can be built through building upon the initial lead.

Each of these benefits can add to the other. Therefore, being first to the market allows a higher initial price to be charged helping to recoup development costs quicker. This revenue will support investment into further developments necessary to retain these initial customers. Meanwhile, the initial product can continue to be sold, generating cash through its high market share. Being first in the market maximises the product life until the time when it becomes obsolete.

An impressive approach to the issue of obsolescence is attributed to Akio Morita, the co-founder of Sony and inventor of the Walkman. He believed that it was his job to make his own products obsolete before competitors did so. In effect, not only was his aim to make innovative products, he also sought to build on this success in the knowledge that if he did not then someone else soon would.

The related argument here is that of *break-even time* rather than break-even volumes discussed in Chapter 3. Traditional break-even analysis focuses on the volume of product needed to be moved before the investment pays off. Given shortening times-to-market and compressed product life cycles (example: from 6 months to 45 days of shelf-life for Nike footwear) the analysis shifts towards the question 'how long before break-even is reached?' Figure 5.1 illustrates the point.

As product life cycles shrink, so the time window of opportunity for making profits also shrinks. This consideration means that a new product must achieve its break-even time more quickly.

Reducing risk by relying less on forecasts

There is a saying in industry that there are only two types of forecast: wrong ones and lucky ones, and there are precious few of the latter! It is certainly true that the further ahead a company tries to forecast, the less likely the forecast is to be correct.

One of the aims of a time-based initiative is often to minimise how much forecasting is needed. By reducing the production lead time, the period when demand is uncertain becomes shorter. Forecasting over a shorter time period results in a more reliable forecast and therefore in less risk of stock-outs or obsolete stock. It also reduces the amount of finished goods stock needed, which frees up working capital.

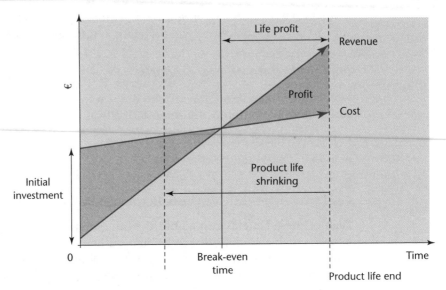

Figure 5.1 **Break-even time**

In product development, risk is also reduced by shortening lead times. This is achieved when the specification for the new product can be fixed with more certainty, thus improving the chances of market success.

The ultimate goal is to reduce production time so it lies within the lead time it has been given by the customer to deliver. In this situation, no forecasting is needed and all production is done in line with actual customer orders. The implications of reducing production time in relation to the demand time of customers are very significant and we have devoted the whole of section 5.2 to addressing them.

5.1.4 Time-based opportunities to reduce cost

The second key element of time-based competition is to reduce cost and therefore improve productivity through the elimination of non-value-added time in processes. This means that wasted lead time and unnecessary tasks that are not actually adding any value in the customer's eyes should be identified and eliminated. Stopping unnecessary tasks and removing wasted time from those that remain reduces cost by:

● reducing the need for working capital;
● reducing the need for plant and equipment capital;
● reducing development costs;
● reducing quality costs.

We address each of these in turn.

Reducing working capital

Increasing the speed of flow through processes by eliminating unnecessary steps and wasted time reduces the amount of money tied up in the system. In the short term the focus will be upon inventory. Here manufacturing lead time is inversely proportional to work-in-progress levels. By focusing on time we decrease raw material, work-in-progress and finished good stocks. Lowered inventory levels result in reduced working capital. As already mentioned, returns on working capital will be improved by reducing obsolescence caused by making to stock and not to order.

Reducing plant and equipment capital

Over the longer term, processes become more visible, inventory levels reduce and opportunities to minimise capital expenses become more visible. These opportunities include the removal of equipment not employed in activities that add value. Initial items to remove will include the racking and pallets formerly used to store inventory. Next will be a purge of unnecessary equipment in offices, stores and production, including the jigging for unnecessary operations of obsolete parts.

In terms of what to do with superfluous items, some may be sold and capital recovered. The remaining items should just be skipped. While it may seem stupid to just throw away equipment given how much some items have cost, these are sunk costs. If the equipment can no longer be used to generate revenue, all it does is incur further costs, such as maintenance, and the floor space it occupies will have many better uses.

As a company embraces time-based competition then success in the marketplace will increase demand for products and services that the customer really values. To make way for these means that space will be at a premium in the company. This is just the driver needed to replace the old with the new.

Reducing development costs

Shortened lead times in product development are achieved in-part by more effective use of development resources through elimination of rework and reduction of distracting superfluous projects. This leads to cost reductions as the time spent on a given project is less.

Reducing quality costs

One of the main elements in improving quality is to reduce the time between an error being made and the problem being detected. The sooner the error is detected the smaller the amount of product affected by it. Reducing lead times has a positive effect on the speed of feedback and hence quality costs are reduced.

In keeping with the total quality movement, time-sensitive organisations will only become consistently responsive if they strive to maintain quality processes. This means that as defects and errors arise they are detected quickly, root causes identified and effective solutions installed to ensure they can not recur.

Activity 5.1

List six applications of responsiveness in an organisation: for example, 'external phone calls answered within five rings'. How many organisations can you think of that compete overtly on time, such as the Vision Express example given in Chapter 1?

5.1.5 Limitations to time-based approaches

Despite the clear benefits of time-based approaches to logistics management described above there are often barriers to its application, as well as limitations to its relevance.

Two basic limitations to the need for time-based logistics management are the need for speed and the degree of speed required. Not all operating environments require speed. Product demand that is very predictable such as high-volume, low-value commodity products can be planned well in advance and processed without a particular speed. Not all customers value speed as they may be able to order well in advance of delivery. Delivery before the parts are needed creates unnecessary inventories. In particular, when there are costs involved in creating speedy delivery, customers may trade that off against ordering in advance. Only selected parcels need to be shipped with express carriers, for example.

A particular issue with the costs involved in speeding up logistics processes in the supply chain is the distribution of those costs between companies in the supply chain. It is well known that JIT deliveries for example may generate significant costs for suppliers whereas the customer may experience most of its benefits (such as low process inventories and rapid delivery). Toyota is capable of manufacturing a car in five days but has decided not to do so because of the pressure it would place on its suppliers and its distribution processes, creating costs that are not expected to be outweighed by revenue opportunities in current market circumstances.

An additional issue is that time-based approaches might lead to superior performance only being achieved on a limited number of occasions. An illustration of this situation is shown in Figure 5.2. In this example a supplier demonstrates that it is able to deliver in only one day. However, it is clear that this was achieved for only a minor portion of shipments, which does not mean that customers can depend on shipments being consistently completed within a day. Rather customers will order seven days in advance, where the required 99 per cent service level for deliveries is achieved. Time-based approaches are not about managing exceptions but managing for speed reliably.

5.2 P:D ratios and differences

Key issues: **What are P- and D-times, and why are they important to logistics strategy?**

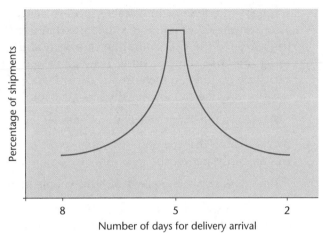

Figure 5.2 Distribution of shipment cycle times in days

P-time and D-time are measures of performance of the supply pipeline. They are explained in section 5.2.2, but let us first look at the importance of time as a performance measure.

5.2.1 Using time as a performance measure

One of the major advantages of a time-based approach to managing processes over one based on cost or quality is the ease with which time is understood as a measure. While cost and quality are open to differences in interpretation, time is an absolute measure. Stalk and Hout (1990) refer to the 'time elasticity of price', where the price that customers are prepared to pay is often related to the delivery speed. For example, Talleres Auto in case study 1.4 was able to charge premium prices for spare parts in breakdown situations because these were 'distress purchases'.

Cost is a more subjective measure that is open to interpretation, three examples of which we saw in section 3.2. Many people have a poor grasp of how costs work in practice, and do not understand how the actions they take affect others. An all too frequent example is saving costs in one part of the supply network only to cause extra costs elsewhere. While quality is an important area for organisations to improve, there are a number of different ways to interpret 'quality'. Garvin (1988) lists eight *dimensions of quality*, which depend on the perspective taken, such as product quality (design), conformance quality (manufacturing), and fitness for use (customer). In order for quality measures to be useful they often require a statistical approach that can easily be misunderstood by those who have not been explicitly trained. Deming's famous Monte Carlo experiments with a funnel and glass marble (Deming, 1986: 327) illustrate the perils of interfering with a stable process:

> If anyone adjusts a stable process to try to compensate for a result that is undesirable, or for a result that is extra good, the output that follows will be worse than if he had left the process alone.

Frequent interference in a stable process increases the variability of its output! Time, on the other hand, is a measure that everyone understands. Every person has access to the exact duration of a second, minute or hour, thanks to clocks using the same units of time. Time allows people across an organisation, with very little training, to measure the performance of a process or activity. Using this measure anyone can answer the key question:

Do we meet the target the customer has set for us?

By comparing this measure with one taken for the performance of competitors, we can easily answer the next key question:

How good are we compared with the competition?

If we take a reason for measuring performance as being to understand the effect of making changes to a process, we can more easily answer the question:

Is our performance getting better or worse?

By using measures that are simple to understand, people can see the big issues more easily. They can measure and quantify the flow of activities directly, and ask themselves whether each of the steps in a process is adding real value or just adding cost. By following the flow through a process we can see where time is lost (see Chapter 3). This allows us to translate the data into time-reduction and cost-reduction opportunities. Looking at cost analyses alone does not tell anyone where to save time.

5.2.2 Using time to measure supply pipeline performance

In the same way that time can be used to measure the performance of a process within a company so it can be used to measure the supply pipeline. Two measures are presented below that are key to understanding supply pipeline performance: P-time and D-time.

P-time

The first measure of performance for the total supply process is to determine how long it takes for a product or service to pass through it. This measure is used to identify the total logistics lead time, also known as the *P-time* or production time.

Just to be clear, the P-time is a measure of the total time it takes for a product to go through a pipeline. Thus it includes procurement lead time, manufacturing lead time and distribution lead time: it is not just the time it takes to supply from stock.

The measure starts the moment a new order is raised. It includes all the time needed to take a product through all the processes necessary to make and deliver that product. It is important to be clear about when these activities start and end in order for the measure to be consistent should you want to measure performance for a number of processes, including those of competitors. For a first attempt at this measure take the starting time as the point when an order is raised.

Consider the total time needed to make and deliver a new product or batch of products. This includes the time needed to procure the longest lead parts and the total manufacturing time. The end of the process is the time when you fulfil an order and send the product to the customer.

When you are competent in measuring this time and creating useful data you should improve the measure you take. Instead of measuring from when you receive the order, measure from when the person in the customer's company realises they have a need. The end point is not when you send the product but when it is received by that person. This measure incorporates the internal process of the customer's company for informing you of the order and the steps they take to receive your delivery and get it to where it is needed. Exploring this process will reveal useful opportunities where you can help the customer to help themselves, thus strengthening your competitive position.

D-time

The time for which a customer is willing to wait to have their demand fulfilled is the *D-time* or demand time. D-time varies considerably. For example, the time a customer is willing to wait for 'fast food' is comparatively short. Assuming you are in a city with plenty of options, once you realise you are hungry you will probably want to be eating within 10 minutes. This D-time will include the time it takes to walk to the outlet/restaurant, wait in a queue, be served and sit somewhere. By contrast, as a customer of an up-market restaurant, you may have travelled for an hour, spend 20 minutes in a reception area over an aperitif and study the menu for 15 minutes, before happily waiting half an hour for the meal to be cooked and served.

In addition to the obvious differences in grade and choice of food, the implication from a supply chain point of view is that the two restaurants must be organised in totally different ways to deliver the food within their customers' D-time. Interestingly, the same customer may visit both restaurants on the same day and accept the two different delivery systems. You do not *expect* to wait at a fast-food counter, but you *do* expect to linger over a meal in a high-quality restaurant.

Similar examples can be found in other industries. Buyers of new premium cars expect to wait a month or two for delivery when they place an order. Some people are not prepared to wait so long, but are prepared to accept a second choice of colour instead of their first, especially if the dealer gives a discount! Manufacturers of vehicles for customers with short D-times face increased supply chain challenges compared with those who have long ones. If it is not possible to make a car to order within the expected D-time, then the manufacturer is forced to carry out some or all of the logistics processes speculatively. The most risky scenario is to make the whole car for stock, hoping that the forecast mix of diesel and petrol, of left- and right-hand drive and so on is correct. But taking such a risk is necessary to cope with the customer who wants to drive away a vehicle the same day he or she enters the dealer's showroom.

It is worth pointing out the parallels in new product development. Some new product development is a race to get new ideas and innovations to market.

Table 5.1 **Getting ideas to market**

	Idea to market	**Meet window of opportunity**
Objective	Reduce lead time for turning idea into cash	Delay commitment of cash; Develop fresher, more fashionable product; Operate within shorter, less unstable forecast period
Examples	Electronics – maximise advantage in a new market segment before competitors respond	Summer clothing – delay outlay on raw materials to improve cash flow and delay commitment to particular designs until last possible time
	Pharmaceuticals – get new drug to market to (1) save life and (2) begin to recover development spending	New car launch in four years' time – delay spend on tooling and delay design freeze so latest technologies can be incorporated

However, others involve hitting specific customer-defined windows of opportunity for getting products to market. This is particularly true for lower-tier suppliers in supply chains. These two concepts have different objectives, as shown in Table 5.1.

Suppose your customer announces their intention for the launch of their new product. They usually give a number of deadlines to would-be suppliers, including:

- date for tenders;
- date for first-off samples;
- date for volume launch.

These are the D-times for each stage of product development. As a potential supplier, you must be able to meet all of these windows. Indeed, each supplier must be capable of meeting all of these deadlines for the product to meet its launch date successfully.

5.2.3 Consequences when P-time is greater than D-time

P-time should be measured for each separate product group, because each will have different internal processes. D-time should be measured for each different market segment that is served, because customers may have different needs (e.g. prepared to wait/not prepared to wait).

Armed with this data, P-times and D-times should be contrasted for each product/customer group to see if P-time is more than D-time. A simple way to do this is by drawing them on a graph as time lines, as shown in Figure 5.3. The length of the two shaded bars shown in Figure 5.3 represents *time*. The bar for the P-time represents the time taken for buy, make and sell processes. The D-time bar represents the time the customer is prepared to wait for an order to be fulfilled.

Comparing the length of the two bars, it can be seen that the time it takes to respond to an order is longer than the customer is prepared to wait. Thus the P-time is greater than D-time. The consequence is that this focal firm is not able to make to order. On the other hand, it may be possible to complete the final 'make' processes such as assembly and test within the customer required D-time. This is basically how Dell manages to supply the computer you want so quickly!

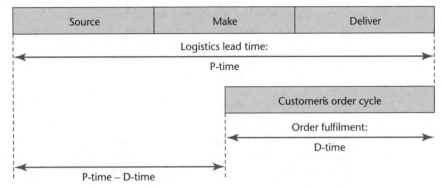

Figure 5.3 **When P-time is > D-time**

Activity 5.2

Assess the benefits and concerns that may arise as a result of the relative sizes of P-time and D-time. Compile your views in the table below:

	P-time greater than D-time	P-time = D-time	P-time less than D-time
Benefits	● ● ●	● ● ●	● ● ●
Concerns	● ● ●	● ● ●	● ● ●

CASE STUDY 5.1

Wiltshire Distribution Transformers

Sid Beckett, the Managing Director of Wiltshire Distribution Transformers (WDT), had concentrated on a new generation of simplified, modular designs that used proven US technology. He had energetically exploited the market advantages this had given. WDT now has two major product ranges:

- TR 100: 3-phase, oil-cooled transformers with a power rating from 200 to 2000 kVA;
- PS 300: packaged substations that utilise TR 100 transformers with appropriate switchgear and LV control panels. Judging by the number of enquiries, the market for both product ranges was now increasing.

The new JIT system

Each product must be individually designed to order. Formerly, this process had taken two weeks, because a design engineer had to develop an entirely new design from scratch based on the customer order. Designs have now been modularised as a result of the new system: that is, a new design is produced from a few hundred standard 'modules' that are held on file. This can be done by a sales engineer in a matter of hours. If a tender is accepted by a customer, it had formerly taken another two weeks to convert the tender information into specifications and drawings for manufacture. Today, it is possible simply to send the accepted tender information to the shopfloor, and to use the set of standard engineering information already held on file to act as manufacturing instructions. The following is a list of the main features of the new JIT system.

Enquiry processing

The engineer enters major design details (kVA rating, voltage ratio, product classification and quantity) into a computerised estimating program. From a list of 700 possible options, the selected ones to suit the tender requirements are added. From a library of material, labour and overhead costs, a tender price is calculated.

Should the customer accept this price, then a customer delivery date is agreed and the tender becomes the works order.

Engineering instructions

WDT's efforts had resulted in the completion of a comprehensive library of standard drawings and instructions that covered all major options. The works order simply calls these up by reference number and description. The one exception is the fabricated cubicle that houses the packaged substations. This has to be individually designed. A simple CAD/CAM system enables the design and associated manufacturing instructions to be completed quickly. Presentations of the panels can be separately worked on and designed. The output is a set of CNC tapes for the relevant machines in the fabrication shop, and a set-up schedule indicating sheet size, clamp positions, list of tools, etc.

Master production scheduling (MPS)

Standard networks are kept on file. Activity durations for each manufacturing process vary according to specific designs, and are picked up from the works order. Only bottle neck operations are scheduled, and can be loaded only up to 100 per cent of their capacity. Given the customer requirement date, the scheduling program works backwards and loads activities to key resources so that the final assembly date will be met. The MPS acts by pulling demand through the manufacturing system (a process called pull scheduling).

Material requirements for each work centre for each order are calculated by means of a modular bill of material, which has been simplified as a result of the modular designs.

Shop scheduling

The MPS generates operation release tickets (ORTs) for each scheduled process. The type and quantity of units required by the next process are withdrawn from the previous one as they are needed. When a work square becomes empty, an ORT is passed back to the preceding work centre to trigger a manufacturing operation. This serves as a signal (*kanban*) to the previous process to produce just enough units to replace those withdrawn.

Work is performed in sequence of ORTs, and is carried out only when an output square is available. Completed operations are marked up on the hard copy of the MPS, which is pinned to the wall of the works manager's office by the supervisors at the end of each shift. The MPS is updated for completed operations and new orders each week.

A combination of four weeks' reduction in the time taken to tender and the time taken to produce a manufacturing design, and a further two weeks' reduction in manufacturing times, has placed WDT in a pre-eminent position in the marketplace. Customers want to place orders for this type of equipment later and later in their own projects, so short lead times are a major benefit to WDT in the marketplace.

Questions

1 Sketch out the main processes between a customer's placing an enquiry and receiving delivery of a WDT transformer. Where has WDT really scored in terms of reducing this time?

2 What are the potential negatives of WDT's new JIT system in terms of limiting customer choice and short-circuiting the design process?

5.3 Time-based process mapping

Key issue: **How do you go about measuring time in a supply network?**

The purpose of supply chain mapping is to generate visibility of the processes within the supply chain. Once this visibility has been achieved it is possible to benchmark similar processes. The processes we need to map are the actual processes that are taking place, not what is supposed to happen. Quality standards based on ISO 9000 require processes to be documented, but within the organisation the actual process undertaken may often differ considerably. When undertaking a supply chain mapping exercise it is the *actual* process that we need to focus on. The key is to track one order, one product, or one person through the process with respect to time. A map is a snapshot taken during a given time period. Workloads may vary during the course of a month, and so may the individual process times. Record the actual times that you observe. Most processes take place in batches, so if you are mapping a trailer being filled with tyres, record the time that the median (middle) tyre waits before being moved. The method of documentation of the process and the symbols to use are illustrated in Table 5.2.

Key operations are visible, but the subprocesses that often consume the most time and generate the greatest inefficiencies (such as waiting for transport) are

Table 5.2 **Example of process document**

Step	Description	Symbol	Time	Notes
1	Machine complete	O	1:37	
2	Inspect	□	0:45	
3	Wait transport	D	5:53	
4	Transport to heat treat	→	0:08	
5	Wait heat treat	D	3:34	
6	Heat treat	O	4:15	

Symbol	Description
→	transport
∇	store
O	operation
□	inspect
D	delay

also revealed. This enables solutions to problems to be generated and the supply chain to be improved.

The following sections give an overview of the key stages involved in the time-based mapping process.

5.3.1 Stage 1: Create a task force

Before the mapping process can be undertaken it needs to be recognised that supply chain processes cross all functions of the organisation. It is therefore important to have all key functions represented. The task force must be assured of top management support. A project champion may also need to be appointed.

5.3.2 Stage 2: Select the process to map

It may not be feasible to map the total supply chain initially. Take an overview of the core processes within the organisation and the time they take before deciding on the priorities for detailed mapping. To get the organisation to 'buy in' to the project, a subprocess may be identified that has been a particular problem. This can act as a pilot for the task force, enabling them to prove that their methods really work. When selecting the process, ensure that there is a generic customer or group of customers that the process serves. A clear start (or trigger) and finish to the process should also be present.

5.3.3   Stage 3: Collect data

The most effective way to collect the data is to follow an item through the process. This is often referred to as *walking the process*. An actual component or order will be followed through all the stages of the process. Identify someone who is actively involved in each part of the process and knows what is really happening within the process; interview these key individuals. Get the interviewee to describe each movement of the item with respect to time. It can be useful to ask the interviewee to describe 'a day in the life of' that product or order. Remember that the steps an item goes through is not just those where something is done: for example, items could be waiting or being moved, or may be sitting waiting for a decision to be made. Identify an appropriate level of detail at which to map the process. Initially it might be better to map at a high level to gain an overview of the process; one can always map in more detail if needed later.

5.3.4   Stage 4: Flow chart the process

Use the data collected by walking the process and the interviews with operators to sketch a flow chart so linkages and dependencies between steps can be clarified before constructing the time-based process map. This flow chart is used by the task force to ensure they have not missed any steps in the process.

5.3.5   Stage 5: Distinguish between value-adding and non-value-adding time

A rough definition of value-adding time is time when something takes place on the item that the end-customer is willing to pay for. The definition of value-adding time requires due consultation, and should be aligned with the overall business strategy. The business strategy should define the markets and segments, and the accompanying order qualifiers and order winners (see Chapters 1 and 2). Once the value-adding criteria at the strategic level have been defined, these can be translated into value-adding criteria at an operational level. The time data collected in stage 3 can then be analysed to identify the value-adding time. Value-adding time is characterised using three criteria:

● whether the process (or elements of the process) physically transforms the material that forms the input to that process;

● whether the change to the item is something that the customer values or cares about and is willing to pay for;

● whether the process is right the first time, and will not have to be repeated in order to produce the desired result that is valued by the customer.

Non-value-adding activity can be split into four categories: delay, transport, storage and inspection, using the categories from Table 5.2.

5.3.6   Stage 6: Construct the time-based process map

The purpose of the time-based process map is to represent the data collected clearly and concisely so that the critical aspects of the supply network can be communicated in an easily accessible way. The ultimate goal is to represent the process on a single piece of paper so that the task force and others involved in the project can easily see the issues. A simple Gantt chart technique can be used to show the process, and different categories of non-value-adding time can be represented on this. These categories will be dependent on the nature of each process. Figure 5.4 shows three operations processes (delivery, production and goods in), with the last one magnified to show four types of waste.

From the interviews and data from walking the process, extract the relevant data. It is sometimes useful to sketch a flow diagram so that linkages and dependences between steps can be clarified before constructing the map. This flow diagram can be used to approximate the total time that the business process consumes.

5.3.7   Stage 7: Solution generation

Once the time-based process map has been produced, the opportunities for improvement are generally all too obvious. The task force can collect ideas and categorise causes of non-value-adding activity using problem-solving approaches

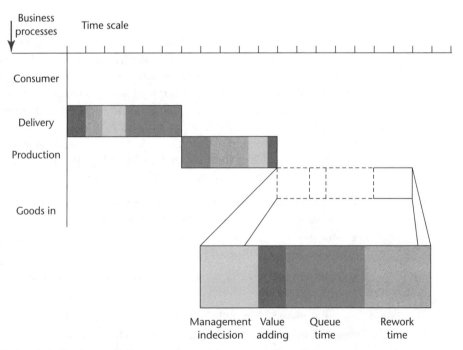

Figure 5.4 Process activity mapping and sources of waste

such as cause-and-effect diagrams. (A helpful condensed guide to problem-solving tools and techniques will be found in Bicheno, 2000.)

The Electro-Coatings case study describes how the above principles were applied to a focal firm that produces electroplated parts for the automotive industry.

CASE STUDY 5.2

Electro-Coatings Ltd

Electro-Coatings Ltd electroplates parts for the automotive industry: for example, the marque badges fitted to the front of prestige cars. Customers were becoming increasingly demanding, resulting in Electro-Coatings' undertaking a review of its internal supply chain. The initial analysis by walking the process identified 12 key processes, shown in Figure 5.5.

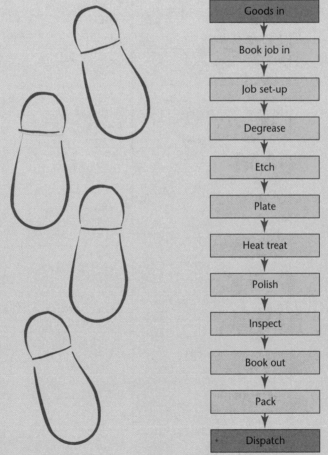

Figure 5.5 Walk the process (12 steps)

Once this initial map has been produced, each step was mapped in detail, and some 60 steps were identified. These steps have been summarised as a flow diagram in Figure 5.6, showing every process step.

An initial analysis of value-adding and non-value-adding time was undertaken. This is shown in Table 5.3, which summarises the total time, wasted time and value-adding time for each of the 12 steps. These data were then used to produce a map with the value-adding (activity) time and non-value-adding (wasted) time shown as the series of 12 steps against total elapsed time in hours (Figure 5.7).

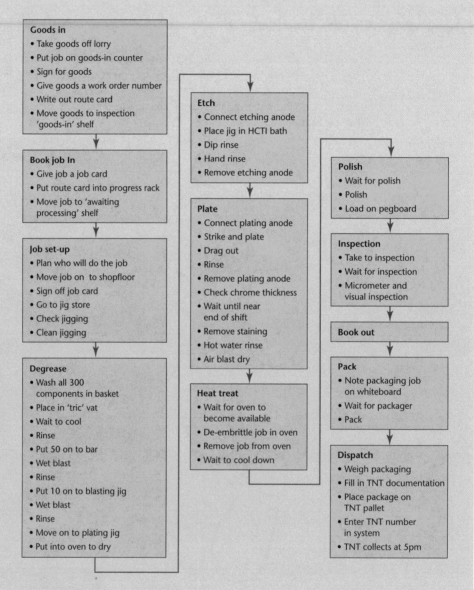

Figure 5.6 Identify every process step

The total process took approximately 70 hours. The project team held an afternoon meeting with those involved in the process, and the results of this brainstorming session produced the cause-and-effect diagram shown in Figure 5.8. This was then used to

Table 5.3 **Time-based analysis data**

	Total time/hours	Wasted time/hours	Activity time/hours
Goods in	0.00	3.91	0.41
Book job in	4.32	20.00	0.41
Job set-up	24.73	5.50	1.77
Degrease	32.00	1.00	0.60
Etch and plate	33.60	8.75	2.20
Heat treat	44.55	0.00	4.50
Polish	49.05	1.95	1.95
Inspect	52.95	9.50	1.00
Book out	63.45	0.00	0.40
Pack	63.85	4.00	0.85
Dispatch	68.70	0.00	0.40

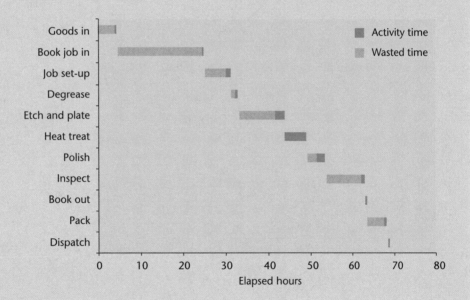

Figure 5.7 **Time-based process map: current**

identify opportunities for improving the process. For example, the analysis revealed that jobs arriving goods inwards at 9.00 am might not be input into the system until 5.00 pm because the operator would undertake the computer inputting in one go at the end of the day. This resulted in manufacturing not having visibility of the updated order book until 9.00 am the following morning. This was easily addressed by combining the booking-in process with the good inwards process, removing a further lead time. Figure 5.9 depicts the re-engineered process.

▶

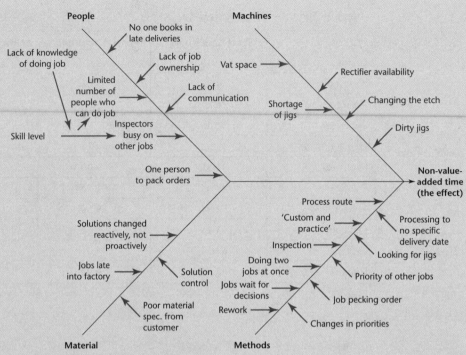

Figure 5.8 Cause and effect diagram

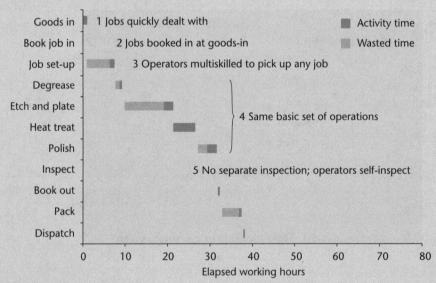

Figure 5.9 Time-based process map: re-engineered

The simple actions undertaken by the company resulted in the total process taking 37 hours. This resulted in a more responsive service being offered to its customers, and increased business.

(Source: Based on a study by Dr Paul Chapman and Dr Richard Wilding, Cranfield Centre for Logistics and Supply Chain Management)

5.4 Managing timeliness in the logistics pipeline

Key issue: **When P-time is greater than D-time, what time-based strategies and practices can help to improve competitiveness?**

5.4.1 Strategies to cope when P-time is greater than D-time

When faced with a D-time shorter than the corresponding P-time, a company has a number of options. In the short term it can attempt to make to order, or to forecast demand and supply from stock.

Making to order in these circumstances is likely to dissatisfy customers. If competitors exist that can deliver within the customer's D-time, or there are substitute products available that will, then the customer is likely to select them. If there are no alternatives then it may be possible to continue supplying to order for the short term. In the longer term it is likely that the customer will seek to develop alternative suppliers, or re-engineer its products to remove the need for yours.

The more common solution is to forecast customer demand, make products to stock, and supply from there. This stock may be held as finished goods if the D-time is very short, or it could be work-in-progress held in the manufacturing process that can be finished in time. This option incurs a number of penalties. The stocks of goods will need to be financed, as will the space needed to store them. There is also the risk that the customer may not order those goods already made within their shelf-life, causing them to become obsolete.

Both make-to-order and make-to-stock have associated costs and risks, so a company should look at ways to reduce these costs and risks in the longer term. Reducing risks can be grouped into three inter-linked areas. These are marketing, product development and process improvement. Each of these areas is analysed below.

Marketing

There are various ways in which you could reduce risk, with customer help. For example, ask the customer to cooperate by supplying more detailed demand information at an earlier stage. Speed up the access to demand data, perhaps by locating one of your people in the customer's scheduling process. Perhaps the customer is prepared to wait longer than stated, if you can guarantee delivery on time.

Product development

There are only so many improvements to the reduction of production time that can be made when a process is based around existing products. With time-based thinking in mind, next-generation products can be designed for 'time-to-market'. Such thinking aims for products that can be made and distributed quickly, and which offer product variety without unnecessary complexity.

Process improvement

Time-based organisations come into their own by changing the way they go about their business. They engineer their processes to eliminate unnecessary steps, and take wasted time out of those that remain. Engineering your key processes means focusing on those things the customer cares about and getting rid of all the rest. Having done this once, the best organisations go on to do it again and again as they learn more about their customers and grow in confidence in what they can change.

5.4.2 Practices to cope when P-time is greater than D-time

There are a number of ways to reduce P-time. These can be summarised as follows:

- *Control* by optimising throughput and improving process capability.
- *Simplify* by untangling process flows and reducing product complexity.
- *Compress* by straightening process flows and reducing batch sizes.
- *Integrate* by improving communications and implementing teams.
- *Coordinate* by adding customer-specific parts as late as possible.
- *Automate* with robots and IT systems.

Control

In any process, lead time depends on the balance between load and capacity. If demand rises above available capacity, lead times will increase unless resource is also increased, for example through overtime or subcontracting work. Therefore in order to maintain or reduce lead time it is necessary to balance this equation effectively by optimising throughput. Similarly, if a process is out of control, and we are never sure whether conforming product will be produced, the focus will be on improving the capability of that process.

Simplify

Simplification is concerned with cutting out sources of process complexity and of product complexity. Process complexity is often caused by many different products *sharing the same process*. This process becomes a bottleneck, and process flows become tangled because they all have to go through this single, central process. In manufacturing, the solutions are based on cellular manufacturing: in distribution, the solutions are based on different distribution channels. Product complexity is often related to the *number of parts*. The more parts there are in a product the more difficult it is to plan, to make and to sell. One way to reduce product complexity is to reduce the number of parts, by integrating several components into one. The other is to reduce the number of parts by standardising them between products.

Compress

Compressing P-time is concerned with squeezing out waste in each process step. There are two main ways to achieve this. First, straighten the process flow by making a linear flow for each product. Second, reduce the batch size so that flow is improved and queuing time is minimised.

Integrate

Integrating different value-adding activities so that they work more closely together helps to reduce P-time. Integration is in turn helped by improving the speed and accuracy of information to the process owner. Important issues are demand information (what to do next?), product information (what is it?) and process information (how is it done?). Ways of speeding up information range from simple, paperless systems such as *kanban*, through simple IT systems such as e-mail, to more complex systems such as making EPOS data available in real time through the Internet. Integration is also helped by forging relationships between departments or organisations that need to communicate. Teams and partnerships help to integrate activities that are otherwise disconnected.

Coordinate

Other approaches to reducing P-time aim to reorganise value-adding activities so that they are done in parallel and/or in the best order. Thus running activities at the same time (in parallel) instead of one after another (in series) will reduce lead times. Sometimes it is possible to reduce lead times by doing the same activities in a different order. This may make it possible to combine activities or allow them to be done in parallel. It may also make better use of resource by fitting an extra job into a shift, or by running long tasks that need no supervision overnight.

Automate

This approach should be used last, once all the others have delivered their improvements (Do not automate waste!). Chiefly it is concerned with reducing lead time through the use of robots and IT systems to speed up processes. Such approaches are best focused on bottleneck steps in the overall process. The aim is to improve process capability and reliability as well as speed.

5.5 A method for implementing time-based practices

Key issue: **How can time-based practices be implemented?**

Becoming a time-based company means that a systematic approach is essential to improve all three measures of cost, quality and time. This approach means identifying and removing the sources and causes of waste in the supply network, rather than merely treating the symptoms. The method shown here will give you a starting point for implementing a time-based strategy.

First, you need to understand the ways in which customers value responsiveness. Then the method (shown in Figure 5.10) takes you through a series of steps that help you to change your processes to be able to deliver what the customer wants.

5.5.1 Step 1: Understand your need to change

The first step in implementing a time-based strategy is to understand whether you *need* to change. This need to change depends on how important responsiveness is to your customers. Here are five key questions that will help to identify the strategic importance of time:

● Is supply responsiveness important to your customers?
● How important is it to them?
● What is the supply D-time target that customers have officially or unofficially set?
● What happens if you do not meet this target?
● What is the total P-time, i.e. the lead time taken from an order's arriving in the company until it is fulfilled and finally leaves the company?

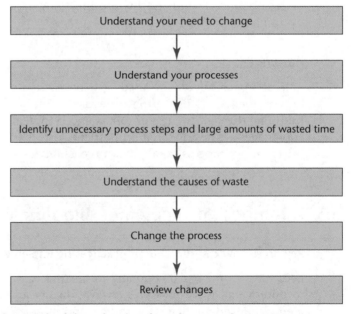

Figure 5.10 A methodology for time-based process improvement

5.5.2 Step 2: Understand your processes

While you may think you already know your current processes, the only way to make sure is to walk the process in the way described in section 5.3 above. Mapping a process involves creating a very simple flow chart. This is best done with a pad of paper, a pencil – and a smile. Start at the point where a customer order comes into the company. This could be with a salesman in the field, over a phone, through the fax or via a computer. Write down the name of this step and draw a box around it. Ask whoever picks this order up what happens next. Very probably it gets reviewed, logged in or put on someone's desk. Any of these options is a step. Write this down on your pad of paper below the first step. Draw a box around it too, then join the boxes with an arrow. Keep going, throughout the company, following that order until a product is finally delivered to the customer. Write down every step you encounter.

During your expedition following the process through the company ask the people who undertake each step how long it takes to work on a single, typical order. You need to find out the *activity time* – the time they spend physically working on it, not the time it spends on their desk or next to their machine.

When you have mapped the whole process, compare the total lead time (the P-time) with the time in which your customers are demanding you respond to them (their D-time). How well do you do? If the P-time is greater than the D-time you have a challenge.

Now add up the activity times for all of the steps in the process. How does this compare with the overall lead time (the P-time)? It is likely to be considerably smaller. How does it compare with the D-time? Possibly it is also smaller. If so, you have a real opportunity to improve your responsiveness and get your lead time within that demanded by the customer through applying the ideas listed above, and without the need for extensive investment in technological solutions.

5.5.3 Step 3: Identify unnecessary process steps and large amounts of wasted time

Using your process flow chart you should work with the other members of the company involved in the process to identify those steps that do not add value to the customers. Also, identify where large amounts of wasted time are added to the overall lead time.

5.5.4 Step 4: Understand the causes of waste

Once again, work with your colleagues and identify the causes of the unnecessary process steps and wasted time. Why do they exist?

5.5.5 Step 5: Change the process

Having understood the process, and the causes of waste in it, choose from the generic solutions described above approaches that will make the process more responsive. Apply these solutions with vigour, going for easy ones that deliver early results first to give everyone confidence that you are doing the right thing.

5.5.6 Step 6: Review changes

Having made changes to the way you go about your operations measure the performance of the process again and find out whether there have been any changes to your performance. Have you become more responsive? If not, why not? Find out and try again. If you have, tell as many people as you can, and have another go at building on your success.

5.5.7 Results

The likely result of the above change programme is a situation such as that graphically displayed in the basic four-step supply chain shown in Figure 5.11. Through the implementation of time-based practices or initiatives, cycle times are compressed throughout the supply chain. As a result, delivery can take place in a timely manner more reliably and faster, while more operations can be performed to order within the service window. As a result, lower asset intensity is coupled with enhanced delivery service as possible input to both lean thinking and agility efforts (see Chapters 6 and 7 respectively).

Note that this approach assumes a supply chain point of view, not just a focus on manufacturing or any other segment of the supply chain. A well-known illustration of the importance of this point is that lean approaches have resulted in automotive manufacturing cycle times being compressed to a matter of hours. After manufacture, however, cars are stored in the distribution pipeline or in dealer outlets for weeks, if not months. Lack of supply network thinking results in all of the cycle time investments in manufacturing being wasted.

This does not mean to say that all operations in the supply chain need to be subject to time compression. In the example shown in Figure 5.11, the new delivery cycle times (shown with a dotted line) actually increase in the new structure. But this suboptimisation is allowable, as traditional distribution from local warehouses here is replaced with direct delivery from the factory, where products are made to order. The transition to make-to-order replaces the need for inventory-holding points, where goods typically are stored for extensive periods of time. Of course this basic example also indicates how time-based initiatives can require structural supply chain redesign, such as the reconfiguration of distribution channels and the adjustment of manufacturing systems and policies.

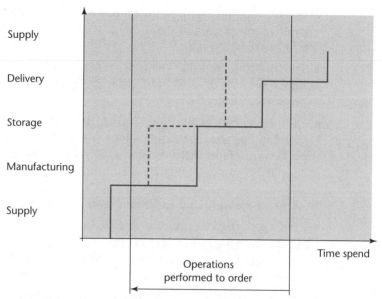

Figure 5.11 Results of time-based change initiatives

5.6 When, where and how?

There are several tactical considerations to be made when planning a time-based strategy. We have grouped these in the form of three questions to be asked:

- *When?* Time-based competition is only as relevant as the customer perceives it to be. Speed for the sake of speed can create unnecessary costs, and can cut corners, leading to poor quality.

- *Where?* D-times are a measure of the importance of speed as a competitive factor, while P-times measure the ability to deliver. The integration of the two measures the point at which the customer order penetrates the supply chain. In Chapter 7 we develop this issue in terms of the customer order decoupling point.

- *How?* The more predictable and lower-priority products and components can be delivered from inventory with less priority given to speed. Shipments of customised products can be assembled from stocks of standard components and modules within the D-time demanded.

Summary

What is the lead-time frontier?

- Competing on time demands a fast response to customer needs. Time-based approaches to strategy focus on the competitive advantage of speed, which helps a network to cope with variety and product innovation, while also improving returns on new products. Speed also means less reliance on long-term forecasts.

- Speed of response also helps to lower costs by reducing the need for working capital, and plant and equipment. It also helps to reduce development costs and the cost of quality.

- The lead-time frontier is concerned with reducing P-time (time needed to produce a product or service) to less than D-time (time for which the customer is prepared to wait).

- Differences between P-times and D-times are referred to as the lead-time gap. The gap has strategic implications for marketing, product development and process development. P-time can be reduced by a six-stage process: control, simplify, compress, integrate, coordinate, automate.

How do we measure and implement time-based strategies?

- Time-based mapping aims to generate visibility of time in the supply network. A six-step approach to mapping involves creating a task force, selecting the process, collecting data, distinguishing between value-adding and non-value-adding activities, constructing the time-based process map and generating a solution.

- Implementing time-based practices can be accomplished using another six-step process involving understanding the need to change, understanding the processes, identifying non-value-adding processes, understanding the causes of waste, and reviewing what has been done.

Discussion questions

1 Why is time important to competitive advantage? Identify and explain six key contributions that speed can make to logistics strategy.

2 Explain the significance of P:D ratios. How can the production lead time be reduced?

3 Sections 5.3, 5.4 and 5.5 all contain step-by-step models for reducing waste and implementing improved logistics processes. Explain why such models are useful in implementing logistics strategy.

References

Bicheno, J. (2000) *Lean Toolbox*, 2nd edn. Buckingham: Picsie Books.

Crosby, P.B. (1979) *Quality is Free: The art of making quality certain*. New York: McGraw-Hill.

Deming, W.E. (1986) *Out of the Crisis*. Cambridge, MA: MIT.

Garvin, D.A. (1988) 'The multiple dimensions of quality', in *Managing Quality*, Ch. 4. New York: Free Press.

Stalk, G. and Hout, T. (1990) *Competing Against Time*, New York: Free Press.

Suggested further reading

Galloway, D. (1994) *Mapping Work Processes*. Milkwaukee, WT: ASQC Quality Press.

Rother, M. and Shook, J. (1999) *Learning to See,* Version 1.3, Brookline, MA: The Lean Enterprise Institute Inc.

CHAPTER 6

Just-in-time and lean thinking

Outcomes

The planned outcomes of this chapter are to:

- explain the philosophy of just-in-time and how that philosophy relates to managing the supply chain;
- identify two methods of applying just-in-time philosophy to the supply chain (vendor-managed inventory and quick response);
- explain how lean thinking can be used to avoid the build-up of waste in supply chain processes.

By the end of this chapter you should be able to:

- distinguish between 'push' and 'pull' scheduling;
- understand how companies can compete by using vendor-managed inventory and quick response methods of controlling material flow;
- understand how lean thinking can be used to improve performance of the supply chain in meeting end-customer demand with no waste;
- identify different ways of reducing waste in supply chains.

Introduction

The discipline of doing things just-in-time – neither too early nor too late – has had a profound influence on the way supply chains are managed. The ideal of materials flowing at a controlled and coordinated rate through the supply network in line with end-customer demand has been widely adopted across many industrial sectors. While the origins of just-in-time are somewhat shrouded (Harrison in Slack, 1997: 85), the company that has made JIT famous across the world is Toyota Motor Company of Japan. Toyota adopted just-in-time as one of the pillars of its production system. The lead in productivity and quality that leading Japanese automotive producers in Japan opened up over Western producers led to the term *lean production* being coined (Krafcik and McDuffie, 1989). Lean production sought to describe a radically different approach to running the business from the traditional *mass production*. Lean production has achieved lower stocks, higher productivity and superior product quality. These contribute to the achievement of logistics performance objectives (Chapter 1) by offering improvements in quality, time *and* cost. This potentially across-the-board improvement to competitive performance has meant that JIT and lean thinking have had an enormous influence on logistics.

Researchers on the International Motor Vehicle Program (IMVP); (Womack *et al.*, 1990:13) described lean production as cutting needed resources in half:

> It uses less of everything compared with mass production – half the human effort in the factory, half the manufacturing space, half the investment in tools, half the engineering hours to develop a product in half the time. Also, it requires keeping far less than half the needed inventory on site, results in many fewer defects, and produces a greater and ever-growing variety of products.

In other words, a lean producer can use its advantages to reduce costs, or to increase product variety, or a combination of both. The concept of 'lean' in the automotive industry has been extended into other sectors using the term *lean thinking* (Womack and Jones, 1996). And instead of lean production, today we refer to the *lean enterprise* to emphasise that lean concepts spread organically from production into design and development and into logistics. The concepts of 'JIT' and 'lean' essentially come from the same stable. This chapter provides an introduction to just-in-time and lean thinking, and shows how these concepts have been extended to the supply network through techniques such as quick response and vendor-managed inventory.

The overall aim of this chapter is to introduce you to methods of coordinating material movements in the supply chain in line with end-customer demand.

<table>
<tr><td>Key issues</td><td>

This chapter addresses four key issues:

1 **Just-in-time:** pull and push scheduling. Different ways of scheduling materials.

2 **Lean thinking:** the seven sources of waste, cutting out waste in business processes.

3 **Vendor-managed inventory:** delegating to the supplier the responsibility for controlling inventories and replenishments.

4 **Quick response:** improving communications between retailers and the rest of the supply network.

</td></tr>
</table>

6.1 Just-in-time

Key issues: What are the implications of just-in-time for logistics? How can just-in-time principles be applied to other forms of material control such as reorder point and material requirements planning?

Just-in-time is actually a broad philosophy of management that seeks to eliminate waste and improve quality in all business processes. JIT is put into practice by means of a set of tools and techniques that provide the cutting edge in the 'war on waste'. In this chapter, we focus on the application of JIT to logistics. This partial view of JIT has been called *little JIT* (Chase and Aquilano, 1992): there is far more to this wide-ranging approach to management than we present here (see for example Harrison, 1992). Nevertheless, little JIT has enormous implications for logistics, and has spawned several logistics versions of JIT concepts.

The partial view of JIT is an approach to material control based on the view that a process should operate only when a customer signals a need for more parts from that process. When a process is operated in the JIT way, goods are produced and delivered just-in-time to be sold. This principle cascades upstream through the supply network, with subassemblies produced and delivered just-in-time to be assembled, parts fabricated and delivered just-in-time to be built into subassemblies, and materials bought and delivered just-in-time to be made into fabricated parts. Throughout the supply network, the trigger to start work is governed by demand from the customer – the next process (Schonberger, 1991). A supply network can be conceived of as a *chain of customers*, with each link coordinated with its neighbours by JIT signals. The whole network is triggered by demand from the end-customer. Only the end-customer is free to place demand whenever he or she wants; after that the system takes over.

The above description of the flow of goods in a supply chain is characteristic of a *pull* system. Parts are pulled through the chain in response to demand from the end-customer. This contrasts with a *push* system, in which products are made whenever resources (people, material and machines) become available in response to a central plan or schedule. The two systems of controlling materials can be distinguished as follows:

- *Pull scheduling:* a system of controlling materials whereby the user signals to the maker or provider that more material is needed. Material is sent only in response to such a signal.
- *Push scheduling:* a system of controlling materials whereby makers and providers make or send material in response to a pre-set schedule, regardless of whether the next process needs them at the time.

The push approach is a common way for processes to be managed, and often seems a sensible option. If some of the people in a factory or an office are idle, it seems a good idea to give them work to do. The assumption is that those products can be sold at some point in the future. A similar assumption is that building up a stock of finished goods will quickly help to satisfy the customer. This argument seems particularly attractive where manufacturing lead times are long, if quality is a problem, or if machines often break down. It is better and safer to make product, just in case there is a problem in the future. Unfortunately, this argument has severe limitations. Push scheduling and its associated inventories do *not* always help companies to be more responsive. All too often, the very products the organisation wants to sell are unavailable, while there is too much stock of products that are not selling. And building up stock certainly does not help to make more productive use of spare capacity. Instead it can easily lead to excess costs, and hide opportunities to improve processes.

6.1.1 The just-in-time system

Companies achieve the ability to produce and deliver just-in-time to satisfy actual demand because they develop a production system that is capable of working in this way. Such a system can be envisaged as a number of 'factors' that interact with each other, as shown in Figure 6.1. This shows JIT capability as founded on layers of factors that interact together to form a system that is designed for flow. Excellence in each of the six factors determines the effectiveness with which JIT capability can be achieved: that is, how easy it is to get to the top of the pyramid.

Factor 1

The top of the pyramid is full capability for just-in-time supply. This is the level at which a focal firm can produce and deliver according to the demand that is placed on it. The relationships operating within and between levels 2 and 3 form the system that ultimately underpins the achievement of JIT. They are complex, and in some cases there is a long time delay between taking actions and seeing the effects.

Factor 2

The two factors *delay* and *inventory* interact with each other in a system of positive amplification: that is, they go up together and they go down together. This interrelationship results in either a virtuous cycle, where things keep getting better, or a vicious cycle, where they keep getting worse. For example, extra delay in a process will result in extra inventory being held to compensate for the delay. Delay and inventory can be reduced by replenishing parts only as needed by *kanban*. Kanban is the Japanese for 'card' or 'signal'. The supply process responds to a kanban card by sending only what is needed immediately (Harrison, 1992). Making sure this relationship operates as a virtuous cycle of reducing delay and inventory depends on the underpinning factors in level 3.

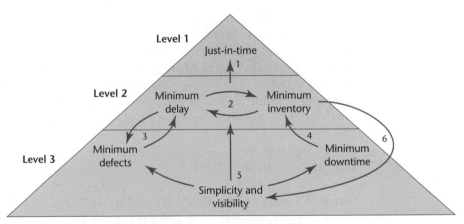

Figure 6.1 The pyramid of key factors that underpin JIT

Factor 3

Defects lead to delays, either through requiring rework or necessitating increased production to compensate for scrap. The likelihood of defects leads to safety stocks being held as a buffer against potential problems. This thinking amplifies quality problems by increasing the time between a defect's occurring and its discovery. Not only is the cause harder to identify, but more production will be affected. The attitude that holding inventory can mitigate the effect of quality problems is fundamentally flawed. It stands in opposition to the only successful approach to defect minimisation, where problems are quickly identified, their causes are traced and permanent solutions are devised and applied.

Factor 4

Machine downtime relates to a number of issues:

- unplanned downtime – that is, breakdowns;
- planned maintenance;
- changeover times.

Downtime, and particularly the risk of unplanned downtime, is a key cause of the need for safety stocks in a process. Other JIT tools and techniques can help to minimise the problems here. For example, *total productive maintenance* (TPM) (Nakajima, 1989) seeks to answer the question 'What can everyone do to help prevent breakdowns?' Regular planned preventive maintenance, closer cooperation between production and maintenance personnel, and equipment sourcing for ease of maintenance are some of the actions that can be taken in response. In other words, increasing planned maintenance costs often results in reduced overall costs of machine downtime. Minimising changeover time is a JIT tool that can be used not only to reduce lost production time but also to improve production flexibility. Inflexible facilities delay the rapid production of customer orders.

Factor 5

Where the flow through a process is easily seen, people in the process will have a better understanding of their colleagues' work and how they themselves affect others. A simple process results from having first *focused* operations around a family of compatible products. Layout is then organised to bring together all the people and equipment needed to undertake the process. These are arranged so that there is a logical flow between the process steps. Arranging the process so that the stations for undertaking the steps are close together not only helps to reduce inventory but also will itself be made easier when inventory is low. A simple process will be more *visible*, allowing it to be better maintained. Not only should there be fewer things to go wrong, they will be more obvious when they do, and will be easier to fix. This attribute helps to minimise both machine downtime and product defects.

Maintenance of the process is underpinned by housekeeping and cleanliness. This starts with designing processes and facilities to create order. There is a place for everything, and everything has its place. Orderliness depends on a thinking workforce that has accepted ownership and responsibility for organising the work place. Attention to detail in terms of 'respect for human' issues is an essential part of JIT philosophy (Harrison and Storey, 2000).

Factor 6

The levels of work in progress and other types of inventory have a significant impact upon the visibility of a process. It becomes increasingly difficult to see the flow of a process as inventory increases. This may be literally true on a shop floor or in a warehouse, where piles and stacks of goods can isolate workers. The same is true in offices when the process flow becomes lost in assorted piles of work on people's desks.

In order to highlight the inadequacies of push production we next consider the case of how a focal firm took a rather traditional approach to responding to new demands being placed on the production process.

CASE STUDY 6.1

Smog Co.

The Smog Co. production system

This is the case of Smog Co., a small supplier of well-engineered components. Smog produces a range of products grouped into families. Production of one of the higher-volume product families has been organised into a flow process made up of four steps, which follow one after the other in sequence. Changeover from one product to another is relatively simple, but takes around 10 minutes per machine. To minimise delays caused by changeovers, products tend to be made in batches. These batches move from one step to the next, where they queue on a first in, first out basis to be worked on, after which they move to the next step. This process is shown in Figure 6.2.

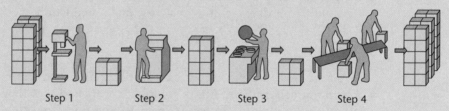

Step 1   Step 2   Step 3   Step 4

Figure 6.2 The Smog Co. production process

Key measures of the performance of this process are the utilisation of people and of machines. The objective is to keep utilisation of both as high as possible. In this situation, if people or machines are idle – and material is available – they are used to make something. Naturally it would not make sense to make anything. Instead the production manager has a feel for what is needed, and uses a forecast from the sales department to make an early start on products that it is considered will be required in the near future.

Fred Hollis, the Smog production manager, felt pleased with performance as he looked out across the factory. He was pleased because his machines and people were busy, there were plenty of finished goods on hand, which the sales team could use to supply customers, and there was stock to call upon if product demand increased. Everything seemed to be under control.

Changes to customer requirements

The motivation to change from the current system has been low in the past, as the process at Smog Co. is a reliable one, which has worked well for the company. The 'big three' customers, who take three-quarters of sales, tend to order the same things in similar quantities one week in advance of delivery. With a production lead time of three weeks Smog Co. uses a forecast to schedule production and make sure that finished goods stocks will be available to meet predicted demand. Consistent demand means that forecasts are often close to real demand, so stockouts are rare. In fact the only time this occurred was an incident a couple of years ago, when a key machine went down and a spare part took a long time to source. Current inventory levels now include safety stock to provide cover against a similar problem in the future.

When the company found that certain finished goods were selling slowly, the sales team was particularly good at finding a way to move them. Sometimes prices were cut; at other times sales used special promotions. If production was too high, or the forecast was a bit optimistic, then there were ways of selling surplus stock, and the sales team seemed to enjoy the challenge.

Recently, however, this well-understood position has begun to change. The main customers have started to use a number of new strategies to compete with each other. First one and now a second of them has announced that it will be reducing the call-off time for its products from one week to two working days. At the same time they are all looking for a 5 per cent cost reduction, and are demanding quality improvements.

A 'traditional' reaction to customer demands for better service

The combination of demands for better services caused Smog management some concern. The obvious response to the changes in ordering patterns was to increase stock levels to cater for unexpected variations in demand. This approach had worked before, when it was used to justify the safety stocks that covered production problems. It seemed worth trying again, so stocks were increased.

Things went well over the first few months, during which time delivery performance remained good, while the customers went ahead with their plan to reduce the order lead time. Keeping up with these orders provided the production manager with a few headaches. Preventing stockouts led to an increase in the number of batches being expedited through the factory. This disrupted the production plan, increased the number of machine changeovers and lowered productivity. As a result, overtime increased in order to maintain output.

The higher level of inventory meant that quality problems were harder to detect. In one case a new operator missed a drilling operation. By the time the first customer discovered the error, nearly two weeks' worth of production had to be recalled and reworked.

The higher inventory levels were also taking up more space. Fred Hollis had submitted a requisition to the finance director to pay for more storage racking. The extra racks were necessary because existing ones were full, and parts stored on the floor were suffering occasional damage in an increasingly cramped factory. Some parts were recently returned by a customer, who felt that damaged packaging indicated damaged products. Naturally, Fred was concerned when his request for more storage space was turned down owing to spending reductions imposed in response to price cuts imposed by customers.

Reflecting on what had happened at Smog, the increase in stock levels had badly affected competitiveness. Smog Co. was experiencing the consequences of trying to forecast demand and using the forecast to determine what to make. Their 'make to stock' approach was responsible for:

- removing the company's ability to be responsive to changes in either quantities or product mix;
- increasing costs and making quality problems worse;
- burying underlying production problems under inventory, and thereby preventing efforts to uncover and resolve them.

In conclusion, while the company had been motivated to change by its customers, the direction it took seemed to have caused many problems.

(Source: After an original by Paul Chapman)

Questions

1 List the actions that Smog Co. took to respond to the new demands being placed on it by customers. Group your responses under the headings of stock levels, level of expediting and storage space. Briefly describe the effects that these actions had on production performance.

2 Use the 'Pyramid of key factors that underpin JIT' to describe the factors that caused these actions to affect the company's ability to respond to the demands being placed on it by customers.

6.1.2 The supply chain 'game plan'

Let us next drill down into the 'plan' process in the SCOR model shown in Figure 3.11 and link it with JIT thinking. The planning process takes demand signals as its inputs. Demand may be true demand in the form of customer orders, or it may be an estimate of future demand in the form of a forecast. Let us take a firm called Victoria SA that makes iced cakes to illustrate how demand is converted into supply. Victoria makes 'fantastically good cakes' from basic ingredients like flour, water and cherries.

Figure 6.3 summarises the supply chain 'game plan'. Demand for Victoria sponge cakes comes from two sources. Some big retailers place their order with the firm two days in advance, while other customers arrive at Victoria's own shops without warning and select from cakes that are on display. This means that some cakes are made in line with orders, while a forecast is also required to predict day-by-day demand.

Demand data is fed into a *master schedule*, which collates sales forecasts and orders. The master schedule is a production plan not a sales plan. It allows for capacity constraints and is a realistic, achievable plan. It tells us *how many* and *when* each type of cake must be available for delivery. Here, it is useful to distinguish between independent and dependent demand:

- *Independent demand* refers to demand for a product that is ordered directly by customers. It is independent in that it does not depend on demand for any other product.

- *Dependent demand* refers to demand for parts or subassemblies (ingredients in this case) that make up independent demand products. It is dependent in that it depends on demand for these products. It does not have to be forecast, but can be calculated from demand for the independent products and the number of parts in each.

The master schedule is then converted into a *material plan* by breaking it down into the individual ingredients that are needed. This is the point at which dependent demand is calculated from independent demand. In order to do this, we need the *recipe*, which is contained in a static file called the *bill of material* (BOM). The conversion of the master schedule into plans for each ingredient is called *material requirements planning*, or MRP. Once we have the requirements for the ingredients, those needed from suppliers are planned by means of *purchase orders*. Mixes and finished cakes that are made internally are planned by means of *works orders*. The outline planning and control 'game plan', sometimes called 'sales and operations planning' (SOP), is shown in Figure 6.3.

While there are many varieties of cake, the bill of material for the famous sponge cake is shown in Figure 6.4.

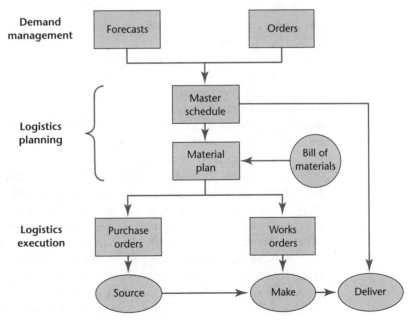

Figure 6.3 The supply chain 'game plan'

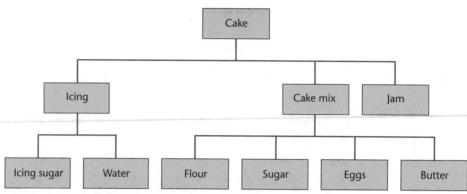

Figure 6.4 The bill of materials (BOM) for sponge cake

When overall demand across the range has been collated, Victoria SA is able to determine how much of each ingredient will be needed to make the right number of cakes. Too many and cakes will have to be thrown away, because the shelf-life is 5–8 days (Victoria does not use stabilisers like potassium sorbate). Too few and sales will be lost. Accurate planning is thus crucial to the efficiency of the whole operation. The ideal situation is that cakes are made and delivered *just-in-time* to meet customer demand.

In an effort to increase sales, Victoria SA decided to increase the product range. Strawberry jam is the traditional filling, but marketing considers that customers would also like other types of filling and decides to try blackberry jam, apricot jam, lemon curd and chocolate. Over the course of the next few months, the experiment appears to be working. Overall sales are up by 10 per cent, with each of the new varieties contributing well. The problem however is that no stable pattern exists in the mix of sales. For example, some days the chocolate-filled cakes sell out while on other days hardly a single chocolate-filled cake is sold. The issue appears to be that offering increased variety has led to less stability in the demand pattern – as well as increased complexity in the production operation. Major retail customers are complaining about wastage and lost sales opportunities.

To fix the unexpected problems, Victoria SA decides on a new way of working. It is recognised that demand is not going to stabilise given the increased product range. The firm decides to adopt a *postponement* strategy. The basic cake is a *standard component*, while the filling is non-standard and represents the source of complexity and variable customer interest. Cakes are therefore kept in the standard form and only turned into the final form by adding the filling once customer orders have been received. Victoria SA has applied postponement to the supply chain and introduced a decoupling point at the end of the process. Upstream of the decoupling point overall demand is forecast to inform sourcing decisions. Standard components are baked each morning. Downstream of the decoupling point, cakes are finished in the shop in line with customer requirements. The time this activity takes has been minimised by setting up a workstation with cakes, filling and spreading tools arranged in a mini flow-line. This brings the production time (P-time, see section 5.2) within the time the customer is prepared to wait (D-time). Carrying out the operation in view of the customer also helps engage them and extends their D-time to a minute or so, long enough to complete the final assembly task.

The flexibility of the new operation means that customers no longer need to place an order two days in advance. Victoria SA can now supply from the new process if orders are received by major customers the day before. An unexpected benefit of the new approach is the ease with which innovations can be test-marketed and adopted.

6.1.3 Demand characteristics and planning approaches

One of the key contributions of just-in-time to logistics thinking has been the understanding of *how many* to order and *when* to order. Determining the most appropriate approach for answering these questions relies heavily on the characteristics of demand for a given part or product. Although advances in techniques such as statistical forecasting, causal modelling and market intelligence can increase the predictability, future demand is rarely certain. Future demand is therefore always likely to include a *probabilistic* element – which is characterised by the forecast error. An approximation to the forecast error that is often used is the level of demand variability.

'Economic' batch sizes and order sizes

The question of how many parts to make at a time has traditionally been answered by reference to a longstanding concept called the 'economic' batch quantity (EBQ) formula. Similar principles are used to determine how many parts at a time to order from suppliers in 'economic' order quantities (EOQs). Both EBQ and EOQ assume that parts are used up at a uniform rate, and that another batch of parts should be ordered when stock falls below the *reorder point*. The principle behind re-order point, which sets out to answer the question when to order, is shown in Figure 6.5.

A buffer (or safety) stock line is shown below the reorder level. Buffer stock acts as a 'safety net' in order to cushion the effects of variability in demand and in lead times. Buffer stock is a function of the service level (risk of stock outs), lead time variability and demand variability. The reorder point is therefore the sum of the forecast demand during the lead time plus the buffer stock requirement. There are various ways of calculating buffer stock (for a detailed coverage, and for details of EBQ and EOQ calculations, see Vollman *et al.* 2004, and Waters, 2003).

In the case of manufacturing, the EBQ is determined by optimising the trade-off between changeover cost and inventory carrying cost:

- *Changeover cost per unit.* The cost associated with changing over a given machine from the last good part from a batch to the first good part from the succeeding batch.

- *Inventory carrying cost.* The cost of holding stock, calculated from the total inventory cost and the annual rate charged for holding inventory.

All too often overlooked when calculating the EBQ is that the higher the changeover cost, the higher the EBQ. The key point here is that the EBQ can

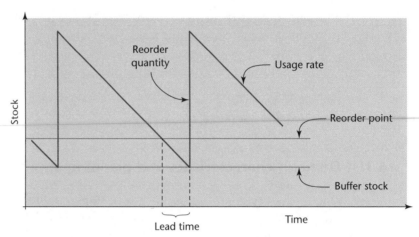

Notes:

1. Reorder point = demand during lead time + safety stock
2. Reorder quantity = economic order quantity
3. Buffer stock = *f*(service level. lead time variability. demand variability)

Figure 6.5 When: the reorder point

therefore be reduced when the changeover cost is reduced. In the ideal case, the changeover activity should be simplified so that it can be carried out in seconds rather than in hours. Where this is achieved, the changeover cost becomes negligible and the EBQ becomes one.

Given zero changeover costs, the EBQ formula obeys the JIT ideal of pull scheduling – only make in response to *actual* demand. We return to the issue of small batch production in section 4 of this chapter. Actual demand is likely to vary from one day to the next, unlike the assumption for demand rate shown in Figure 6.3 earlier. Pull scheduling is more sensitive to demand changes, because only what is needed is made.

Similar considerations have resulted in the concept of the economic order quantity (EOQ). Here, the calculation addresses the question 'how many parts will we order?' The trade-off this time is between the cost of placing an order and inventory carrying cost, where:

> *Cost of placing an order* = **All order related costs, including purchase department costs, transportation costs from the supplier and goods-in inspection and receiving.**

EOQ again increases in line with the cost of placing an order, and reduces in line with the inventory carrying cost. Again the trade-off can be changed. If the cost of placing an order can be simplified to a routine basis whereby parts are ordered by paperless systems such as cards, and collected on regular pickup routes called 'milk rounds', the EOQ can again be reduced towards the JIT ideal. EOQ principles are still widely used for ordering 'independent demand' items that are not directly used to manufacture products, such as automotive spare parts, class 'C' parts in retail and office supplies.

Periodic order quantity and target stock levels

EOQ models generally relate to a given order size being placed whenever the inventory level falls below the reorder amount. The effect upon suppliers is that although a regular amount is ordered, the time the order is placed can vary enormously. An EOQ system finds it very difficult to cope if demand goes up or down rapidly. If demand goes up rapidly, then an EOQ system would tend to make replenishments that lag the demand trend.

To illustrate, let us assume a sequence of 10 weeks where demand fluctuates between 100 and 1,000 units. The EOQ has been established as 1,000 units, and the safety stock at 100 units. Inventories at the start and end of each week can then be calculated as shown in Table 6.1.

An alternative way to deal with variable demand is to use the periodic order quantity. Here, the reorder quantities are revised more frequently. The method uses mean time between orders (TBO), which is calculated by dividing the EOQ by the average demand rate. In the above example, the EOQ is 1,000 and the average demand 410. The economic time interval is therefore approximately two. An example shown in Table 6.2 illustrates the same situation as in Table 6.1 in terms of demand changes and safety stock level. However, the reorder quantity is based on total demand for the immediate two weeks of history. This reorder method is called *periodic order quantity* (POQ).

POQ normally gives a lower mean inventory level than EOQ in variable demand situations. In this example, the average inventory holding has fallen from 5,150 to 4,150. The same number of orders (Chase and Aquilano, 1992) have been used, but the order quantity varies from 200 to 1,800.

Table 6.1 Economic order quantity example

Week no.	Demand	Order quantity	Inventory end	Inventory start	Inventory holding
1	100	1,000	900	1,000	950
2	100	0	800	900	850
3	200	0	600	800	700
4	400	0	200	600	400
5	800	1,000	400	200	300
6	1,000	1,000	400	400	400
7	800	1,000	600	400	500
8	400	0	200	600	400
9	100	0	100	200	150
10	200	1,000	900	100	500
Sum	4,100	5,000	5,100	5,200	5,150
Average	410	500	510	520	515

Table 6.2 Periodic order quantity example

Week no.	Demand	Order quantity	Inventory end	Inventory start	Inventory holding
1	100	200	100	200	150
2	100	0	0	100	50
3	200	600	400	600	500
4	400	0	0	400	200
5	800	1800	1000	1800	1400
6	1000	0	0	1000	500
7	800	1200	400	1200	800
8	400	0	0	400	200
9	100	300	200	300	250
10	200	0	0	200	100
Sum	4100	4100	2100	6200	4150
Average	410	410	210	620	415

A widely used model for inventory control in retailing is *periodic review*. This works by placing orders of variable size at regular intervals – the *review period*. The quantity ordered is enough to raise stock on hand plus stock on order to a target level called the target stock level (TSL):

Order quantity = Target stock level – Stock on hand – Stock on order

The TSL is the sum of cycle stock (average weekly demand over the review period and replenishment lead time) and the safety stock. An example of the way the TSL is calculated is:

TSL = cycle stock + safety stock
$$= D*(T+ LT)+ Z*\sigma*(T+ LT)$$

where D = average weekly demand per sku, T = review period in weeks and LT = lead time in weeks. Z = number of standard deviations from the mean corresponding to the selected service level, and σ = standard deviation of demand over T + LT.

6.1.4 JIT and material requirements planning (MRP)

Material requirements planning (MRP) was conceived in order to answer the questions *how many?* and *when?* in ordering parts that are directly used to manufacture end products as described above. MRP systems are widely used in manufacturing companies for planning materials, and MRP logic is one of the pillars of current *enterprise resource planning* (ERP) systems.

MRP is a logical and systematic way of planning materials. It links downstream demand with manufacture and with upstream supply. It can handle detailed parts requirements, even for products that are made infrequently and in low volumes.

On the other hand, MRP is based on a centrally controlled, bureaucratic approach to material planning. Although it is based on a pull scheduling logic, it instructs processes to make more parts whether or not the customer (the next process) is capable of accepting them. Typically, MRP adopts push scheduling characteristics. It remains insensitive to day-to-day issues at shop floor level, and continues to assume that its plans are being carried out to the letter. In other words, MRP is good at planning, but weak at control.

Meanwhile, JIT pull scheduling is good at handling relatively stable demand for parts that are made regularly. It is sensitive to problems at shop floor level, and is designed not to flood the next process with parts that it cannot work on. On the other hand, JIT pull scheduling is not good at predicting requirements for the future, especially for parts and products that are in irregular or sporadic demand. JIT is good at control, but weak at planning. There are clear opportunities for putting together the strengths of both systems, so that the weaknesses of one are covered by the strengths of the other. For example, even in systems with great variety, many of the parts are common. So JIT can be used to control those parts, while a much downsized MRP plans what is left.

JIT has become associated with the Japanese way of cutting out waste, doing the simple things well and getting better every day. The pillars of Toyota Production System (TPS) are JIT and *jidoka*. *Jidoka* means humanising the man–machine interface so that it is the man who runs the machine, not vice versa. MRP has become associated with the Western way of automating a way out of trouble, and by investing in bigger and better systems that competitors cannot afford to match. Let us next review how these two different approaches apply in motor manufacture by comparing Ford (which has developed its own version of TPS called Ford Production System, FPS) and Toyota.

CASE STUDY 6.2

Ford and Toyota

A car assembly plant is built around a simple sequence of tasks that starts in the press shop and ends as a car rolls off the final assembly line. Figure 6.6 shows these basic tasks in summary form.

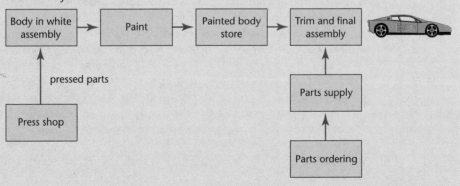

Figure 6.6 Basic tasks in a car assembly plant

While these basic tasks are the same for both Ford and Toyota, the way they are managed by the two firms is quite different. We compare policies and practices in relation to small cars like the Ford Fiesta and the Toyota Yaris:

- Ford is driven by a long-term strategy in Europe. It has invested heavily in fixed assets, and does not seek an early return on them. Currently, it is struggling with a capacity that was designed for a 15 per cent market share when current share is only 9 per cent. It seeks to make a step change in the production process through high capital investment. Its investment policy has therefore been technically oriented, seeking the 'best' technical solution for each task. For example, Ford's body shop is almost fully automated with robots that are flexible across different parts. When production is changed between one part and another, the robots must be reprogrammed. This places high emphasis on technical support for the software, and makes Ford dependent on given equipment suppliers. The layout is designed around the robots, and for fixed volumes.

- Toyota has expanded cautiously in Europe. Its investment policy has been step-by-step and it has sought to make early returns. Key to Toyota Production System (TPS) are process and quality disciplines through JIT and *jidoka*. Toyota's philosophy is more people-oriented: shop floor people are heavily involved in improvement activities as well as in production work. Toyota's body shop has maybe one-third the number of press shop robots as Ford, and tends to use simple multi-welders at low initial cost. It is relatively easy to swap suppliers. Tooling must be changed when production is changed between one batch and another, but people are trained to go for fast set-ups and to improve the process. The layout is designed around people and volume flexibility.

Ford has done much to reduce product complexity. This is basically measured by the number of different body styles that are possible. Both Ford and Toyota have three basic body styles, But Ford limits variation to left-hand/right-hand drive and sunroof/no sunroof versions. Since these are multiplicative, 12 body shells are possible. Toyota in addition has variations to allow for different engine types and air conditioner types, together with spoiler/no spoiler versions. In total, this means that Toyota has over 70 body shell variations. When multiplied again by the number of painted body colours (say 10 for both firms), Toyota ends up with hundreds more painted body options than Ford. This contributes to a surprising difference when it comes to building the car:

- Ford treats the painted body as a commodity. Once they have been painted, bodies are kept in the painted body store, which is a buffer between the body shop and final assembly. The Ford system calculates the number of each painted body type that should be in the store to meet forecast final assembly requirements. The trouble is that the store can be full of the wrong bodies, which means that it is impossible to build the current orders. Up to this point in the sequence, the emphasis is on numbers, not on the end-customer. Bodies are not given a vehicle identification number (VIN) – which allocates the body to a particular customer order – until the painted body is removed from the store and dropped onto the trim and final assembly line.

- Toyota treats the body shell as a customer's car from the start. The VIN is added as the first process at body in white assembly, when panels are welded together to make the shell. In turn, this drives discipline and focus in the paint shop, and helps to improve first time through (FTT) in the paint process. The sequence of bodies through trim and final processes is thereby more predictable, allowing more precise material control downstream.

The parts ordering process for automotive assembly is particularly challenging, because some 2,000 individual parts are needed for each vehicle. Most of these parts are added at the trim and final assembly stage. TPS already has a number of advantages when it comes to this task. First, the more predictable sequence of painted bodies into trim and final means that there are few last minute schedule changes. Second, TPS sets stable lead times that are fixed at certain times for each part. Third, supplier lead times are allowed for. Ford on the other hand leaves schedules uncommitted until parts are collected. The Ford call-off quantities are set on the day of collection, and do not allow for supplier lead times. Figures 1.8 and 1.9 compare what happens from a supplier point of view – there are huge differences between scheduled and actual demand.

Question

1 What changes would you propose to both TPS and to FPS in order to cope with customer demands for increasing product variety and more rapid model changes?

6.2 Lean thinking

Key issues: What are the principles of lean thinking, and how can they be applied to cutting waste out of supply chains?

As stated in the introduction to this chapter, *lean thinking* (Krafcik and MacDuffie, 1989) developed as a term used to contrast the just-in-time production methods used by Japanese automotive manufacturers with the mass production methods used by most Western manufacturers. Suffering shortages and lack of resources, Japanese car manufacturers responded by developing production processes that operated with minimum waste. Gradually the principle of minimising waste spread from the shop floor to all manufacturing areas, and from manufacturing to new product development and supply chain management. The term *lean thinking* refers to the elimination of waste in all aspects of a business.

Lean thinking is a cyclical route to seeking perfection by eliminating waste (the Japanese word *muda* means waste) and thereby enriching value from the customer perspective. The end-customer should not pay for the cost, time and quality penalties of wasteful processes in the supply network. Four principles are involved in achieving the fifth, seeking perfection (see Figure 6.7):

● specifying value;
● identifying the value stream;
● making value flow;
● pull scheduling.

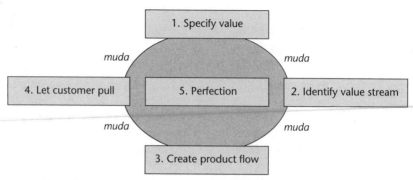

Figure 6.7 Principles of lean thinking
(Source: After Womack and Jones, 1996)

Specify value

Value is specified from the customer perspective. In Chapter 3 we discussed value from the shareholder perspective. From the end-customer perspective, value is added along the supply network as raw materials from primary manufacture are progressively converted into finished product bought by the end-customer, such as the aluminium ore being converted into one of the constituents of a can of cola (see Chapter 1, section 1.1.1). From a marketing and sales perspective the can of cola should be 'always within reach of your thirst'. That is an attempt to define value from the end-customer perspective. Another is Porter's concept of the *value chain* (Porter, 1985), which sees two types of activity that are of value to the customer. The first is the primary value activities of transforming raw materials into finished products, then distributing, marketing and servicing them. The second is support activities, such as designing the products and the manufacturing and distribution processes needed to underpin primary activities.

Identify the value stream

Following on from the concept of value, the next principle is to identify the whole sequence of processes along the supply network. The principles of time-based mapping are discussed in sections 5.4 and 5.5 of Chapter 5.

Make value flow

In essence, this means applying the pyramid of key factors that we outlined in section 6.1. Minimising delays, inventories, defects and downtime supports the flow of value in the supply network. Simplicity and visibility are the foundations to achieving these key factors.

Pull scheduling

Enforce the rules in section 6.1: make only in response to a signal from the customer (the next process) that more is needed. This implies that demand information is made available across the supply chain. Where possible, supply from manufacturing, not from stock. Where possible, use customer orders not forecasts.

While some of these concepts may be distant from current practice, lean thinking shares the philosophy of 'big JIT': seek perfection. This is the fifth principle, and is achieved by gradually getting better at everything, squeezing waste out at every step. We continue this section by considering the sources of waste, and the way in which lean thinking can be applied to enriching value in business processes.

6.2.1 The seven wastes

In Chapter 5 we saw how any activity that does not add value is a form of waste. By mapping processes through the supply chain, it is possible to sort value-adding and non-value-adding activities (transport, store, inspect and delay). Lean thinking goes further by adding three more types of 'waste' to make seven in all:

- *The waste of overproduction*: making or delivering too much, too early or 'just in case'. Instead, the aim should be to make 'just-in-time' – neither too early nor too late. Overproduction creates unevenness or lumpiness of material flow, which is bad for quality and productivity. It is often the biggest source of waste.

- *The waste of waiting*: takes place whenever time is not being used effectively. It shows up as waiting by operators, by parts or by customers.

- *The waste of transporting*: moving parts around from one process to the next adds no value. Double handling, conveyors and movements by fork-lift truck are all examples of this waste. Placing processes as close as possible to each other not only minimises the waste of transport but also improves communications between them.

- *The waste of inappropriate processing*: using a large, central process that is shared between several lines (e.g. a heat treatment plant) is an example of this type of waste. Another example is a process that is incapable of meeting quality standards demanded by the customer – so it cannot help making defects.

- *The waste of unnecessary inventory*: inventory is a sign that flow has been disrupted, and that there are inherent problems in the process. Inventory not only hides problems, it also increases lead times and increases space requirements.

- *The waste of unnecessary motions*: if operators have to bend, stretch or extend themselves unduly, then these are unnecessary motions. Other examples are walking between processes, taking a stores requisition for signature, and decanting parts from one container into another.

- *The waste of defects*: producing defects costs time and money. The longer a defect remains undetected (e.g. if it gets into the hands of the end-customer), the more cost is added. Defects are counteracted by the concepts of 'quality at source' and 'prevention, not detection'.

Lean thinking invites us to analyse business processes systematically to establish the baseline of value-adding processes and to identify the incidence of these seven wastes. The aim is to get parts and data to flow through business processes evenly and in harmony. The more detailed analysis prompted by the concept of seven wastes encourages a greater analysis and understanding of processes and their relationships than is made by supply chain mapping. This analysis should first start with key business processes such as the supply pipeline. Working back from the customer, a business should consider the following processes in the first instance:

- order to replenishment;
- order to production;
- product development.

In each of these processes, the application of lean thinking involves examining the process, quantifying waste within it, identifying root causes of the waste, and developing and implementing solutions. Examining the process involves mapping it using a variety of techniques such as flow charting, depending on the nature of the process. Performance is quantified by taking measures of the different kinds of waste. For a first attempt, using the time-based measures of lead time and value-adding time often reveal the main incidences of waste. Having identified waste, lean thinking applies the problem-solving tools associated with total quality control (TQC) to identify root causes and develop solutions.

   The application of lean thinking is the means by which many companies bring their processes under control. Following a systematic approach to tackling waste, they seek to minimise defects, to minimise downtime and to maximise simplicity and visibility.

6.2.2 Application of lean thinking to business processes

Order to replenishment

The order replenishment cycle concerns the time taken to replenish what has been sold. Lean thinking seeks to manage the order replenishment cycle by replacing only what has been sold within rapid replenishment lead times. These points are taken up in sections 6.3 and 6.4 of this chapter, on vendor-managed inventory and on quick response.

Order to production

The order to production cycle is the series of steps that are followed to respond to an order, organise and undertake production, and deliver the product to the customer. This 'make to order' process may be contained within a company or can extend down the supply chain.

Product development

Product development delivers new products or services that can be sold. This process is essential if an organisation is to have future success. Lean thinking can be applied to this process to make it more effective by supporting the development of products with desirable attributes and features and achieving this on time. It can also make the process more efficient and ensure that products are developed to cost.

6.2.3 Role of lean practices

Lean thinking is associated with a number of operational practices that help to deliver the aim of waste minimisation. Two of the most significant are:

- small-batch production;
- rapid changeover.

These two practices are closely associated with each other, but are considered separately here to aid clarity.

The target in small-batch production is a batch size of one. The traditional logic behind large batches is to take advantage of reduced costs through economies of scale (see EBQ in section 6.1 above). This approach is often flawed, as batch size decisions generally consider only production costs, and overlook the costs of inventory and lack of flexibility that is caused by large batches. Lack of flexibility is a major contributor to poor quality of service to the end-customer. The rationale behind small batches is that they can reduce total cost across a supply chain, such as removing the waste of overproduction. They help to deliver products that the end-customer wants within the expected lead time (D-time – Chapter 5, section 5.2).

The contribution of rapid changeover was graphically shown by the changeover of press tools used to make car body panels. These cumbersome pieces of equipment can weigh up to 10 tonnes, and historically took up to eight hours to change within the large presses. The consequence of these long changeover times was that component production runs were long, often going on for days before the press tools were changed so that another component could be made. Extensive work, again led by Toyota, was undertaken on press design, tooling design and component design over a number of years to help to reduce changeover times. The effect has been to reduce changeover times for tools for large pressed parts to around five minutes. Consequently, practices that reduce changeover times are often known as *single minute exchange of dies* (SMED) (Shingo, 1988). The ability to undertake rapid changeovers allows a batch of each different body panel to be produced each day in line with current demand instead of having to produce to forecast.

The lesson from the automotive industry is that even very large pieces of equipment can be developed to allow rapid changeovers. This effort may take a number of years, and is reliant upon developments in machinery and product design, but it can be done. The effect is to provide the flexibility to make possible small-batch production that responds to customer needs.

Small-batch production associated with rapid changeover allows productivity to be maintained by taking advantages of economies of scope. Instead of economies of scale, where quantities of the same thing are made, economies of scope lower costs when quantities of similar things that use the same production resources are made.

6.2.4 Design strategies

Underpinning the application of lean thinking is the need to influence design. Many of the wastes uncovered in the replenishment, make to order and product development cycles cannot be removed because they are inherent in the design of products, systems, processes and facilities. The design strategy employed in lean thinking is to incorporate the ability to undertake lean practices across the total life of a product or facility and also include flexibility to deal with unpredicted events. These issues are described more fully below.

6.2.5 Lean product design

Products can be designed with a number of lean attributes. These include:

- a reduction in the number of parts they contain and the materials from which they are made;
- features that aid assembly, such as asymmetrical parts that can be assembled in only one way;
- redundant features on common, core parts that allow variety to be achieved without complexity with the addition of peripheral parts;
- modular designs that allow parts to be upgraded over the product life.

6.2.6 Lean facility design

The facilities within which new products are developed and existing ones are made and delivered should be designed with lean attributes. Among these are:

- modular design of equipment to allow prompt repair and maintenance;
- modular design of layout to allow teams to be brought together with all the facilities they need, with the minimum of disruption, and then subsequently to be dispersed and reassembled elsewhere;
- small machines, ideally portable, which can be moved to match the demand for them;
- open systems architectures (both IT and physical ones) that allow equipment to fit together and work when it is moved and connected to other items.

6.2.7 Lean thinking summary

Lean thinking is based around the simple philosophy of eliminating waste. This concept can be applied to almost all business processes in almost any company.

A simple method to help companies achieve this is for them to pursue the goal of single-piece flow, where the batch size passing through the processes of a company is a single item. Problems encountered during progress towards this goal reveal the areas that need to be resolved in order to become leaner.

To aid waste elimination, a number of practices have been developed. Key ones such as rapid changeover, presented here, provide standard solutions that are widely applicable and help most companies to reduce costs and improve quality.

6.3 Vendor-managed inventory (VMI)

Key issue: How can suppliers help to reduce waste in the customer's process?

Sections 6.3 and 6.4 continue the theme of just-in-time and lean thinking by considering how these principles have been applied to retailing supply chains in the form of *vendor-managed inventory* and *quick response* logistics (section 6.4). Vendor-managed inventory (VMI), is an approach to inventory and order fulfilment whereby the supplier, not the customer, is responsible for managing and replenishing inventory. This appears at first sight to counter the principle of pull scheduling, because the preceding process (the manufacturer) is deciding when and how many to send to the next process (the retailer). In practice, the basis on which decisions will be made is agreed with the retailer beforehand, and is based on the retailer's sales information. Under VMI, the supplier assumes responsibility for monitoring sales and inventory, and uses this information to trigger replenishment orders. In effect, suppliers take over the task of stock replenishment.

Automated VMI originated in the late 1980s with department stores in the United States as a solution to manage the difficulties in predicting demand for seasonal clothing. Prior to this *manual VMI* had been around for many years – particularly in the food industry. Under manual VMI, the manufacturer's salesman took a record of inventory levels and reordered product for delivery to the customer's store, where the manufacturer's representative would restock the shelves. As product variety has increased and life cycles have shortened, manual VMI has been replaced by automated VMI.

6.3.1 How VMI works

The supplier tracks product sales and inventory levels at their customers, sending goods only when stocks run low. The decision to supply is taken by the supplier, not the customer as is traditionally the case. The supplier takes this decision based on the ability of the current level of inventory to satisfy prevailing market demand, while factoring in the lead time to resupply.

The smooth running of VMI depends on a sound business system. It also requires effective teamwork between the retailer and the manufacturer. In order for both parties to gain full benefit from the system, appropriate performance measures need to be used. The top priority measure is that of product availability at the retailer. It is in both parties' interests to maximise product availability, avoiding lost sales in the short term and building customer-buying habits in the long term. By emphasising the supplier's responsibility for maximising product availability, VMI aims to achieve this with minimum inventories. In order to combine both of these apparently conflicting goals, it is necessary to have access to real-time demand at the customer.

The most widely used technology for broadcasting demand data from the customer is *electronic data interchange* (EDI). This provides the means for exchanging data from customer to suppliers in a standard format. Internet-based applications using EDI protocols are increasingly popular, providing the same facility at lower cost. Customer demand and inventory data are often processed through software packages to automate the application of decision rules and identify stock lines that need replenishment.

6.3.2 Potential benefits

The immediate benefit to a supplier engaged in VMI is access to data on:

- customer sales;
- inventory levels at the customer.

The assumption is that the supplier can use these data to provide better control of the supply chain and so deliver benefits for both the customer and themselves.

Having the supplier take the decision on replenishment aims to minimise the impact of *demand amplification*, which is discussed in Chapter 7. This critical problem erodes customer service, loses sales and increases costs. The ability to dampen demand amplification caused by infrequent, large orders from customers is key to the success of VMI. The surplus capacity and excess finished goods held by suppliers to counteract such variation can then be reduced.

In the longer term, suppliers should integrate demand information into their organisation and develop the capability to drive production with it. This helps to replace the traditional push scheduling, based on forecasts and buffer stocks, with pull scheduling, based on meeting known demand instantaneously out of manufacturing.

Activity 6.1

There are several different ways in which the use of VMI can benefit the supplier and the customer. Make a list of those benefits you think exist under the headings of 'supplier benefits' and 'customer benefits'.

6.3.3 Potential problems in setting up a VMI system

Other than the practical difficulties of setting up a VMI system, a number of problems can prevent the attainment of the above benefits, five of which are listed below:

Unwillingness to share data

Retailers may be unwilling to share their marketing plans and product range strategies with manufacturers. This is particularly true in the United Kingdom, where supermarkets have strong own brands that compete with those of the manufacturers.

Retailers continue to be the owners of information on actual demand passing through their tills. An inability to forward this information, whether due to reluctance or to procedural and technical problems, will prevent suppliers from responding effectively, leading to the need for buffer stocks and increasing the risk of stockouts.

Seasonal products

The benefits of VMI are quickly eroded in fashion and seasonal products, especially apparel. VMI in these cases can involve suppliers making to stock based on a pre-season forecast with little scope for manufacturing in season. Small quantities are delivered from this stock to the retailers over the season. Naturally the forecast is regularly at odds with actual demand, so products will be frequently understocked or overstocked. In effect all that has happened is that the burden of owning inventory and disposing of excesses has been moved onto the supplier.

Investment and restructuring costs

Adopting a VMI approach incurs a high investment by the customer and supplier. Setting up the processes and procedures for undertaking this new way of working takes time and effort. The customer will need to close their materials management function if they are to make cost savings, while the supplier will need to develop the capability to take over this task.

Retailer vulnerability

The process of outsourcing materials management to suppliers makes the retailer more dependent on them.

Lack of standard procedures

The practicalities of the processes and procedures that underpin VMI may not be transferable from one customer to another. Customers may ask for different tagging methods or bespoke labelling. With many industrial products there is no bar-code standard.

System maintenance

Errors creep into inventory records due to incorrect parts counts, mislabelling, damage, loss and theft. These records need to be maintained through manual methods such as stock counts.

6.4 Quick response

Key issue: **How can capabilities across the supply chain be aligned to meet end-customer demand?**

Another application of just-in-time and lean thinking is *quick response logistics*. Quick response (or QR for short) is an approach to meeting customer demand by supplying the right quantity, variety and quality at the right time to the right place at the right price. This concept originated in the US textile and apparel industry in response to the threat posed by overseas competitors. The concepts behind QR are based on taking a total supply chain view of an industry. From this perspective it is possible to understand overall performance and the causes of poor performance, and to identify opportunities for improvement.

Understanding overall performance involves mapping the processes needed to convert raw material into final product (see Chapter 5). The performance of the process is also assessed to determine its effectiveness. In the case of the apparel industry, mapping followed the process of converting raw material into fibre, then into fabric, then into apparel and finally delivery to the retailer. Key measures of the process were lead times, inventory levels and work in progress.

This investigation found that the total process of converting raw material into clothing took 66 weeks. A basic analysis of the process identified that 55 weeks were taken up with product sitting in various stores as inventory. The principal cause of the need for this inventory was identified as being lack of communication between the organisations in the supply network.

Such analysis is similar to that described in Chapter 5, with the process considered in this case being the whole supply chain from end to end. There are two main differences between QR and a time-based approach to improvement. First, there is an emphasis on using actual customer demand to pull products through the distribution and manufacturing system. Second, there is extensive use of information technology as the preferred way to achieve pull. These two issues are explored in more detail below.

6.4.1 JIT/QR relationship

Quick response has much in common with the principles behind just-in-time described in section 6.1. The same principle of making only to demand is applied to different parts of the supply network. QR applies the pull principle to the front-end process of distribution management between the retailer and the supplier. JIT applies this principle throughout the supply network. In the case of QR, items are supplied to the retailer in response to consumer demand. Deliveries are made just-in-time for them to be sold. Delivery to the retailer triggers the supplier to produce another item, so pulling further parts through the supply chain in a JIT manner.

This process is very different from the traditional approach of the apparel industry. It has been commonplace to make the whole of a season's forecast demand in advance, and to deliver to store in line with the forecast. While a true 'make to demand' approach has not been achieved, applying QR has led the industry to make two important changes:

- Development lead times have been compressed. This allows designs to be released later, and thus more in line with the latest fashion trends.

- Production lead times are shorter. This allows smaller pre-season inventories to be built up. Instead, high-demand items are supplemented by production during the season. The effect is to maintain high availability of popular lines while minimising stocks of items that prove to be less popular and which would otherwise have to be discounted.

6.4.2 Role of enabling technologies

High variety in clothing markets – due to different sizes, styles and colours – and in grocery markets has led these industries to use information technologies as a means of enabling QR. These technologies are based around the use of uniform product codes and electronic data interchange (EDI). The process involves collecting merchandise information at the point of sale from the product bar-code. Data are sent to the supplier via EDI, where they are compared with an inventory model for the store concerned. When appropriate, production is ordered for the specific items needed to restock the store to the requirements of the model. Once these items have been made, the cycle is completed when they are packed, shipped to the store and delivered to the shelf.

This process has enormous implications for links across the supply chain. With each retailer having a range of suppliers and each supplier servicing a number of retailers there is the need for common bar-code standards across the industry. The retailer needs to have a scanning and data capture system to identify the item being sold. It will need to have a reordering system that links the item to its manufacturer, and which places an order. Information needs to be exchanged between the parties in a common data format, which can be read by different IT systems. The high volume of transactions means that the systems handling the data exchange need to be robust and reliable. Having been informed of the sale, the supplier inputs this information to its manufacturing planning system in order to schedule production and the ordering of supplies.

It is hardly surprising that it is extremely difficult to achieve this integration across the whole of a supply network. There are significant implications for small businesses, which have difficulty justifying the cost of the IT system and the associated training. These set-up costs can deter new companies with innovative products from being able to supply. Recent developments in Internet-based applications are helping to resolve this situation because the implementation and data transfer costs are much lower.

Summary

What is JIT, and how does it apply to logistics?

- JIT is a broad-based philosophy of doing the simple things right and gradually doing them better. As applied to logistics, JIT can be conceived as a pyramid of key factors that centre on minimum delay and minimum inventory.

- 'How many?' and 'when?' to order are key questions that impact on delay and inventory. JIT contributes to the answers to these questions by cutting down the sources and causes of waste in logistics. Specific contributions include the reduction of changeover times and simple, paperless systems of material control.

- Long-standing approaches to material control, such as reorder point stock control (ROP), economic order quantities (EOQ) and material requirements planning (MRP), can be made far more responsive by the application of JIT principles. Examples are reducing batch sizes and reorder quantities, and reducing lead times. Synergies can be delivered, too: JIT pull scheduling works best for control, MRP for planning.

What is lean thinking, and how can it be applied to logistics?

- Lean thinking seeks perfection by gradually reducing waste from each of four areas: specifying value from the customer perspective; identifying the value stream (through time-based mapping); making the product flow through the supply network (by applying JIT principles); and letting the customer pull (through pull scheduling).

- Lean thinking focuses on how the seven wastes can be used to support lean principles. Lean thinking follows JIT principles via the concept of 'one piece flow'. Lean thinking extends these principles into product and facility design.

In what ways have JIT and lean thinking been applied to supply networks?

- Two of the ways in which JIT and lean thinking principles have been applied to logistics are covered in this chapter. Others follow in later chapters in this book.

- Under vendor-managed inventory (VMI), suppliers take responsibility for monitoring sales and inventory in the retailer's process. This information is used to trigger replenishment orders. VMI is facilitated by willingness to share data, the use of integrated systems and standard procedures. It is made more difficult by such factors as long replenishment lead times, inaccurate data, and unwillingness by either party to invest in systems support.

- Quick response (QR) logistics take the lead from time-based mapping, and adopt a total supply chain view to following sales trends: for example, in the fashion industry. Instead of making a season's product in advance, QR aims to be responsive to market trends. This has had the effect of compressing development lead times and shortening production lead times to greatly improve the responsiveness of the supply network as a whole.

Discussion questions

1 Dealers have criticised the way automotive assemblers use JIT as an excuse for buying parts from the inbound supply network 'so that their costs are kept down'. They then dump finished vehicles onto the dealer by matching '*their* perceptions of a marketplace demand with *their* constraints as a manufacturer, i.e. what they've produced' (adapted from Delbridge and Oliver, 1991). Referring to the Ford/Toyota case in case study 6.2, comment on the trade-offs implied in these comments from disgruntled dealers.

2 What matters more: value to the customer or value to the shareholder? Refer to section 3.4 of Chapter 3 in formulating your response. How does this question affect the philosophy of lean thinking?

3 Explain the thinking behind quick response (QR) logistics. How can QR help a retailer to plan and control product lines for a new fashion season?

4 What is meant by the term *overproduction*? Why do you think this has been described as the biggest waste of all?

5 Explain the difference between pull scheduling and push scheduling. Under what circumstances might push scheduling be appropriate?

References

Chase, R.B. and Aquilano, N.J. (1992) *Production and Operations Management: A life cycle approach*, 2nd edn, Homewood, IL: Irwin.

Delbridge, R. and Oliver, N. (1991) 'Just-in-time or just the same? Developments in the auto industry: the retailers' views', *International Journal of Retail and Distribution Management*, Vol. 19, No. 2, pp. 20–6.

Harrison, A.S. (1992) *Just in Time Manufacturing in Perspective*. Hemel Hempstead: Prentice Hall.

Harrison, A. and Storey, J. (2000) 'Coping with world class manufacturing', *New Technology, Work and Employment*, Vol. 13, No. 3, pp, 643–64.

Krafcik, J.F. and MacDuffie, J.P. (1989) *Explaining High Performance Manufacturing: The international automotive assembly plant study*. MIT, Boston, MA: International Motor Vehicle Program.

Nakajima, S. (ed.) (1989) *TPM Development Program: Implementing total productive maintenance*. Cambridge, MA: Productivity Press.

Porter, M.E. (1985) *Competitive Advantage: Creating and sustaining superior performance*. New York: Free Press.

Schonberger, R.J. (1991) *Building a Chain of Customers: Linking business functions to build the world class company*. New York: Free Press.

Shingo, S. (1988) *Non-Stock Production*. Cambridge, MA: Productivity Press.

Slack, N. (ed.) (1997) *Blackwell Encyclopedic Dictionary of Operations Management*. Oxford: Blackwell.

Vollman, T.E., Berry, W.L., Whybark, D.C. and Jacobs, F.R. (2004) *Manufacturing Planning and Control for Supply Chain Management*, 5th edn. Singapore: McGraw-Hill Higher Education.

Waters, D. (2003) *Inventory Planning and Control*, 2nd edn. Chichester: John Wiley.

Womack, J. and Jones, D. (2003) *Lean Thinking*, 2nd edn. New York: Simon & Schuster.

Womack, J., Jones, D. and Roos, D. (1990) *The Machine that Changed the World*. New York: Rawson Associates.

CHAPTER 7

The agile supply chain

Outcomes

The planned outcomes of this chapter are to:

- introduce the concept of the agile supply chain as a broad-based approach to developing the time advantage;
- explore the challenges and difficulties of coping with volatile demand situations;
- explain how capabilities can be developed and specifically targeted at thriving in conditions of market turbulence.

By the end of this chapter you should be able to understand:

- that different strategies are needed for different volume/variety conditions in the supply chain;
- the distinctions between lean and agile mindsets, and how the two can work together;
- the type of market conditions under which agile strategies are appropriate and how they can be operationalised.

In Chapter 9 we consider another key aspect of the agile supply chain – the virtual organisation.

Introduction

In the previous two chapters, we reviewed just-in-time, quick response and other time-based approaches to developing the capabilities needed to support the speed advantage. While such logistics capabilities are important enablers to lean and responsive supply chains, the 'agile supply chain' takes the argument a significant step further. Market places of the twenty-first century are often characterised by proliferation of products and services, shorter product life cycles and increased rates of product innovation. Simply responding quickly and at the right time are not enough to meet the needs of such marketplaces.

The mission of modern logistics is to ensure that it is the right product – to meet exact end-customer needs – that gets delivered in the right place at the right time. Such a mission means that the *end-customer comes first.* This chapter proposes the agile supply chain as an approach that elevates speed capabilities in a given supply chain to much higher levels than would be possible using the tools and techniques discussed so far.

In Chapter 6, we looked at the concepts of 'lean production', and the wider concept of the 'lean enterprise'. The focus of the lean approach has essentially been on the elimination of waste. A common view is that lean thinking works best where demand is relatively stable – and hence predictable – and where variety is low. But in situations where demand is volatile and customer requirement for variety is high, the elimination of waste becomes a lesser priority than the need to respond rapidly to a turbulent marketplace.

It is also important to recognise that no single approach offers a solution to every supply chain situation, a point we made in section 1.4.3.

Key issues *This chapter addresses two key issues:*

1 **The concept of agility:** the dimensions of the agile supply chain and the environments that favour agility.

2 **Agile practices:** addressing the challenges of market turbulence, rapid response logistics and managing low-volume products.

7.1 The concept of agility

Key issue: **what are the dimensions of the agile supply chain?**

Figure 7.1 sets out our view of the agile supply chain (Harrison *et al.*, 1999). First, the agile supply chain is *customer responsive*. By customer responsive we mean that the supply chain is capable of reading and responding to end-customer demand. Most organisations are forecast-driven rather than demand-driven. In other words because they have inadequate real-time data and cannot react fast enough anyway, they are forced to make forecasts based upon past sales or shipments and convert these forecasts into inventory. The breakthroughs of the last decade in the form of such advances as efficient consumer response (ECR – see Chapter 8, section 8.2) and the use of information technology to capture data on demand direct from the point-of-sale or point-of-use are transforming an organisation's ability to hear the voice of the market. This throws down the challenge of how to develop the capabilities needed to respond.

Second, the supply chain should be viewed as a *network* of partners who have a common goal to collaborate together in order to respond to end-customer needs. In Chapter 1, we introduced the term 'network' to refer to the cross-linking of partners that forms the basic model used in this book. Individual partners are viewed in terms of their contribution to the value being generated for the end-customer. Competitive strength comes from focusing the capabilities of a network of partners onto responding to customer needs.

The third component of agility is viewing the network as a system of *business processes*. Nesting the capabilities of these processes creates power and synergy for the network. 'Stand alone' processes that do not support material flow create penalties in terms of time, cost and quality for the whole network. As we said on p.12, 'all processes within the network need to be understood in terms of how they interact with other processes'.

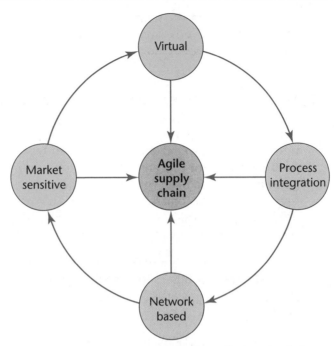

Figure 7.1 **An integrated model for enabling the agile supply chain**

Fourth, use of information technology to share data between buyers and suppliers creates, in effect, a *virtual* supply chain (see Chapter 9, section 9.5.2). Virtual supply chains are information-based rather than inventory-based. Conventional logistics systems seek to identify optimal quantities of inventory and their spatial location. Complex formulae and algorithms exist to support this inventory-based business model. Paradoxically, what we are now learning is that once we have visibility of demand through shared information, the premise upon which these formulae is based no longer holds. Electronic data interchange (EDI) and the Internet have enabled partners in the supply chain to act upon the same data – real demand – rather than being dependent upon the distorted and noisy picture that emerges when orders are transmitted from one step to another in an extended chain.

As proposed in Figure 7.1, enabling the agile supply chain requires many significant changes. As an example of such changes, consider the position of Li and Fung, the largest export trader in Hong Kong. The organisation coordinates manufacturers in the Far East to supply major customers like *the Limited*, mostly in the United States. Chairman Victor Fung says that one of the key features of his approach is to organise for the customer, not on country units that end up competing against each other.

> So customer-focused divisions are the building blocks of our organisation, and we keep them small and entrepreneurial. They do anywhere from $20 million to $50 million of business. Each is run by a lead entrepreneur (Magretta, 1998: 109).

And capabilities of the supply networks are 'all about flexibility, response time, small production runs, small minimum order quantities, and the ability to shift direction as the trends move'.

7.1.1   Demand characteristics and supply capabilities

The 'agile supply chain' is an essentially practical approach to organising logistics capabilities around individual end-customer demand. It is about moving from supply chains that are structured around a focal company and its operating guidelines (for example, Ford Production System) towards supply chains that are focused on end-customers. The key here is to organise logistics from the customer order back – or 'outside in' – as opposed to pushing product-service offerings into the market – or 'inside out'. Requirements for that change in mindset include:

- a relentless focus on drivers of customer value in all logistics processes;

- developing capabilities for responsiveness and flexibility in advance;

- using those capabilities to align supply chains operations in a dynamic manner.

Mason-Jones *et al*. (1999) developed a helpful comparison between agile and lean supply, shown in Table 7.1.

We have extended such ideas into our comparison of characteristics of lean and agile supply, shown in Table 7.2.

There is no reason why there should be an 'either-or' approach to logistics strategy. Thus, many supply chains can adopt a 'lean' capability up to a given downstream process, and then adopt an 'agile' capability thereafter. This enables high-productivity, low-cost processes to start with, followed by responsive processes to allow high levels of customisation thereafter. Such a strategic choice has

Table 7.1 Comparison of lean supply with agile supply: the distinguishing attributes

Distinguishing attributes	Lean supply	Agile supply
Typical products	Commodities	Fashion goods
Marketplace demand	Predictable	Volatile
Product variety	Low	High
Product life cycle	Long	Short
Customer drivers	Cost	Availability
Profit margin	Low	High
Dominant costs	Physical costs	Marketability costs
Stockout penalties	Long-term contractual	Immediate and volatile
Purchasing policy	Buy materials	Assign capacity
Information enrichment	Highly desirable	Obligatory
Forecasting mechanism	Algorithmic	Consultative

(Source: Mason-Jones *et al.*, 1999)

Table 7.2 Comparison of characteristics of lean and agile supply

Characteristic	Lean	Agile
Logistics focus	Eliminate waste	Customers and markets
Partnerships	Long-term, stable	Fluid clusters
Key measures	Output measures such as productivity and cost	Measure capabilities, and focus on customer satisfaction
Process focus	Work standardisation, conformance to standards	Focus on operator self-management to maximise autonomy
Logistics planning	Stable, fixed periods	Instantaneous response

been referred to as 'leagility' because it combines the benefits of both supply capabilities. The concept of leagility is close to that of postponement, which we discuss later in this chapter.

The comparisons in Tables 7.1 and 7.2 help us to place 'agile' in relation to 'lean', and thus to complement our earlier concept of logistics performance objectives. In Table 1.1, we considered the issue of competing through logistics. The relative importance of the four ways of competing through logistics (quality, time, cost and dependability) can be assessed with the help of order winners and order qualifiers (see Chapter 1, section 1.3.2). *Order qualifiers* comprise the factors that are needed to gain entry into a given market. To actually win orders demands that performance of the focal firm on one or more factors must be superior, so that products win orders in the marketplace because performance of competitors on these factors is not as good. These are called *order winners*. The specification of order qualifiers and order winners helps in the development of logistics strategy. Order winners and qualifiers can *change over time* (Johnasson *et al.*, 1993), for example, as a result of changes in the product life cycle. Thus it is essential to revisit the specification of order winners and qualifiers regularly to ensure that they reflect current market characteristics.

A study of the personal computer supply chain over a 15-year period shows an evolution of order winners from quality and cost to availability and lead time (Christopher and Towill, 2000). Table 7.3 shows four stages in this evolution.

The supply chain has evolved from mainly lean capabilities in the 1980s to increasingly agile characteristics in the 1990s. This has been in response to changes in drivers of customer value as end-customers became more knowledgeable about the product.

The agile mindset aims to align supply capabilities with end-customer demand, so we can view demand characteristics as placing the challenges that supply capabilities must meet. Figure 7.2 describes demand characteristics in terms of market predictability, while supply capabilities describe how quickly the supply chain can respond.

Let us now examine demand characteristics and supply capability in more detail. Both of these strategic considerations needs to be applied to major market segments, a topic that we explored in Chapter 2.

Table 7.3 **Transitions in the personal computer supply chain**

Supply chain evolution phase	I	II	III	IV
Supply chain time marker	early 1980s	late 1980s	early 1990s	late 1990s
Supply chain philosophy	Product driven	Market oriented	Market driven	Customer driven
Supply chain type	Lean functional silos	Lean supply chain	Leagile supply chain	Customised leagile supply chain
Orders winners	Quality	Cost	Availability	Lead time
Order qualifiers	(a) Cost (b) Availability (c) Lead Time	(a) Availability (b) Lead time (c) Quality	(a) Lead time (b) Quality (c) Cost	(a) Quality (b) Cost (c) Availability
Performance metrics	(a) Stock turns (b) Production cost	(a) Throughput time (b) Physical cost	(a) Market share (b) Total cost	(a) Customer satisfaction (b) Value added

(Source: After Christopher and Towill, 2000)

Demand characteristics

In Chapter 5, section 5.2.2, we defined D-time as the time that the customer is prepared to wait to have their order fulfilled. D-time may be measured in time-related measures from months to minutes. Essentially, this sets time objectives for the supply chain. Response in minutes means that there is no time to procure materials or to process them. Therefore, inventories of finished product are inevitable. However, as D-times reduce in turbulent markets, holding inventories becomes an increasingly risky option, and in turn places increasing pressure on supply capabilities. A firm may decide to respond to such pressure by reducing the range on offer, and by increasing the commonality of parts between different

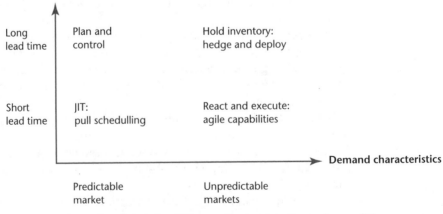

Figure 7.2 **Lean and agile under different demand and supply conditions**
(Source: After Christopher and Towill, 2000)

skus. At the other end of the scale, if the customer is prepared to wait for a long enough period to enable design and procurement processes to be completed, a relatively high level of customisation may be possible.

Forecast error (measured by the *mean absolute deviation* between actual and forecast demand for a given time series) provides clear objectives for developing supply capabilities. Forecast error ties in with the logistics need to align mid- to longer-term capacity decisions with demand. In Chapter 5, we argued that reducing P-times reduces the need to rely on forecasts. But clearly there is a limit to how far this ideal can be pushed. Being able to respond immediately to actual demand means that logistics capabilities have been put in place to do so. In particular, it is still necessary to make mid- to longer-term forecasts – for example to allow for advanced orders to suppliers, long cycle time production processes and to expand facilities.

It is also tough in logistics terms to support high levels of *volume variation* of demand across a given time period in a given supply chain. Constraints such as capacity limitations and fixed order quantities and lead times inhibit what may be done. Building *buffer capacity* into the supply chain (in the form of inventories or spare production capacity) may be too costly. Instead, it helps to analyse the causes of volume variation. Two main factors are the differences between peaks and troughs of demand, and the frequency with which peaks and troughs occur. A standard seasonal pattern may have just one peak (summer for garden furniture, for example), whereas fashion industries may have six seasons or more. Retail promotions may create peaks every other week, which lead to volume variations of 60–70 per cent of 'normal' demand. We analyse these points further in section 7.2. Figure 7.3 shows how demand characteristics can be analysed.

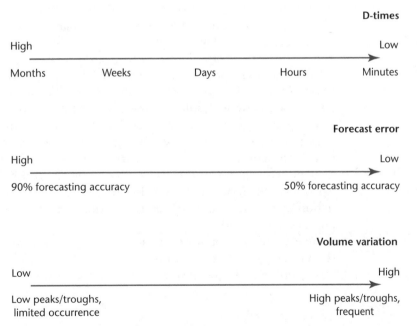

Figure 7.3 **Analysing the influence of demand characteristics on a supply chain**

Supply capabilities

Now let us look at the supply capabilities that are needed to meet the above demand characteristics. Allocation of finished goods to given customer orders is a familiar way of responding quickly to demand – for example, selling cars from a dealer forecourt. But this approach to supply means that inventories of finished goods must first be built up. The problem is that they must be built up in anticipation of *unknown* demand. If stocks pushed by a manufacturer onto its dealer network are too high, they will have to be discounted. If they are too low, sales are lost to competitors. Delaying the exact specification of the car until the customer order is known, and then delivering it within an acceptable D-time, is called *form postponement*. The concept of 'postponement' is now increasingly widely employed by organisations in a range of industries (van Hoek, 1998). For example, the aim of the '3-day car' project is to complete paint, trim, final assembly and delivery of a car to dealer within three days (Holweg and Miemczyk 2002). Many less ambitious form postponement applications delay packaging, labelling, adding documentation or product peripherals until an order is received. If the decision is limited to peripherals such as type of power supply to a printer, or to whether the number of cans in a pack is 6 or 12, we call this *logistical postponement*.

The appearance of wide customer choice can be created while keeping source, make and deliver processes as simple as possible. This is the thinking behind the principle of *design for logistics*. Creating an agile supply chain requires more than revising logistics and distribution management: it goes all the way to product design. A favourite trick of computer manufacturers like Dell is to make common electronic boards and to package them in many ways to create different options. While parts of a board are redundant on many of the finished products, this is more than offset by savings in inbound and manufacturing logistics.

Individual companies in an agile supply chain need to align their operations by redesigning the flow of goods, information and management practices. The aim is the *virtual organisation*, where groups of supply chain partners agree common terms for working together. There are several possible stages in the evolution of a virtual organisation. Traditional sourcing and contract logistics imply an interface between trading partners that is limited to buy–sell transactions. JIT sourcing is an example of a broader interface with sharing of demand data and alignment of logistics processes. Integrated contract manufacturing – in which a third party controls most of the make processes – attempts the integration of demand with supply in the way suggested by Figure 1.7. 'Fourth-party logistics' is close to this model in that a third party takes over organisation and coordination of the entire flow of goods, information and management of the entire logistics (Figure 7.4).

We explore these approaches further in section 7.2. Meanwhile, case study 7.1 shows how Xerox developed a 'next generation' logistics strategy by injecting fresh thinking into the position outlined in case study 1.2.

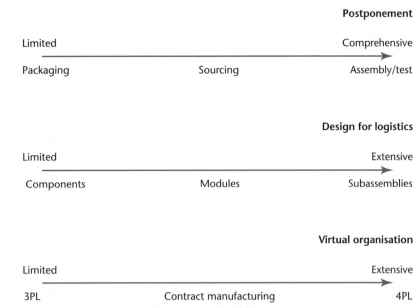

Figure 7.4 Supply capabilities supporting the agile supply chain

CASE STUDY
7.1

Segmenting the supply chain at Xerox

By the middle of the 1990s Xerox had integrated its European manufacturing and logistics processes and organisations developing an end-to-end approach to its supply chain. This had delivered massive financials benefits to the company both in terms of inventory reduction and operating cost. At the time it was to launch a new range of products and to extend its market coverage and it was recognised that the predominantly 'one size fits all' approach to customer fulfilment was not competitive. The company embarked on a programme of asking customers about their requirements for overall fulfilment and understanding supply chain competitive performance.

Based on market/customer expectations the company segmented its supply chain into four different streams across the total source–plan–make–deliver process. The segmentation of the market/customer expectations are shown in Figure 7.5 and the supply chain response in Figure 7.6. *Volume* represents the number of orders/shipments; *variety* reflects the combination of product variation and day-to-day demand variability.

The organisation and the processes of the supply chain needed to operate differently since the priorities of the market and customers were different. Different performance measures and targets were established for each segment and cultures and incentives put in place to drive the change. In all cases the company operated with outsourced partners as part of the supply chain operations but the balance between outsourced and in-house varied depending on the skills and flexibility required. As 'adding customer uniqueness as late as possible' was a key element in the process design, collaboration with the product design teams and suppliers became essential to engineer supply-chain-friendly products.

In particular in the high-volume/high-variety segment the customer order is directed to the integration centre at the end of the line, which has fewer than five days to finalise the product and deliver to the end consumer. This could only be achieved by engineering the

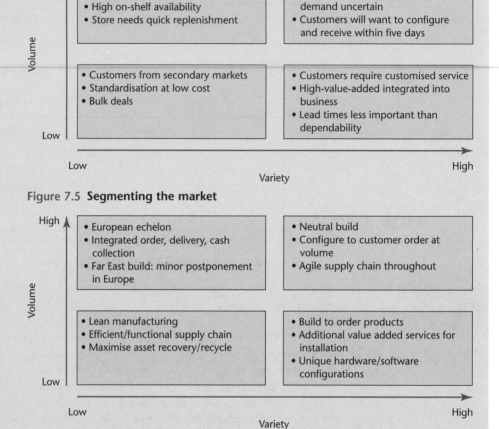

Figure 7.5 Segmenting the market

Figure 7.6 Supply chain response

product to a modular design with final configuration from stock of 'neutral' modules and adding customer-unique options. This capability required flexibility and agility in all areas of the supply chain. In turn, this meant investing in the skills needed for planning demand and supply so that capacity and inventories could meet the variable load.

At the time the segmentation approach allowed the company to fulfil the majority of its European customer orders from a European supply, with the exception of the high-volume/ low-variety segment which supplied customers through distributors and retailers.

This approach not only improved measures of customer responsiveness but also improved inventory turns, so reducing the need for stocks below the European level and overall supply chain costs. Inherent in the design was not only the flexibility in operation but the ability to create and restructure the segments depending on changes to market and customer needs. This configuration of the Xerox supply chain segmentation had a life of approximately four years.

(Source: Graham Sweet)

Question

1 Map the Xerox segments and market response (Figures 7.5 and 7.6) onto demand influences and supply capabilities in Figures 7.3 and 7.4 as far as you can, making assumptions where necessary. How closely does the 'actual' match 'theoretical'?

7.1.2 Classifying operating environments

Figure 7.7 offers a classification of operating environments based on the above demand and supply characteristics. This classification places agility in the context of alternative logistics strategies. First, A, B and C products are positioned. This is based on a Pareto analysis of an organisation's product range (for an example, see Figure 2.1). Typically, class 'A' products comprise 80 per cent of sales value taken on just 20 per cent of orders. They tend to be the more standardised, have lower forecast errors and lower volume variation. Lean logistics methods are therefore often appropriate. Class 'B' products on the other hand are often subject to higher forecast errors, and have higher volume variations. They are often better served by agile approaches.

Quick Response (p. 180) and ECR (p. 224) approaches often favour logistics environments where demand characteristics have a particular impact on delivery and distribution operations.

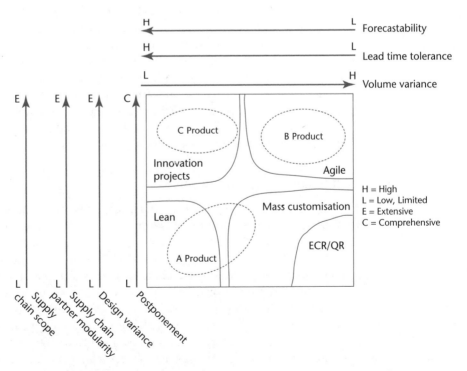

Figure 7.7 **Classifying operating environments**

7.1.3 Preconditions for successful agile practice

In addition to the above supply capabilities within the supply chain, there is another set of factors that need to be in place for the agile principles and practices described in section 7.2 to pay off or work at all. These are cross-functional alignment and enterprise-level focus on the contribution of logistics management and strategy. If revenue-generating functions in particular do not adopt at least a base-level understanding of agile principles, all efforts within logistics may be wasted. And if there is not an enterprise-wide focus on the value potential of logistics, agile efforts are not going to be recognised for what they are worth – and might not provide a compelling enough case for possible investment in them to be made. We propose an *enterprise-level reality check* and a *cost of complexity sanity check* before investing in agile capabilities. We also argue that complexity should be controlled, and that agility will not take away the need for forecasting accuracy.

Enterprise-level reality check

Starting with the enterprise-wide context, most senior managers know that turning to logistics and the supply chain is a 'good call' when times get tough. Logistics probably gets most mentioned in earnings reports when cost cutting is a response offered to poor performance. In spite of its potential to contribute to cost-saving programmes, the value of logistics should not be seen as a first port of call when the bottom line needs to be improved. Agility is centred around the notion of winning in the marketplace based upon service and responsiveness. While such a strategy can be aimed at doing more for less, it may actually – and more importantly – be doing less to earn more. Top-line improvement can flow from outperforming competitors through responsiveness to customer needs. Delivery speed and reliability can be such important sources of productivity to customers that we can earn more of their business. Practices described in section 7.2 will show how this can be achieved in an efficient way; doing less to earn more. An enterprise-level recognition of the contribution of logistics is a precondition for any business case based on agile practices.

Cost of complexity sanity check

The value potential of logistics can only be capitalised on if other functions comply with another key precondition: lowering the cost of complexity where differentiation has no competitive value. As much as agility principles are based on the notion that differentiation is good and 'doable', it does not mean that revenue groups should be given a 'carte blanche' to create proliferating service, product assortments and promotions. There are limits to how much value that variety creates, and the extent to which these demands can be met without cost of complexity spiralling out of control, even for the most agile supply chain. The key point is not to exceed the capability of the supply chain to deliver the marketing promise.

While differentiation of logistics service can generate short-term gain, the question that revenue-enhancing proposals need to answer is 'will it do so profitably?' Adding a product feature, offering special delivery service and timetables, and engaging in a special promotion might help close a deal in the market in the short term. But . . . such deals can also create added logistics and supply chain costs that are not compensated for by the added revenue. One executive from a manufacturing company put it well:

> When we showed the financial impact of certain deals our sales teams had closed, it made them realise there were certain deals we should have walked away from.

Even though it may be hard to assess economic gain or pain from product/service differentiation, reality can be checked by asking questions such as:

- Do customers *really* want fast delivery, or is reliable delivery more important even when slower?
- Do customers *really* want delivery whenever they ask for it, or could a shared forecasting process help to avoid last minute panics?
- Do we need product proliferation for short-term gain, or because we add sustainable revenue to the business?
- Is there a limit to the number of product variations that the market can recognise and absorb?
- Did we offset added warehousing and distribution costs – even when just directionally right – against added revenue potential?

Heineken, the brewer, offers a powerful example of the last point. During a recent Christmas season it introduced a special product for promotion in the market – the magnum bottle. This seasonal promotion and product won several marketing prizes, and created a lot of buzz (or fizz, even!) in the marketplace. It was also a product that suffered from substantial added shipment, packaging and production costs because different production line setups, bottles, labels and boxes were needed for a very limited demand window. Was it worth the effort and focus of the responsive capabilities that were needed?

Another powerful illustration of the issue is a tactic that one executive calls the 'warehouse dust test':

> We take our sales people through our warehouse when they come to us asking for new products and promotions and show them the dust levels on other promotional products and product variations that we stock. We ask them 'which products can be discontinued when we introduce a new product?' or 'do we need the new product to begin with?'

Lowering the cost of complexity: avoiding overly expensive agility

The purpose of responding to customer demand is fundamental to the role of logistics. In this sense, agility is a natural goal. A key qualification is:

> not at any cost, nor to compensate for mismanagement elsewhere in the organisation.

Many organisations face challenges related to the risk of driving responsiveness over the top in the wrong areas of focus. Three examples illustrate the cost of complexity:

- Product, packaging and stock keeping unit proliferation leading to extremes of 80 per cent or more of products not even generating 1 per cent of revenue.
- Delivery speed is too high, resulting in increased costs for the customer because products arrive too early. This increases handling, storage and related costs.
- Promotions and special events that cause upswings in demand based on sales efforts, not on true customer demand. This leads in turn to downswings shortly thereafter (see section 7.2.1).

In general, complexity in the supply chain is made worse at an organisational level because of aggressive global and international sourcing of materials and products. This reduces the cost of goods sold. However, complexity adds substantial distance, time and dependence on the international logistics pipeline. These increase the risk of supply chain failures.

There are two key issues at stake here. First, agile capabilities are not the excuse for other functions (such as sales) to ignore supply capabilities in running the business. Second, agility should not be driven by the need for supply chains to compensate for mismanagement in other parts of the business. Cost of complexity is the term that captures the negative consequences of agility in poor organisational contexts. It refers to the resulting costs from unnecessary complexity in the supply chain that agility can reduce. But the key questions are:

- Where is the *value* in this complexity to begin with?
- What customer need does it address to have warehouses with products and materials from old promotions collecting dust?
- Does every shipment really need to be a rush shipment or can some shipments be allowed a bit more time and consolidation with other shipments in cheaper modes of transportation?
- Are promotions and resulting short-term peaks in demand a way to boost short-term revenue, or a way to raise long-term sustainable revenue growth?

Here are some examples of actions to help reduce non-value-added costs of complexity:

- Has the organisation conducted an analysis of revenue contribution by sku?

  – *Consider using a revenue threshold for maintaining a given sku.*

- Does the organisation have a process for reviewing the product portfolio at least annually?

  – *One-off sku reductions do not address the ongoing tendency to proliferate skus over time.*

- Are there hard revenue forecasts related to promotion request that can be evaluated?

  – *Revenue upside potential is most often used to justify adding events and skus; reviewing real impact after some time or after the event helps force discipline.*

- Are people ordering shipments aware of the cost of rush orders and are they asked to organise shipment around real and explicit customer requests?

– *Ticking the 'ASAP' ('as soon as possible') box on a shipment form may become standard behaviour, irrespective of customer need.*

In addition to such actions, driving forecast accuracy will assist in avoiding inventories of unsaleable product and panic shipments.

Forecasting; reducing the need for last minute crises

As important as fast response may be, organisations cannot make all of their operational decisions in real time and in response to events already taking place. Some advanced preparation and planning is required. Hence, even in the most agile supply chains, forecasting is needed and can be used to avoid expensive panic shipments against orders that could have been anticipated.

Based upon assessment of market potential of new and existing products, promotions and services a demand forecast can be developed. This can be used to prepare and offer input to several internal forecasts.

The financial forecast (communicated to financial markets) is affected by operational demand forecast and the plan for capacity and asset utilisation. The capacity plan is used in both mid- (example: which warehouse will hold which products from the assortment) and short-term (example: how many products can we make tomorrow) situations. Asset footprint/forecast is the mid- to long-term plan for capacity needed in the supply chain to cope with volume of demand and nature of demand for services (example: how many warehouse spaces do we need in Europe?).

The better the demand forecast, the better a company can prepare in advance of demand occurring, avoiding the need for last minute response to unexpected demand as well as the cost of preparing for demand that might never occur. However, it is probably impossible to fully correctly anticipate demand at all time horizons and in all markets, for all products and services, even if revenue groups used fully tried technology (forecasting tools, enterprise resource planning software, etc.). There are several management approaches to forecasting that will enhance its accuracy and relevance. These include:

- A *'one forecast' approach*: aggregating product/market specific forecasts to a single global forecast allows the 'big picture' to be developed. It also forces differences in local forecasts to be discussed and resolved. Further, it ensures that the firm executes against a single number, not against several.

- *Ensure forecast accountability*: most often, revenue groups will be asked to develop the demand forecast. These groups have limited incentives to drive forecast accuracy. They do not have to live with the consequences, so underforecasting makes it easier to hit sales targets. So one mechanism to drive forecast accountability is to add a review of forecast quality and accuracy to performance evaluation.

- *Make forecasting business relevant*: in addition to the above, linking demand and operational forecasts to financial forecasts and effort to drive business improvement (such as long-term cost savings) adds relevance to the forecasting process.

● *Use one process*: establishing a single forecasting process for the global supply chain (allowing for minor local variations if need be) allows for consistency in approach, interpretation and measurement.

Summary

This section offers insights into the questions 'when' and 'where' agile capabilities should be considered in a supply chain management. Our framework offers both insights and diagnostics for developing logistics strategies. Some supply chains will be better positioned to serve the markets they serve by means of lean approaches – for example in low-variety, high-volume situations. An increasing number of markets will be better served by agile strategies that require responsiveness – for example, because variety is increasing and volumes are decreasing. The next section addresses the question of what capabilities are needed to support this responsiveness in more detail.

7.2 Agile practices

Key issue: How can we use agile practices to benefit from turbulence in the marketplace?

In this section we propose further actions that support the migration towards greater levels of agility in supply chains. Three characteristics of supply chain operations can be earmarked as directly related to becoming agile:

● mastering and benefiting from variation in demand;
● very fast response to market opportunities;
● unique or low volume response.

Each of these characteristics is difficult to achieve under traditional ways of organising supply chains because they obstruct stability, lead to smaller batches, and reduce the ability to plan in advance. This section presents progressive levels of practices within each of these three characteristics. All three are seen as opportunities by agile-oriented companies, because they use the characteristics to create competitive advantage over organisations that continue to focus on reducing demand variation, increasing time windows and raising volumes.

7.2.1 Benefiting from variance

Amplification of demand changes has been called the *bullwhip effect*. This principle recognises that changes in demand get amplified from one tier to the next in the supply chain. For example, the retailer may order only in full truck-loads from its suppliers. Instead of understanding the actual end-customer demand, the suppliers see huge swings in orders that are essentially due to the retailer's desire to minimise transport costs. This has the unfortunate impact of increasing manufacturing costs at the suppliers, because they are asked to make large quantities at irregular time intervals. What may originally have been stable demand through the till becomes heavily distorted.

Figure 7.8 shows an example of the bullwhip effect. Demand through the till is relatively stable, but orders on the supplier are anything but stable! The original range of variation has been amplified into something much worse. The only way in which the supplier can respond is to hold stocks – and even those vary enormously from one week to the next. Uncertainty about customer demand leads to large up-and-down swings in the need for capacity and in inventory levels. This effect ripples through the supply chain. Batching rules at the supplier make things even worse for tier 2 and 3 suppliers upstream.

Information exchange and postponement have been suggested as solutions to the wastes and uncertainties that are created. Delaying actions until orders have been received and sharing demand information are important ways to lower uncertainties. Better coordination of the supply chain helps to get rid of the bullwhip effect. But the question then remains: how do we cope with the remaining uncertainty in demand?

Three sources of demand uncertainty can be identified:

- *seasonality*: some products sell more during summer than winter;
- *product life cycles*: parts volumes for original equipment such as cars are much higher than volumes for spare parts after the model has been changed;
- *end-customer demand*: a residual uncertainty always exists. For example, we go to the supermarket at different times from week to week to suit ourselves.

There are various levels at which seasonality of demand can affect the supply chain. Examples are provided in Table 7.4. These differ in terms of number and

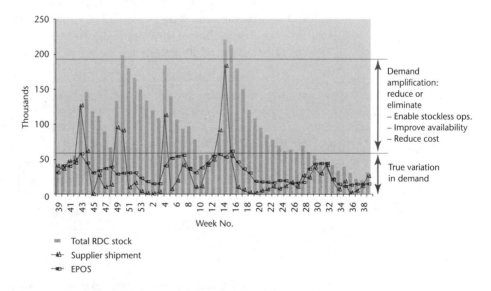

Figure 7.8 **The bullwhip effect at work**

Table 7.4 **The impact of seasonality**

Number of seasons	Example business	Level of postponement	Supply chain scope impact
1 (summer)	Garden furniture	–	One peak for which inventory is built up in advance
2 (summer and Christmas)	Ice cream	Semi-packaging	Limited; two peaks for which inventory is built up, while final packaging (label etc.) can be done once ordered
4 (2 mains and 2 shorts)	Fashion	Semi-manufacturing	Wide; take in orders from collection then plan, make and deliver before season starts

length of seasons, businesses involved, relevant level of postponement and scope of impact on the supply chain. Semi-postponement (that is, postponement to retailer order, not end-customer order) is used to cope with the uncertainty resulting from seasonality. 'Finalisation' or manufacturing is based on retail orders. These are used in addition to the main practice – that of *seasonality swapping*. The common two-season pattern is displayed in Figure 7.9(a). The peaks in the seasons are demanding in terms of the ability to meet demand from capacity and within competitive service windows. In order to ensure delivery, manufacturing can be swapped across the season in order to ensure a safety stock (for example, based upon information exchange regarding pre-season demand expectations from the retailer, or based upon historical demand analysis), which will lower the impact of variance on the operations. This is displayed in Figure 7.9(b).

A second and less predictable type of variance is that driven by product life cycles. Here information exchange and (semi-)postponement is relevant but far from sufficient. The traditional four-stage life cycle passes through several quad-

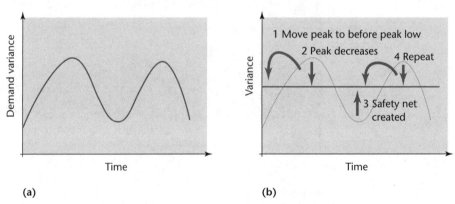

(a)   (b)

Figure 7.9 **Seasonality swapping: (a) two-season pattern   (b) two-season after swapping**

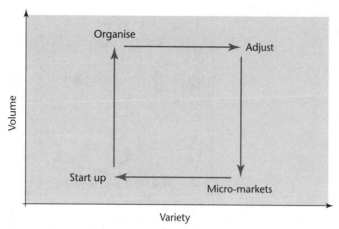

Figure 7.10 The impact of product life cycles

rants of variance, as displayed in Figure 7.10. During the introduction or start-up phase little volume and variety is in place. Volume increases in the growth phase, and the supply chain has to get organised, formalised and structured to cope with the market. In the maturity phase variety increases as a response to decreasing market growth in the main product lines, and the supply chain has to be adjusted accordingly. In the decline stage variety continues to increase as market segments scatter into micro-markets while overall market size declines.

What this pattern implies is that agile entrepreneurial responsiveness is mostly needed in the first and last stages of the cycle. It is in these two stages that market opportunities are most readily captured. In the other two stages, particularly the second, lean efficiency and structured standardisation are more important to cope with growth and high volume in a relatively stable product/service proposition. Figure 7.11 displays this pattern of *reversed life cycling*.

Agile practices have much to offer to this pattern of operational challenges. Such practices facilitate the mastering of uncertainty by managing product life cycles as a loop. The 'loop' works between the identification of a market opportunity in phase 1, letting those opportunities develop, and then rapidly exploring the market for additional and new opportunities at an increasing pace. This means a particular focus on phases 1, 3 and 4 – from identification through constant adjustment to micro-markets as a basis for identifying new opportunities.

The focus on these stages contributes to the third level of uncertainty, that of demand fluctuations. If micro-markets and unique market opportunities become the main fluctuations, then shifts of demand can propel uncertainty sky-high. Simple swapping or reversing of the life cycle focus are then no longer sufficient. The product life cycle focus can be transformed to a customer life time value approach. Ultimately, a market opportunity in micro-markets boils down to individual customers. A solution to the uncertainty they create, as well as an opportunity to exploit it, is the concept of *prosuming*, the opposite of *consuming*. This means involving customers proactively in supply chain design and in developing the product/service proposition. It involves asking customers to specify their demand by selecting from options and constructing the most relevant response together. Information exchange and postponement are taken to higher levels.

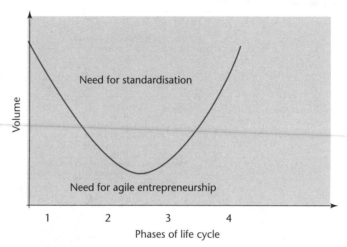

Figure 7.11 Reversed life cycling

The customer determines how sets of information will flow through the supply chain. Postponement becomes real customer-driven postponement, potentially throughout the entire supply chain.

7.2.2 Benefiting from short time windows

With ever-decreasing time windows for product/service fulfilment, delivery dependability achieved by means of mastering uncertainty becomes another major concern. This can be experienced at three levels, each requiring different levels of agility:

- speed of replenishment;
- upstream time sensitivity;
- information dissemination and alignment.

The need for *speed* traditionally starts at the end of the supply chain, driven by end-customer demand. In Chapter 5 we referred to speed of response to customer demand as *D-time*. In a recent survey of distribution patterns it was found that the time sensitivity of shipments in outbound flows is nearly twice as great as it is for inbound flows. Time sensitivity at the end of the chain can be attributed to the urgent need of customers. The solution to this can be helped by supplier-involved replenishment programmes such as vendor-managed inventory (Chapter 6). More important, however, is the urgent need for delivery given narrow windows of opportunity. Where customer demand is invisible upstream, rapid response to the end-customer is limited to what can be done downstream. Vendor-managed inventory (VMI) and quick response (QR) are two examples – described in Chapter 6 – of such partial attempts at supply chain integration.

Cross-docking and in-transit merging are related approaches within distribution. When cross-docking, the warehouse is still in place in the delivery pipeline; the inventory just does not get stored, but only passes by and goes through rapid unloading, deconsolidation/reconsolidation and reloading. With in-transit merging the delivery pipeline is still in place as well, but individual shipments are grouped on the way to the point of delivery. An example of both types of approach is provided by the core depot operation of Marks & Spencer for boxed goods at Coventry in Britain, operated by Exel as third-party logistics provider. Suppliers are instructed daily to make up loads for each of the retail stores. Each box is labelled by bar-code with product specification and store destination. Loads from each supplier are collected daily on a 'milk round' system and merged with those of other suppliers in the round. At the core depot in Coventry the boxes are unloaded from the trailers in two inbound bays, and are automatically routed to the correct outbound trailers. The outbound trailers are arranged in 24 outbound bays for destinations around the United Kingdom and mainland Europe. The whole sortation process (the process of sorting products by destination) takes place with bar-code readers and sortation equipment like baggage-handling equipment at an airport. Coventry is a *living warehouse* operation: no goods are stored between supplier and local distribution centre.

There are various reasons for extending rapid response upstream. For example, JIT and *kanban* approaches aim to align supply with production and ultimately with demand (see Chapter 6). These can be useful in case of resource scarcity or turbulent supply markets. Consider mobile telephones: both Ericsson and Philips have recently indicated that a drop in sales was caused by a shortage of parts, particularly microprocessors. Both companies were unable to supply sufficient products because of parts shortages. Capacity at SE Thompson, a microprocessor manufacturer, is booked for the next five years. Furthermore, rapid price fluctuations in parts pushed electronics manufacturers into delayed purchasing and local sourcing. Such actions help to avoid the necessity of shipping finished products through a lengthy pipeline while prices fluctuate rapidly.

These examples indicate how there can be separate reasons for upstream time sensitivity. Over-focus on ensuring supply, however, should not lead to an underfocus on the end-customer. And in more advanced upstream, time-based approaches the customer order really works its way further upstream. 'Semi-postponement' is no longer sufficient in these situations, and JIT is no more than semi-postponement. Fewer intermediate hold-ups and less consolidation/cross-docking and reconsolidation increase speed. Let us next consider the three-week fulfilment cycle in the Smart car supply chain.

CASE STUDY 7.2	The Smart car

Micro Compact Car AG (MCC), a Mercedes-Benz company, introduced a new vehicle concept, named Smart. The car is a so-called two-seater mini car (smaller than the Fiat 500), developed mainly for in-city use. Both the car itself and the processes needed for producing and distributing the car to the final customer are focused on increasing the responsiveness to customer demands as much as possible. In general, three stages in the supply chain are involved in actually achieving customisation.

▶

First, the generic car is assembled in the plant at Hambach in Elzas-Lothringen, France (referred to as Smart Ville). The car is based on an integral body-frame (called Tridion) to which modules are attached/assembled. The car consists of five main modules: the platform, the powertrain, the doors and roof, the electronics and the cockpit, containing submodules and components. The modules are supplied, in sequence for final assembly, by a small number of first-tier suppliers of which seven suppliers are fully integrated in the final assembly plant. These seven companies are located at the same site as MCC and supply 'supermodules' based on a postponed purchasing approach. Modules are bought by the original equipment manufacturer (OEM) only when they are needed in the final assembly process (postponed purchasing). For example, a complete rear, including wheels, suspension and engine, is preassembled by one supplier which maintains the module in its possession until it is needed on the assembly line. The same is true for the doors and for the dashboard system. Together these seven suppliers deliver 50 per cent of the total value of the purchased goods.

In order to maintain a smooth flow of goods within the plant, the car is moved along the work stations of the assembly line, which is laid out in the form of a cross (Figure 7.10). In this way, the integrated suppliers are able to supply their finished products directly to the final assembly line from their workshop in the factory. The effect of this enlarged role for the supermodule suppliers is that MCC is able to assemble the car in 4.5 hours. Apart from short lead times the benefit of the product design and flexible manufacturing system is that, at a module level, parts can be combined into a wide variety of products.

Also, other activities traditionally considered to be core activities of manufacturers, such as the pressing of body-parts, the painting process, and even the coordination of internal logistics, are no longer performed by MCC. Not only is there a close participation of the suppliers in the final assembly of the car, but the suppliers are also strongly involved in the development, planning and launching of the product. What can be said about the outsourcing of components and modules manufacturing is also true for supporting services such as transportation, and it applies to ownership of the production buildings and site management.

As a second stage of the supply chain the distribution system is geared totally towards responding quickly to ever-changing customer needs. The car is sold at life style centres located in shopping centres and other highly frequented places in urbanised areas. These franchise organisations use multimedia systems to enable clients to 'build' their car in the showroom, and to forward the order for the car to the distribution centres. The customer can thus be involved in the design process, and sales can become more consultative, based on a direct dialogue with individual customers. Within an order-to-delivery lead time of less than one day, five interregional distribution centres in Europe supply the dealer with the requested car. Some of the final assembly tasks, such as adding special features or light final assembly, are performed at these distribution centres. This is an example of postponed manufacturing. In order to perform final finishing, the distribution centre stores cars and changeable modules.

Finally, the modular concept of the car enables the customer to renew and upgrade the product completely during its lifetime, based on adding product features and rapidly replacing body parts. As a result the car is more of a consumption product than a fixed capital good, and customers can be kept for life.

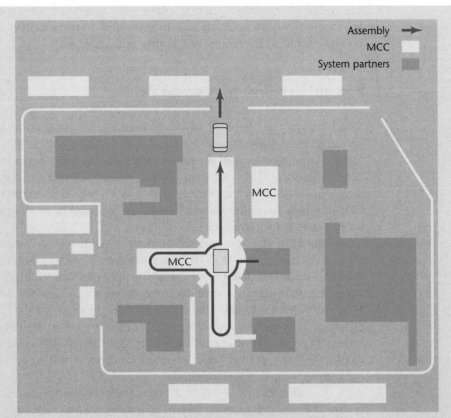

Figure 7.12 **Factory lay-out at Smart**

Question

1 How has SMART speeded up the process from customer order to customer receipt of the ordered vehicle?

A further impact of time sensitivity is that it not only works its way upstream, requiring channel adjustments, but also calls for dissemination and alignment of information flow through information decoupling. Time sensitivity does not just mean speed of information flow. It also means that the flow should take place accurately, and that fluctuations in response times required to link end-customers with the rest of the chain should be understood by all concerned. The dissemination takes place through information exchange throughout the supply chain, in which the information decoupling point actually penetrates deeper and wider into the supply chain. For example, information exchange formats can be shared – as can customer profiles and market intelligence. A free flow of information can to some extent be expected to harm competitive positions in supply chains. However, because the players in the chain are dependent on each other there is a further reason. The actual creation of market intelligence and information alignment is a competence in itself, whatever information is shared. A timely and accurate response to customer demand is developed in advance through superior information exchange. These approaches are in addition to the transactional information exchange that is often also practised in rapid replenishment approaches, where point of sale information triggers delivery (see for example vendor-managed inventory in Chapter 6, section 6.3).

7.2.3 Benefiting from small volumes

Small volumes are a result of micro-markets, customisation and rapid responsiveness. They represent a threat under the traditional model, structured as it is around large batches, full container loads, standardisation and frozen production runs. There are three areas in which small volumes can be used within the dynamic contingency approach, which is leveraged to benefit from agile capabilities. These are: changeover flexibility, modularity at the network level, and service- and information-based solutions.

Starting with the first area (changeover flexibility), techniques such as single-minute exchange of dies (SMED) see Chapter 6, section 6.2.3), flexible automation and milk run deliveries (where a supplier makes multiple deliveries from a single load) are among the well-known answers to a need for smaller volume outputs and fulfilment. They have proved their value from the JIT era and before, although it is still common among manufacturers to challenge their value in terms of economics of output. In reality this discussion is one between different mindsets. If the market value of small volumes is not important, tools such as these tend to have a lower priority.

In the second area (modularity), smaller volumes approach the level of craft/one-piece production, requiring greater agility and mass customisation at the supply chain level. This requires modularity applied at the product and process level to be extended to the supply chain level. Even when it is difficult to modularise products or processes, supply chains can still be organised into distinct functional, geographical and organisational zones. The supply network coordinator can cherry-pick from such zones when needed from an end-customer point of view. While individual players in the network can achieve scale and standardisation by participating in multiple supply networks, the output of the individual supply network can be tuned to a given micro-market. Organising for supply networks involves:

- stipulating interfaces between elements;
- creating a shared coordination and information exchange infrastructure;
- building the portfolio of elements in response to market opportunities;
- developing network relations with those market opportunities that are temporal and partial rather than exclusive, rigid and volume-based.

On these grounds it is possible to avoid complete craft production without the sophistication and economics of modern supply chains (see Figure 7.13).

The third area, characterised by even lower volumes, demands attention to information flow as well as to material flow. The Batman case study 2.5 in Chapter 2 showed how the service and information content of a product could be increasingly customised while the physical content remained unchanged.

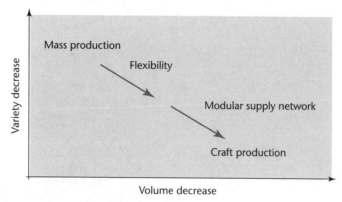

Figure 7.13 **Towards smaller volumes**

Services are customised around *mini projects*, each designed around a specific customer requirement. This can further increase the value proposition for small-volume products. Regarding information and knowledge content, it is well-known that the average user of a word-processor uses only about 5 per cent of its built-in features regularly. This means that the end-customer can benefit from many unique features, whereas the next end-customer can do so as well. They both apply the product for their specific requirements, even though the product is the same.

Figure 7.14 integrates the practices in one framework for moving forward with agility.

7.2.4 Conclusion

It is becoming increasingly apparent that competitive advantage derives from the combined capabilities of the linked organisations that we now refer to as the supply network. This is a fundamental shift in the traditionally held view of a business model based upon a single firm. It has also become apparent that markets today are increasingly volatile and hence less predictable, and so the need for a more agile response is increasing. Putting these two ideas together leads us to the conclusion that a prerequisite for success in such markets will be the agile supply chain.

What we have proposed in this chapter is a framework for agility that is contingent upon the context in which the business operates. Thus we have sought to bring together lean and agile mindsets, not just to highlight the differences but also to show how they might be combined for enhanced competitiveness. Increasingly, managers need to understand how market conditions and the wider operating environment will demand not a single off-the-shelf solution, but hybrid strategies that are context specific. In Chapter 9, we consider another key aspect of the agile supply chain – the virtual organisation.

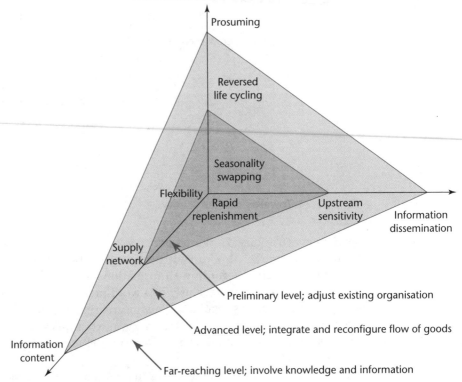

Figure 7.14 Progressive agile practices

Summary

What is agility, and how does it contribute to competitiveness of the supply network?

- Agility is a supply-chain-wide capability that aligns organisational structures, information systems, logistics processes and, in particular, mindsets. It means using market knowledge and a responsive supply chain to exploit profitable opportunities in a volatile marketplace. Agile supply is concerned with developing capabilities proactively to position a supply chain to benefit from marketplaces in which product life cycles are shrinking, product variety is increasing, and the ability to forecast demand is reducing.

- Lean thinking (Chapter 6) is concerned primarily with the elimination of waste. The order winners that are supported by this mindset are cost and quality. Agility is concerned primarily with supporting order winners of service levels and customer value. Time compression is a fundamental requirement for leanness, but only one of the enablers of agility.

- A key difference in logistics strategy is that lean thinking is concerned with placing orders upstream for products that move in a regular flow. Agile supply is concerned with assigning capacity so that products can be made rapidly to meet demand that is difficult to forecast.

- Three ways to develop supply strategies that support agile demand characteristics are postponement, design for logistics and the virtual organisation.
- The integrated model for enabling the agile supply chain envisages a combination of postponed fulfilment and rapid replenishment at level 1 supported by level 2 programmes such as quick response and agile supply, and level 3 actions such as process management and cross-functional teams. Supply chain managers need to be change managers in order to handle the massive implications of change.

What are the agile practices that help to underpin the agile supply chain?

- First, to understand the sources and causes of uncertainty in demand, and to take steps to position the supply chain to benefit from this uncertainty. The easy option is high-volume, low-variety, low-demand uncertainty. The tough option is the opposite of all three. Agility seeks not only to eliminate the bull-whip effect (amplification of demand uncertainty upstream), but also to create capabilities for dealing with seasonality, stages in the product life cycle, and end-customer demand uncertainty.
- Second, to develop capabilities for dealing with shrinking time windows for customer demand fulfilment. Speed of replenishment is usually much better downstream than upstream. Developing upstream time sensitivity is therefore a major enabler. And information dissemination and alignment bring capabilities of dealing with rapid and accurate response using supply-chain-wide dissemination and exchange.
- Third, to facilitate servicing the 'market segment of one' by investing in flexible processes, modularity at the product and process level, and capabilities to support the information and knowledge content of products and services.

Discussion questions

1 Suggest order winning and order qualifying criteria for the following product environments:
   a reprocessing nuclear fuel;
   b upstream petroleum refining;
   c downstream manufacture of petroleum products;
   d high-value automotive products such as Land Rover Defender or BMW 5 series.

   To what extent would lean and agile mindsets contribute to the support of such products in the marketplace?

2 Figure 7.14 shows a demand series for a high-volume grocery product with a comparatively stable demand. The vertical lines mark the end of each trading week, which is Sunday midnight.

   Suggest key features of this trading pattern. The retailer now wishes to implement two stock-replenishment 'waves' each day from the supplier: one in the morning (75 per cent of volume) and the other in the afternoon (25 per cent of volume).

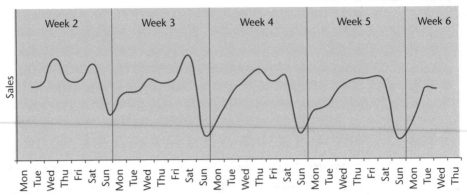

Figure 7.15 Demand series for a high-volume grocery product

Previously, only one replenishment delivery was made per day. What are the potential benefits to the retailer, and what are the likely risks to the supplier?

3 Explain the difference between surge and base demands. Multi Electronique SA (ME) produces a range of electrical connectors for the automotive industry. Currently, the six production lines at its factory in Toulouse are fully loaded, operating a three-shift system for five days per week. One of ME's major customers wants to place an order that would add loading equivalent to a seventh production line, but only for the summer months (May–September). Sales are keen to accept the new order, but it would need to be taken at prices that are no higher than for current business. Suggest options for how ME might manage this order if it were accepted.

4 Refer back to Figure 2.1 in Chapter 2: it shows a Pareto curve for the sales per sku of a book stockist. A small number of 'hot sellers' constitute most of the sales, while there is a lengthy tail of slow-selling lines and new introductions. The operations people are pressing for the 'tail' to be chopped in half, arguing that it adds cost, not value, to the business. They argue that each order is taken at fixed cost, regardless of size. Sales order processing and pick and dispatch from the warehouse are examples of such fixed costs. 'Instead, we should focus on the core of the business: 90 percent of our business comes from just 10 per cent of the titles', the operations director argues. 'We could chop our costs in half and only lose 5–7 per cent of the business. Think of the effect on margin!' Sales, on the other hand, are reluctant to give up any of the titles, arguing that it is customer choice that drives the business. 'We have built up this business on the strength of our product range', the sales director argues. 'Retailers come to us because we are a one-stop shop. If we haven't got it in stock, we get it.' Explain the above in terms of a lean versus agile debate, using the concepts of market winners and qualifiers and benefiting from small volumes.

References

Christopher, M. and Towill, D.R. (2000) 'Supply chain migration from lean and functional to agile and customised', *International Journal of Supply Chain Management*, Vol. 5, No. 4, pp. 206–13.

Harrison, A., Christopher, M. and van Hoek, R. (1999) *Creating the Agile Supply Chain*, Corby: Institute of Transport and Logistics.

Holweg, M. and Miemczyk, J. (2002) 'Logistics in the "three-day car" age: assessing the responsiveness of vehicle distribution logistics in the UK', *International Journal of Physical Distribution and Logistics Management*, Vol. 32, No. 10, pp. 829–50.

Johansson, H.J., McHugh, P., Pendlebury, A.J. and Wheeler, W.A. (1993) *Business Process Reengineering: Breakpoint strategies for market dominance*. Chichester: John Wiley.

Magretta, J. (1998) 'Fast global and entrepreneurial: supply chain management Hong Kong style', *Harvard Business Review*, September/October, pp. 102–14.

Mason-Jones, R., Naylor, B. and Towill, D.R. (1999) 'Agile, or leagile: matching your supply chain to the marketplace', *Proceedings of the 15th International Conference on Production Research*, Limerick, pp. 593–6.

van Hoek, R. (1998) 'Reconfiguring the supply chain to implement postponed manufacturing', *International Journal of Logistics Management*, Vol. 9, No. 1, pp. 95–110.

Suggested further reading

Cusumano, M. and Nobeoka, K. (1998) *Thinking Beyond Lean*. New York: Free Press.

Goldman, S., Nagel, R. and Preiss, K. (1995) *Agile Competitors and Virtual Organisations*. New York: Van Nostrand Reinhold.

Part Three

WORKING TOGETHER

In a supply network, no organisation stands on its own. Nor does it compete on its own. A focal firm depends on its network partners for components to assemble, for products to sell, for the movement of goods, and so on. While Part Two focused on the central logistics task of ensuring responsiveness to customer demand, most organisations cannot achieve this without the support of their network partners. Complete vertical integration of industries has become a largely obsolete logistics strategy. Functional specialisation of suppliers on those parts of the value proposition in which they excel, coupled with integration into the supply network, is common wisdom nowadays.

This is becoming especially relevant today. Some manufacturing organisations, for example in the electronics and automotive industries, add only 10–20 per cent of total added value internally. The rest is created in the supply base – by commodity suppliers, by co-designers and co-manufacturers, by main suppliers and by partners. Chapter 8 offers approaches to integration and collaboration in the supply chain, and Chapter 9 offers specific approaches to managing different types of relations and the supply base.

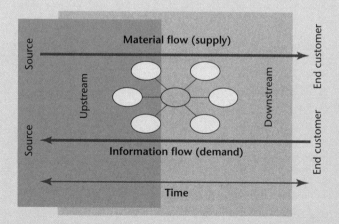

Integrating the supply chain

Outcomes

The planned outcomes of this chapter are to:

- explain the need for aligning processes and collaborating between organisations within supply chains;
- show how the management of supply chains can be leveraged by improving new product introductions, promotions, product ranges and replenishment;
- identify methods for implementing collaborative planning between supply chain members;
- develop a framework for managing the supply chain.

By the end of this chapter you should be able to understand:

- the benefits of collaboration within supply chains;
- ways to improve responsiveness to the end-customer;
- key aspects of managing the supply chain.

Introduction

Chapters 6, on lean thinking, and Chapter 7 on creating the agile supply chain, dealt with two ways of managing the supply chain. They show how supply chain processes can be prepared for better performance by eliminating the sources of waste. Cutting out waste in this way offers the opportunity to produce and deliver goods cheaper, faster and with better quality. This chapter draws on these ideas and suggests a vision of *flow* logistics, whereby only the end-customer is free to place an order whenever he or she wants. After that, the system takes over. Flow logistics offers the customer:

immediate availability of products at the point of sale

or

rapid configuration and delivery of customer-specified products.

The overall aim of this chapter is to show how the supply chain can be managed to maximise the opportunities of integrated, waste-free processes to achieve superior quality of service.

Key issues

This chapter addresses five key issues:

1 **Collaboration in the supply chain:** the benefits of internal collaboration and external collaboration.

2 **Efficient consumer response:** the total supply chain working together with an objective to fulfil the demands of the end consumer.

3 **Collaboration planning, forecasting and replenishment:** an approach to effective supply chain and organisational strategy.

4 **Managing supply chain relationships:** the objective of deeper, closer relationships in the supply chain and the factors for achieving them.

5 **A framework for managing the supply chain:** six building blocks to help managers to overcome obstacles and position organisations for supply chain success.

8.1 Integration in the supply chain

Key issue: **How can we integrate internally, externally and electronically?**

What drives integration in the supply chain? It is the conviction that working together to meet end-customer demand beats arm's-length relationships by a long way. As an illustration, the following are four principles of Procter & Gamble's supply chain strategy:

- Produce every product that needs to be produced every day through short-cycle production.
- Communicate with suppliers in real time – suppliers with whom we have built long-term relationships.
- Draw demand data from the point nearest to the customer – in this case, the retail cash register.
- Let innovation and new technologies drive the implementation.

The first three principles are about integration – both internal and external. The fourth principle is about using IT developments to enable even closer collaboration.

Evidence that increased integration (both upstream and downstream) leads to improved performance for the supply chain as a whole has been found by survey research for firms in fabricated metal products, machinery and equipment manufacturing (Frohlich and Westbrook, 2001). 'Integration' was measured across eight variables as follows:

1 Access to planning systems.

2 Sharing production plans.

3 Joint EDI access/networks.

4 Knowledge of inventory mix/levels.

5 Packaging customisation.

6 Delivery frequencies.

7 Common logistical equipment/containers.

8 Common use of third-party logistics.

The authors found that the broadest integration strategies led to the largest rates of significant performance improvements. They pictured this in terms of 'arcs of integration', our version of which is shown in Figure 8.1. We can propose that broader integration reduces uncertainty of material flow through the supply network. In turn, this improves efficiency and reduces the 'P'-time (Chapter 5, section 5.2).

8.1.1 Internal integration: function to function

Another survey – this time of over 300 organisations in the United States – probed collaboration between marketing and logistics functions within a focal firm (Stank *et al.* 1999). More frequent collaborative behaviour between marketing and logistics resulted in better performance and better interdepartmental effectiveness. This may seem obvious, but the improvements in performance included cycle time reduction, better in-stock performance, increased product availability levels, and improvements in order-to-delivery lead times.

Firms with higher internal integration demonstrated higher relative logistics performance compared with less integrated firms. There was no difference between 'high' and 'low' integration firms on basic service: that is, consistent delivery on request data and advance notification of delays and shortages. However, on the 'higher value' service elements, such as delivery reliability, there was a significant difference. High-integration firms had greater performance in

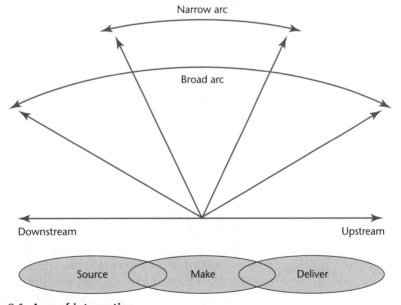

Figure 8.1 Arcs of integration
(Source: After Frohlich and Westbrook, 2001)

terms of meeting customer needs, accommodating special customer requests and new product introductions. This resulted in an enhanced customer perception of the organisations.

The implications of this research are that organisations should continue to work at improving internal integration. For example, functional barriers between purchasing, manufacturing and distribution may lead to the following scenario:

- Purchasing buys castings on the basis of low price, but the supplier has a poor record for delivery reliability and quality. Manufacturing is faced with uncertain deliveries and high reject rates.

- Manufacturing aims to keep machine and labour productivity high, so batch sizes are kept high. Distribution is faced with poor availability, especially of class B and C parts.

- Distribution wants to maintain a warehousing operation with fast throughput, so resists carrying out any post-manufacturing operations. Manufacturing is faced with the additional complexity of customising products.

Internal integration is the starting point for broader integration across the supply chain. As Robert Lynch said,

> **For some reason alliance professionals find it easier to create alliances with their major competitors than with other divisions in their own companies. We don't deal with our own internal integration. How can we integrate externally if we can't do it internally?' (Kirby, 2003: 68)**

Activity 8.1

Taking your business (or one well-known to you) as an example, how well do the internal functions integrate? Consider the purchasing–manufacturing–distribution example above and develop a scenario for the company, using the company's names for the functions concerned. What impact does your scenario have on material flow?

8.1.2 Inter-company collaboration: a manual approach

If significant improvements can be achieved by internal collaboration and integration, the potential for the benefits of external collaboration are potentially even higher. This was demonstrated by the Bose Corporation (a US-based manufacturer of hi-fi equipment) in the early 1990s when they developed the *JIT2* concept. Bose recognised that, if the traditional buyer–supplier relationship were to be made more effective, more people would be required in their organisation. However, budget constraints meant that no additional people could be employed in this role. This acted as a driver to develop the JIT2 concept.

A logical extension of the just-in-time concept described in Chapter 6 is to place customer and supplier processes closer together. The JIT2 approach goes a stage further by eliminating the buyer and the salesman from the customer–supplier relationship, thus fostering increased communication between the parties. The principle is simple: a supplier employee who resides full-time in the customer's purchasing office replaces the buyer and supplier. This *supplier-in-plant* is empowered to use the customer's scheduling system to place orders with their own company. The supplier-in-plant also does the material planning for the materials supplied by his company.

The 'supplier-in-plant' is also part of the production planning process, so production is planned concurrently with the supplier organisation. This form of collaboration streamlines the supply process by removing the multi-level planner–buyer–salesman–supplier's plant process by making this the responsibility of one individual. This dramatically reduces the demand uncertainty experienced by the supplier organisations. The benefits of this streamlining have also resulted in major business improvements for Bose. These include:

- 50 per cent improvement in terms of on-time deliveries, damage and shortages;
- 6 per cent reduction in material costs;
- 26 per cent improvement in equipment utilisation;
- major reductions in inventory holdings.

The Bose supplier-in-plant concept demonstrates how collaboration and integration can benefit the supply chain. The supplier-in-plant can, to a large degree, be superseded by today's electronic collaboration techniques.

Activity 8.2

What are the opportunities for the JIT2 supplier-in-plant principle in your chosen company? Could the principle help to improve collaboration, either by a company representative working in the customer's organisation, or by representatives from major suppliers working in your chosen company?

8.1.3 Electronic collaboration

Much of the pioneering work for electronic collaboration has been in the fast-moving consumer goods (FMCG) business. Therefore, most of the leading examples have been developed by retailer–manufacturer collaboration. The traditional way to exchange orders and delivery information has been by means of electronic data interchange (EDI). But EDI systems are generally incompatible with each other, and have high development and installation costs. Technologies based on the Internet, which we review in Chapter 10, offer world-wide connectivity and relative ease of access.

Trading partners can collaborate electronically in three ways: transactional, information sharing and collaborative planning.

Transactional: the electronic execution of transactions

This is usually found in business to business (B2B) e-commerce, with the trading partners focusing on the automation of business transactions such as purchase orders, invoices, order and advanced shipment notices, load tendering and acknowledgements, and freight invoices and payments. These transactions involve the electronic transmission of a fixed-format document with predefined data and information fields.

Information sharing: the electronic sharing or exchange of information

This occurs where trading partners are given access to a system that has shared information on it. Often, however, one partner transmits shared information to the other partner. The information is sent on a 'for your information' basis; the recipient uses the data as they stand, and no feedback is given. Shared information may include product descriptions and pricing, promotional calendars, inventory levels, shipment tracking and tracing. This type of arrangement only supports independent planning done by each partner. Uncertainty is reduced by each partner becoming aware of the other partner's activities. However, trading partners do not have the opportunity to comment on or change the plan in any way.

Collaborative planning: strategic, tactical and operational exchange

Collaborative planning embraces electronic collaboration at all levels: strategic, tactical and operational. This is the most sophisticated form of electronic collaboration. It enables trading partners to work together to understand future demand better and to put plans in place to satisfy such demand profitably. The trading partners collaborate on new product planning, demand forecasting and replenishment planning, and work closely to align their organisations' plans.

The discussion on collaborative planning is developed later in section 8.3. Here, the concept of information sharing is developed by means of a case study in *continuous replenishment* (CR). Continuous replenishment logistics is a pioneering approach to using developments in IT to replenish demand quickly from the manufacturer. Using electronic point of sale (EPOS) data to track customer demand through the till, CR shares data from retailer to supplier. The aim is for the supplier to replace quickly what has been sold today, so that stock availability on the shelf is maintained at the retailer. Case study 8.1 gives a view of where fashion logistics is heading.

| CASE STUDY 8.1 | **Continuous replenishment in the apparel industry** |

Case study 4.2 describes some of the competitive pressures in the apparel industry and trade-offs in developing global 'vertical' supply strategies. (Vertical strategies aim to emulate retailers like Zara, who source everything from set manufacturing plants that are situated close to their retail outlets in Europe). Setting up a similar operation in the United States would be problematic – for a start, there is not much left of the apparel manufacturing base because it went overseas long ago for cost reasons. Competitive pressures are constantly increasing: 80 per cent of the industry is fashion driven – and fashion changes every 6–8 weeks. Thus, time-to-market is increasingly important. But lead times from catwalk to customer for such a fast-moving industry are often a leisurely six months or more. Average mark-downs increased to 30 per cent, and missed sales opportunities go unrecorded. Chappel (in Lewis, 2001) states, professional buyers are often measured on the difference between buying and sell-ing prices; merchandisers on maximising sales of a fixed amount of stock, and dis-tribution professionals on achieving the lowest unit cost. No-one takes the overall supply chain into account and creates a balanced view of the trade-offs between bought-in product cost, achievable sales, the cost of mark-down and the cost of operating the supply chain from end to end.

Retailers drive the industry, and in a fragmented and very competitive marketplace, they are moving quickly to address its long-standing logistics problems. Increasingly, they are turning to suppliers to respond faster to better quality information. Kuhel (2002: 19) quotes Agit Patel, an executive at Chico a fast-growing designer and retailer of women's apparel and accessories:

> We're in the stone age right now, but we're going to convert this place and bring it into the 21st century. Today, our suppliers don't have much visibility except for what we provide them through our current communications technology – and that hap-pens to be e-mail primarily. But going forward they will be able to see exactly what we have and what's selling and what's not, and we'll be able to see where they are within a production cycle for any particular order.

Kuhel proposes an apparel supply chain of the future that is based on continuous replenishment, which we have adapted. Let us assume a designer and retailer of fashion apparel is situated in the north-eastern United States. A new range has been designed and early sales are encouraging. These early sales figures are used to refine forecasts quickly, and to prime the logistics pipeline with a flow of product that matches expected demand. After this, it is essential to regulate the flow of finished goods to match actual demand. This is how it is done.

As soon as an item is purchased, the retailer collates the EPOS data from its stores and sends the data upstream. The 'pull' signal (Chapter 6) goes back all the way to the yarn manufacturer. Figure 8.2 represents the path that a garment might take from concept to delivery. Six stages are involved.

1 **Planning**: apparel retailer determines design for a product, evaluates costing and then sends demand data and forecast upstream. These signals set the supply chain in motion. Later, once the product has gone to market, a web-based link from the retailer's EPOS system to the manufacturer triggers replenishment responses.
2 **Raw material**: suppliers respond to demand signals via phone, fax or e-mail. Raw cotton is compressed into bales, and fitted with RFID tags (see Chapter 10) to spec-ify source and type.
3 **Fabric**: manufacturers weave and ship product in response to demand from the retailer. Inventory/shipment tracking starts here. In-transit data is passed down-stream via the Internet.
4 **Assembly**: fabrics and trims come together at the final assembly plant, which in this example is situated in the Caribbean. (Manufacturers situated within short shipping times of the United States are favoured over Far East suppliers). The plant has an ERP system that processes orders received electronically. Finished goods are assembled and bar-coded by store prior to despatch. All suppliers to the apparel retailer use compatible systems.
5 **Distribution**: product is shipped by container to the retailer's national distribution centre (NDC). Here, store orders are cross-docked using the bar-code to identify the

▶

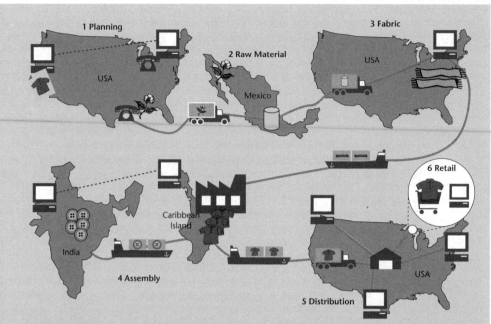

Figure 8.2 Continuous replenishment in the apparel industry

destination store. They are then forwarded to regional distribution centres (RDCs) that serve 50–100 stores.

6 **Retail**: as items are purchased, EPOS triggers replenishment responses.

Questions

1 Summarise the 'current state' problems that are typical of the apparel industry, and their implications for supply chain integration.

2 Identify potential barriers to executing the proposed apparel 'supply chain of the future'.

8.2 Efficient consumer response

Key issue: How can collaboration be extended across the supply chain to focus on meeting consumer demand?

Established as a grocery industry initiative, *efficient consumer response* (ECR) is designed to integrate and rationalise product assortment, promotion, new product development and replenishment across the supply chain. It aims to fulfil the changing demands and requirements of the end-customer through effective collaboration across all supply chain members, in order to enhance the effectiveness of merchandising efforts, inventory flow and supply chain administration.

The origin of ECR can be traced back to work carried out by Kurt Salmon Associates (in the United States) for the apparel sector (Salmon, 1993) and, later, the grocery sector (Fernie, 1998). Since then, ECR has increased industrial awareness of the growing problem of non-value-added supply chain costs.

Within the consumer products industry, ECR emerged partly because of the increased competition from new retail formats entering the traditional grocery industry in the early 1990s, as well as through the joint initiatives developed between Wal-Mart and Procter & Gamble. In Europe, ECR programmes commenced in 1993 with the commissioning of a series of projects, for example the Coopers & Lybrand survey of the grocery supply chain (Coopers & Lybrand, 1996).

The focus of ECR is to integrate supply chain management with demand management. This requires supplier–retailer collaboration – but in spite of the apparent emphasis on the end consumer, a lot of the early ECR studies focused on the supply side. Subsequent increased focus on demand and category management, however, has led to the adoption of a more holistic view of the supply chain when discussing ECR initiatives. In addition, ECR has also stimulated collaborative efforts that have increased companies' emphasis on key areas such as EDI, cross-docking (see Chapter 7 section 7.2.2) and continuous replenishment.

Other examples of studies of ECR initiatives include the Coca-Cola survey evaluating supply chain collaboration within 127 European companies; PE International's 1997 survey, and IGD's 1997 report (Boitoult, 1997). Generally, ECR initiatives aim to promote greater collaboration between manufacturers and retailers. Effective logistics strategies as well as administrative and information technology are essential for its successful implementation. These required techniques are available within most organisations, but the main problem facing most organisations is ensuring that people use these existing tools differently in order to secure or achieve their maximum potential.

The main areas addressed under ECR initiatives are category management, product replenishment and enabling technologies. These can be broken down into 14 areas where individual as well as well-integrated improvements can be made in order to enhance efficiency (see Figure 8.3).

8.2.1 Category management

As demand management principles have become more important to supply chain initiatives, the category management process has increased in popularity. With an objective of preventing stockout situations and improving supplier–retailer relations, category management aims to balance retailers' product volume and variety objectives. Activities included in the category management process include the capture and utilisation of knowledge of the drivers behind consumer attitudes and choices.

By focusing on category management and measuring promotional efficiency, ECR enables organisations to utilise their joint resources to reduce supply chain inventory levels, streamline product flows, and exploit cross-dock options where appropriate. Thus category management represents a focus on the development of at least some of the following capabilities:

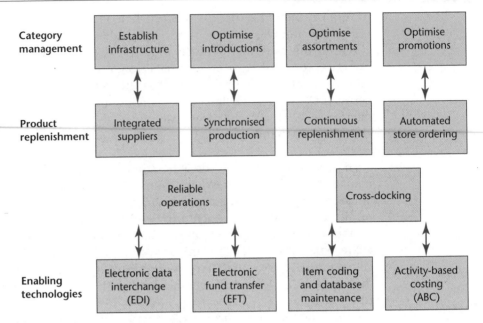

Figure 8.3 ECR improvement categories
(Source: After Fernie, 1998, p. 30)

- account management;
- demand management;
- multifunctional selling teams;
- price list restructuring;
- effective and customised promotions.

8.2.2 Continuous replenishment

Continuous replenishment offers both retailers and their suppliers the opportunity to manage their inventory in a more efficient manner (Mitchell, 1997; PE International, 1997). Each of the six stages that make up the product replenishment process (illustrated in Figure 8.3) represents a link that integrates the supply chain from product suppliers right through to end consumers. In addition, effective replenishment strategies require development of the following capabilities:

- joint inventory management;
- cross-dock operations;
- continuous replenishment;
- effective logistics strategies and product flows;
- quick response.

8.2.3 Enabling technologies

These drive ECR and make it work. They include scanning data, data warehousing and data mining, which have facilitated an understanding of customer requirements. Examples include EDI, which is increasingly about synchronising trading data among supply chain partners in advance of doing business as it allows the transmission of forecasting data back up through the supply chain. Other capabilities required by organisations in order to implement an effective ECR initiative include:

● effective information sharing;
● automated order generation;
● bar-coding and the use of other scanning technology.

In addition, the data to be shared and communicated at various stages in the supply chain depend on what will provide the most overall benefit. These data should include:

● demand/consumption/sales information;
● cash flow;
● stocks of finished goods/work in progress;
● delivery and output status.

However, many of the problems in sharing and using these data and implementing EDI networks are related to difficulties in achieving a critical mass of companies sufficient to generate substantial benefits.

| CASE STUDY 8.2 | ECR in the UK |

Dutchman Paul Polman did a stint as General Manager of Procter & Gamble UK and Eire from 1995 to 1999. While admiring the United Kingdom's advanced retailing systems, he saw opportunities for all four of the 'pillars of ECR' – range, new items, promotions and replenishment. The following is extracted from the text of a speech he made to the Institute of Grocery Distribution.

Range

The average store now holds 35 per cent more than five years ago, yet a typical customer buys just 18 skus on a trip. A quarter of these skus sell less than 6 units a week! The number of skus offered by manufacturers and stores has become too large and complex. My company is equally guilty in this area. No question, we make too many skus. I can assure you we are working on it. Actually, our overall sku count in laundry is already down 20 per cent compared to this time last year. What is more, business is up. Clearly, we have an opportunity to rationalise our ranges. As long as we do this in an ECR way – focusing on what consumers want – we will all win. The consumer will see a clearer range. Retailers and manufacturers will carry less inventory and less complexity. The result will be cost savings across the whole supply chain and stronger margins.

▶

New items

There were 16,000 new skus last year. Yet 80 per cent lasted less than a year. You don't need to be an accountant to imagine the costs associated with this kind of activity. And look how this has changed. Since 1975, the number of new sku introductions has increased eightfold. Yet their life expectancy has shrunk from around five years in 1975 to about nine months now. We can hardly call this progress.

Promotions

In promotions it's the same story. Take laundry detergents. This is a fairly stable market. Yet we're spending 50 per cent more on promotions than two years ago, with consumers buying nearly 30 per cent more of their volume on promotions. This not only creates an inefficient supply chain, or in some cases poor in-store availability, but, more importantly, has reduced the value of the category and likely the retailers' profit. We're all aware of the inefficiencies promotions cause in the system, such as problems in production, inventory and in-store availability. They all create extra costs, which ultimately have to be recouped in price. But there's a higher cost. As promotions are increasing, they are decreasing customer loyalty to both stores and brands by 16 per cent during the period of the promotion. We commissioned a report by Professor Barwise of the London Business School. He called it Taming the Multi-buy Dragon. The report shows us that over 70 per cent of Laundry promotional investment goes on multi-buys. The level of investment on multi-buys has increased by 60 per cent over the last three years. There's been a 50 per cent increase behind brands and a doubling of investment behind own labels. Contrary to what we thought, most of this volume is not going to a broad base of households. It is going to a small minority – 71 per cent of all multi-buy volume is bought by just 14 per cent of households. Just 2 per cent of multi-buy volume goes to 55 per cent of households. We really are focusing our spending on influencing and rewarding a very small minority of people indeed.

Replenishment

Based on the escalating activity I've just [referred to], costs are unnecessarily high. There are huge cost savings also here, up to 6 per cent, by removing the non-value-added skus and inefficient new brand and promotional activity.

Questions

1 Cutting down on range, new items and promotions is presumably going to lead to 'everyday low prices'. Is this lean thinking by another name?

2 Procter & Gamble's major laundry brand in the United States is Tide. This is marketed in some 60 pack presentations, some of which have less than 0.1 per cent share. The proliferation of these pack presentations is considered to have been instrumental in increasing Tide's market share from 20 per cent to 40 per cent of the US market in the last five years. Clearly, this is a major issue within P&G. What are the logistics pros and cons of sku proliferation?

8.3 Collaborative planning, forecasting and replenishment

Key issue: **How can collaboration be extended to strategic as to well as operational levels?**

Collaborative planning, forecasting and replenishment (CPFR) is aimed at improving collaboration between buyer and supplier so that customer service is improved while inventory management is made more efficient. The trade-off between customer service and inventory is thereby altered.

The CPFR movement originated in 1995. It was the initiative of five companies: Wal-Mart, Warner-Lambert, Benchmarking Partners, and two software companies, SAP and Manugistics. The goal was to develop a business model to collaboratively forecast and replenish inventory. An initial pilot was tested between Wal-Mart and Warner Lambert using the Listerine mouthwash product and focusing on stocks kept in the retail outlets. The concept and process was tested initially by exchanging pieces of paper. This generated clear visibility of the process required and the requirements for the IT specification. The two companies later demonstrated in a computer laboratory that the Internet could be used as a channel for this information exchange.

In 1998 the Voluntary Inter-industry Commerce Standards Committee (VICS) became involved in the movement, which enabled it to make major strides forward. VICS was formed in 1986 to develop bar-code and electronic data interchange standards for the retail industry. The involvement of VICS meant that other organisations could participate in the validation and testing of the CPFR concept. With VICS support, organisations including Procter & Gamble and Kimberly Clark undertook pilots to test the idea of sharing information to improve inventory handling. One of the pilots in the UK grocery sector is described in case study 8.3.

CASE STUDY 8.3

CPFR trials in the UK grocery sector

CPFR pilots have been a popular diversion in the UK grocery sector. Often, they show – as in this case – that considerable opportunities for improvement exist, but that the problems of scaling up the pilot are too great. The scenario for this pilot, researched by one of our Masters students Alexander Oliveira, was a manufacturer that supplied a major grocery retailer in the United Kingdom. Figure 7.15 shows the typical demand series for one of the 10 products in the study, all of which were in the high-volume ambient category. Total sales through the till (EPOS) for a given week were really quite stable. While there is apparent high demand variation, most of this is due to predictable behaviour such as that due to different store opening hours. The day-by-day demand for this product was actually relatively stable over the course of a year. Figure 8.4 places the pilot in context. The manufacturer's national distribution centre (NDC) supplied one of the retailer's regional distribution centres (RDCs), which in turn served 10 stores in the pilot.

The starting situation that Alexander found was that forecasting methods were based on a history of the last 2-3 months. While this gave the correct day-by-day pattern, it was insensitive to actual demand during a given week. As can be seen in Figure 7.15, ▶

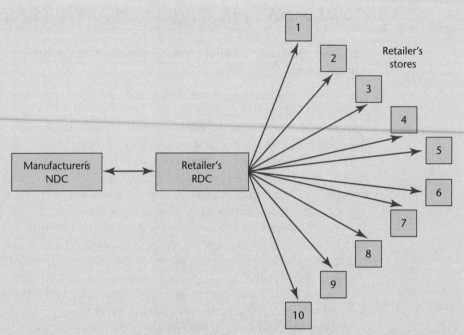

Figure 8.4 A collaborative planning pilot

the actual demand pattern varies from day to day across the series due to a proportion of randomness in the pattern. The replenishment cycle was unresponsive because daily deliveries were based on forecasts. This resulted in high safety stocks and poor on-shelf availability. Figure 8.5 provides an inventory profile across the supply chain.

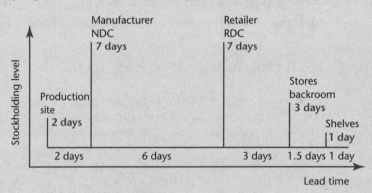

Figure 8.5 Pipeline map at start

The sum of the vertical (average days of stock) and horizontal (average lead time in days) gives the total time for a new batch of product to progress from manufacturing site to shelf. This totals a massive 4–5 weeks!

Alexander coordinated the provision of forecast data from both manufacturer and supplier. Both forecasts were posted on a website, and he was asked to provide instructions as to how much product the manufacurer should supply each day. Stock for the 10 stores was 'ring fenced' at the retailer's RDC – that is, it could not be supplied to any other than the 10 stores in the pilot.

Alexander soon found that current forecast data did not take daily fluctuations into account, and was based on far too long a history period. By tracking daily demand, it was possible to allow for the randomness without anything like the current quantity of safety stock in the system. He developed a new replenishment algorithm that was based on the daily error between forecast and actual, and which added an extra day's buffer stock. It soon became obvious that it was possible to run the system on far lower stock levels at the retailer's RDC, as shown in Figure 8.6.

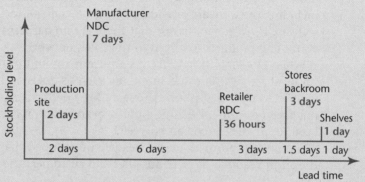

Figure 8.6 **Pipeline map at end of pilot**

Alexander's work had shown the potential for reducing the stock level at the RDC from 7 days to 36 hours. In spite of the huge potential savings, the retailer did not go ahead with scaling up the pilot. This can be attributed to several factors. First, many other improvement initiatives were under way. The CPFR initiative would have needed further scarce resources. Second, scaling up would have required a different operating routine at all RDCs and the supporting IT infrastructure would need to have been changed. Third, what worked with one relatively efficient manufacturer may not have worked with others. Nevertheless, Alexander came up with the following five enablers for CPFR implementation (Barratt and Oliveira, 2002):

1 *Define single point of contact for each trading partner*: to ensure that information is neither lost nor deteriorates during the exchange.
2 *Define agenda for collaboration (short- medium- long-term)*: to stabilise the collaborative goals over time.
3 *Expand collaborative projects (scope and complexity)*: to gain critical mass.
4 *Ensure continuous sharing of information*: a key enabler of collaborative planning.
5 *Development of trust*: this takes time. Smaller problems are gradually removed from the CPFR process to help partners develop confidence that the long-term goal is achievable.

Questions

1 Suppose that the retailer's total sales were €20 bn, and that the ten skus together accounted for 0.4 per cent of these sales. Calculate the approximate savings in inventory to the retailer.

2 Do you consider that the reasons given for not scaling up the pilot are valid?

3 Would there be any benefits to the manufacturer?

In autumn 1999 VICS published a tutorial for CPFR implementation. This is available in hard copy, or can be accessed on its website at www.cpfr.org. This 'road map' offers organisations a structured approach to CPFR implementation based on the experiences of the companies involved in the CPFR pilots.

Having shown that the CPFR concept can have bottom-line impact on their businesses, companies are looking to expand the programmes from the handful of items involved in the pilots to the hundreds or thousands of items covered in most trading relationships. This has been a challenge for all organisations, including the software providers, for whom a major focus has been to ensure that software is scaleable: that is, that there are no barriers to the number of organisations and products involved in the CPFR network.

When implementing CPFR, a significant amount of time and effort is required up front to negotiate specific items such as goals and objectives, frequency of updates to plan, exception criteria and key performance measures. The result is a published document defining the relevant issues for each organisation that has been jointly developed and agreed.

A nine-step business model has been developed that provides an insight into the effort required by both supplier and customer. The model is as follows:

1 Develop front-end agreement.
2 Create joint business plans.
3 Create individual sales forecasts.
4 Identify exceptions to sales forecasts.
5 Resolve/collaborate on exception items.
6 Create order forecast.
7 Identify exceptions to order forecast.
8 Resolve/collaborate on exception items.
9 Generate orders.

In summary, CPFR focuses on the process of forecasting supply and demand by bringing various plans and projections from both the supplier and the customer into synchronisation. CPFR requires extensive support in the form of Internet-based products, which can result in major changes to the key business processes. An academic survey of the success of CPFR (Oliviera and Barratt, 2002) found a significant correlation between companies with high information systems capabilities and the success of CPFR projects. The firms with high levels of CPFR implementation use information systems capable of providing timely, accurate, user-friendly and interfunctional information in real time. Skjoett-Larsen *et al.* (2003) propose that CPFR should be seen as a general approach to integrating supply chain processes, and not as a rigid, step-by-step model as proposed by VICS.

8.3.1 Benefits of electronic collaboration

Nestlé UK states that the benefits of collaborative systems are significant, and lists the following benefits:

- There is improved availability of product to the consumer, and hence more sales.
- Total service is improved, total costs are reduced (including inventory, waste and resources) and capacities can be reduced owing to the reductions in uncertainty achieved.
- Processes that span two or more companies become far more integrated and hence simple, standard, speedy and certain.
- Information is communicated quickly, in a more structured way, and is transparent across the supply chain to all authorised users. All users know where to find up-to-date information.
- An audit trail can be provided to say when information was amended.
- E-mail prompts can update users of variance and progress, and can confirm authorisations.
- The data that are in the system can be used for monitoring and evaluation purposes.
- The process can be completed in a quick timescale, at a lower total cost.
- All trading partners become more committed to the shared plans and objectives. Changes are made with more care, and are immediately visible to all.

Many of these benefits are being experienced by those implementing the CPFR philosophy. Wal-Mart and Sara Lee experienced sales increases of 45 per cent and a decline in weeks-on-hand inventory of 23 per cent. The benefits experienced by Procter & Gamble and its retail partners include a reduction in replenishment cycle time of 20 per cent. The increased visibility of the supply chain resulted in a reduction of in-store availability from 99 per cent to 88 per cent being detected with sufficient lead time to respond. This saved 3–4 days of stockouts for the retailer. Forecast accuracy improvements of 20 per cent have also been experienced.

8.4 Managing supply chain relationships

Key issue: How can broader-based relationships be formed between trading partners in the supply chain?

8.4.1 Creating closer relationships

The traditional supplier–customer relationship has been limited to contact primarily between the customer's buyer and the supplier's salesperson. Other functions, such as information systems, are kept very much at arm's length. Indeed, the customer's buyer argues that dealings with the supplier should only go through him or her: in that way, sensitive communications such as those affecting price, are limited to a single channel.

This traditional style of relationship ('bow tie') is contrasted with the multiple-contact model ('diamond') proposed in Figure 8.7. Here, contacts between different functions are positively encouraged, and the arm's length relationship is replaced by active relationship management and supplier development processes. This is exemplified by the remarkable changes in the supplier portfolio at the UK high street retailer BhS. In the early 1990s BhS had over 1,000 suppliers. Now it has just 50. But the nature of the relationship with the 50 is quite different. There are now multilevel connections between the supply chain players and a high level of electronic collaboration. There is also a much greater involvement by the remaining 50 suppliers in high-level strategy development at BhS.

However attractive such processes of bonding may appear, in practice the organisational boundaries and vested interests inhibit the rate at which relationships deepen. These have been described as a series of factors as a result of research in the automotive industry.

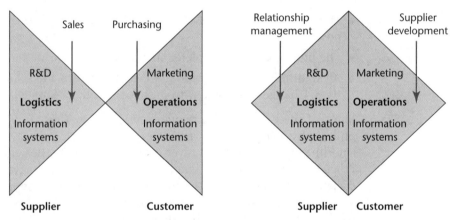

Figure 8.7 **Creating closer relationships**

8.4.2 Factors in forming supply chain relationships

Lamming (1993) proposed nine factors for analysing customer–supplier relationships, which have been modified and extended below:

● *What the order winners are*: for example, price, product range, technology advantage, superior product quality.

● *How sourcing decisions are made*: is it, for example, competitive tender, auctions, supplier accreditation and sole source?

● *The nature of electronic collaboration*: is it transactional, information sharing or collaborative?

- *The attitude to capacity planning*: is this seen as the supplier's problem, as a problem for the buyer (tactical make/buy/additional sources), or as a shared strategic issue?

- *Call-off requirements*: does the customer (for example) alter schedules with no notice, require JIT delivery against specified time windows, or require synchronised deliveries of major subassemblies to the point of use?

- *Price negotiations*: are price reductions imposed by the buyer subject to game playing by both parties, the result of joint continuous improvement projects, etc.?

- *Managing product quality*: does the customer help the supplier to improve process capability? Are aggressive targets (e.g. 50 ppm defects) set by the customer? Is the supplier responsible for quality of incoming goods and warranty of the parts in service?

- *Managing research and development*: does the customer impose new designs and have the supplier follow instructions? Does the supplier become involved in new product development? Is the supplier expected to design and develop the complete product for the next model?

- *The level of pressure*: how far does the customer place pressure for improvement on the supplier to avoid complacency (e.g. 30 per cent price reduction in the next two years)?

Within the European automotive industry at present, the most significant factor seems to be the last. Over-capacity among the assemblers has created massive pressures for cost reduction. The supply chain accounts for 70–80 per cent of an assembler's costs, so this is the primary target. Figure 8.8 shows the inventory profile for volume assemblers in Europe.

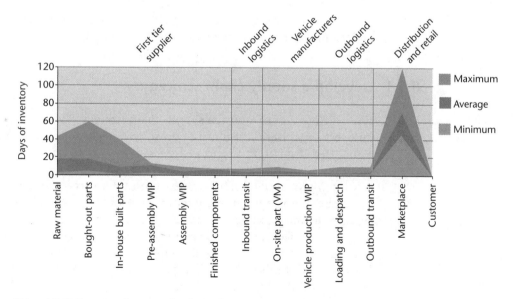

Figure 8.8 Automotive supply chain: inventory profile
(Source: After Holweg and Miemczyk, 2002)

It is apparent that assemblers have been using their power in the supply chain to optimise inventories around their own processes. Meanwhile, component manufacturers upstream and dealers downstream are carrying huge inventories. Dealer networks are holding some €18bn of stock in disused airfields around Europe! While long-term mutually beneficial relationships are often talked about, the reality can be very different.

Activity 8.3

Select an industry of your choice and, within this, review the nine factors listed in section 8.4.2. How would you classify the state of supply chain relationships in this industry?

8.5 A framework for managing the supply chain

Key issue: **What are the management implications of logistic supply chain strategies?**

The supply chain is the conduit for getting products from source to ultimate customer. As a result, it is affected by almost every function within the organisations that it comprises. If managed effectively, the supply chain provides one of the greatest opportunities for improving customer satisfaction, and a major source of competitive advantage.

If we examine the above statement further, it is obvious that we need to manage the supply chain more strategically and holistically than ever before. The management of the supply chain requires an approach that is driven by the organisation's objectives, and combines strategy, people, processes and systems. To further develop our understanding of how to manage the supply chain more effectively, and to realise the opportunities that effective supply chain management can offer, here are six key building blocks (see Figure 8.9) that help in understanding how supply chains can be managed.

8.5.1 Develop a supply chain strategy

The development of a formal supply chain strategy is a critical step to undertake for every organisation. Failure to do so will mean that the significant resources committed (capital, time and people) will be wasted, and the potential benefits of supply chain management will never be realised.

Not only is a supply chain strategy critical for success, it also provides a framework for defining and prioritising initiative for business process redesign, systems enhancements and organisational restructuring. Many organisations deploy numerous projects aimed at becoming more customer-focused and efficient, but in most cases without fully understanding their customers' service expectations. The outcome of this is that the projects simply become cost-cutting exercises that rarely deliver the expected benefits.

What constitutes a comprehensive supply chain strategy? The following elements must be incorporated:

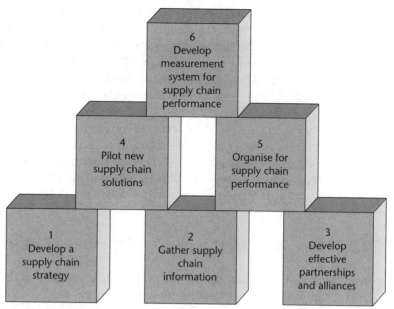

Figure 8.9 Six building blocks for effective supply chain management
(Source: Adapted from Derocher and Kilpatrick, 2000)

- customer service requirements;
- plant and distribution centre network design;
- inventory management;
- outsourcing and third-party logistics relationships;
- business processes;
- organisational design and training requirements;
- performance metrics and goals.

If the strategy is to be effective, it must be linked with the overall business strategy, so aligning the supply chain to fulfil the vision for delivering value to the customer. Having developed the supply chain strategy, the next step is to translate this into a tactical plan, which can be used to traverse the gap between existing supply chain capabilities and those capabilities required to support the business's future direction. This tactical plan identifies and prioritises the business and system initiatives needed to serve the customer more effectively.

8.5.2 Gather supply chain information

If the organisation is to make effective supply chain decisions, then it needs to ensure that there is an accurate, timely flow of information across the supply chain as a whole. If companies are to achieve this, they need to ensure that they have a set of systems that are capable of viewing the entire supply chain process. This would include everything from supplier inventory positioning through levels of true customer demand to delivery modes.

Organisations have counted on *enterprise resource planning* (ERP) systems to facilitate the flow of information across their organisation. Many organisations have gone through considerable 'implementation pain' with their ERP systems, which has generated significant cynicism and disaffection with systems in general. To make the broader-based decisions demanded by SCM, organisations require a capability that extends far beyond the scope of ERP systems alone.

Some organisations have already made this leap of faith and are implementing claimed 'supply-chain-wide solutions', such as those offered by software vendors such as Manugistics and i2. These pioneers are reporting significant early benefits, but as the scope of the solutions spreads across the entire supply chain these benefits are likely to grow further still.

8.5.3 Develop effective partnerships and alliances

There is a growing recognition that organisations on their own cannot maintain all the necessary capabilities required to succeed in the highly competitive environments in which they compete. It has become recognised that it is supply chains that compete, rather than individual companies. To do this effectively the organisation must be able to develop alliances, partnerships and joint ventures with its suppliers and customers, and possibly even with some of its competitors. It is by this extension of the supply chain that better decisions are made possible, in terms of procurement, production, inventory and fulfilment.

When organisations seek to manage the extended supply chain, they run into an initial problem. Despite all the readily apparent benefits of partnering, suppliers and customers are not always ready to collaborate. This reluctance arises from the fact that some organisations are unable to establish relationships that serve the business objectives of both parties. Another problem is that such relationships take a considerable amount of time to develop and nurture.

A further major barrier to such a collaborative approach is that, while organisations readily seek improved business performance, they shy away from sharing information and risk. Such an attitude will simply prevent those organisations from ever becoming the leading companies in their chosen markets. For every link in the supply chain, the relationships between the two organisations that form that link must be as strong as possible. Processes must be aligned and systems integrated to allow the fast and accurate flow of products and information.

Relationships may probably not be formed with all suppliers and customers. Only key suppliers and customers will be chosen for this approach. It would not be possible to develop close relationships with all suppliers and customers, owing to the time and resources required. With the advent of the Internet as a means of sharing information across the supply chain quickly and cheaply, the appropriate levels of relationships must be in place.

8.5.4 Pilot new supply chain solutions

Most organisations tend to be bastions of conservatism when it comes to supply chain innovation: they perceive a significant risk attached to being seen as leading edge or first movers into a new market. The risk of possible mishaps and potential harm to existing relationships is enough for most short-term-thinking managers not to get involved with new projects. Organisations need to recognise the importance of pilot projects within the change management process. Piloting initiatives on a small scale reduces risk, and can encourage buy-in from others within the organisation or supply chain.

Real breakthroughs in supply chain management have come about only when organisations are prepared to question the status quo and participate in a number of projects that appear on the surface to be leaps of faith.

The smart companies will be the ones that implement a number of small, relatively risk-free (if not at least greatly reduced in terms of risk) pilot projects, to test their ideas prior to a broader roll-out if successful. The projects that do fail will be seen as learning experiences, so that similar mistakes are not repeated. Another reason for the pilot projects is that in today's highly competitive environment supply chains that do not function properly will not survive long. Pilot projects help in the fine tuning of supply chain solutions before they are rolled out. New processes are perfect candidates for pilot projects, so as to avoid damaging customer relationships while new processes are implemented on a broad scale.

Successful supply chain improvements may arise from including all the following elements in any such pilot projects:

- Involvement of key stakeholders, suppliers, customers and employees.
- Selection of scope and environment: which site, business, group of items, or customers should be host to the pilot? This activity should focus on avoiding risk while ensuring exposure to a wide range of business scenarios.
- Identification of the key questions that the pilot must answer: what are the critical success factors?

It becomes critical to measure the results of pilot projects carefully. This should ensure that the expected benefits are achieved and any adjustments are made before rolling out the project more broadly across the organisation.

8.5.5 Organise for supply chain performance

If we look at most organisational structures we shall see that a clear majority of the organisations have one thing in common: functionally based structures that run counter to the seamless efficiency demanded of today's supply chain. These organisational structures lack cross-functional objectives and do not support teamwork. Each of the functional areas (such as procurement, production planning and accounts payable) can undermine overall supply chain effectiveness, as each seeks and is motivated to focus on its own success. This is a critical weakness of the functional structure, as one decision may be right for a functional area, but detrimental to the supply chain as a whole. Along with the myriad of corporate initiatives ongoing in most if not all organisations, the implementation of business process changes becomes extremely difficult if not sometimes impossible.

A skill shortage in terms of being able to manage the flow of materials, information and funds across the supply chain is another major weakness common in most organisations. Many supply chain managers lack strategic planning skills and financial literacy. The outcome of this is that most supply chain initiatives are purely cost-focused. Few organisations adopt a value-based perspective, one in which the impact of the initiative on revenues, costs, investments and cash flows – the drivers of shareholder value – is considered. If supply chain performance is to improve, then organisational change seems to be the obvious answer.

8.5.6 Develop measurement systems for supply chain performance

The complexity of supply chains has increased significantly in recent years. At the same time technology has created a change in the ways in which companies can plan, synchronise and execute their supply chain plans. However, many companies have not adapted their performance measurement regimes to align them on supply chain performance. Traditional performance measurements within the organisation have a number of significant deficiencies. They are often function-focused, tracking individual activities: this can promote the optimisation of the function rather than of the complete supply chain system.

A survey of supply chain measures by the management consultants Arthur D. Little found that 64 per cent of companies were focused on procurement measures, 27 per cent on order fulfilment measures, and only 9 per cent on systems that spanned the complete breadth of the supply chain.

There is a clear need for cross-supply chain measures. As a general rule, effective measures should have the following characteristics:

- simple to understand;
- no more than 10 in total number;
- representative of a significant causal relationship;
- have an associated target;
- capable of being shared across the supply chain.

Relatively few measures are needed to cover the supply chain. The following have been found to be useful in most situations, and can be adapted to focus on issues experienced in specific industries:

- *on time in full, outbound*: a measure of customer orders fulfilled, complete and on time, conforming to specification;
- *on time in full, inbound*: a measure of supplier deliveries received, complete and on time, conforming to specification;

- *internal defect rates*: a measure of process conformance and control (rather than inspection);
- *new product introduction rate*: a measure of supply chain product responsiveness;
- *cost reduction*: a measure of sustainable product and process development;
- *stock turns*: a measure of supply chain goods flow (this measure is useful only when applied to specific products and their supply chains);
- *order to delivery lead time*: a measure of supply chain process responsiveness;
- *fiscal flexibility*: a measure of how easy it is to structure the supply chain for financial advantage (with international supply chains, channelling operations through low-tax locations for purposes of gaining supply chain cost benefits should be considered).

The main benefits of these measures are that they are applicable to all levels in the supply chain, and they can increase visibility and control for all players.

Activity 8.4

Using the six building blocks identified for effective supply chain performance, undertake an audit for any organisation of your choice. How does your selected organisation address each building block? Describe activities that can be undertaken to improve the way the organisation undertakes the six building blocks.

Summary

What are the benefits of collaboration in the supply chain?

- Collaboration within the organisation leads to improved results according to a recent US survey. More frequent collaboration between marketing and logistics results in better performance in areas such as cycle times, inventories, product availability and order-to-delivery lead times.
- Benefits of electronic collaboration listed by Nestlé UK include improved availability of product to the consumer, and hence more sales. The total service is improved, total costs are reduced (including inventory, waste and resources) and capacities can be reduced owing to the reductions in uncertainty achieved. In addition, processes that span two or more companies become far more integrated and hence simple, standard, speedy and certain. Trading partners become more committed to the shared plans and objectives.
- Replacement of the single point of contact (bow-tie relationship) by the multiple-contact model (diamond relationship) suggests an arm's length process being replaced by a broad-based, cross-functional process. In spite of such ideals, research in the automotive industry indicates that massive downward cost pressures on suppliers limit the progress at which relationships deepen.

How can collaboration be put into practice?

- JIT2 aims to achieve intercompany collaboration manually by placing customer and supplier together as supplier-in-plant.

- Electronic collaboration can be undertaken in three ways: transactional (the transmission of fixed-format documents with predefined data and information fields); information sharing (a one-way process of providing access to information such as product description and pricing, sales information, inventory and promotional calendars); and collaborative planning (electronic collaboration at strategic, operational and tactical levels).

- Efficient consumer response (ECR) aims to integrate and rationalise product range, new product introductions, promotions, and replenishment across the supply chain. It is an industry-wide initiative that has many followers in retailing and manufacturing of fast-moving consumer goods across Europe and the United States. ECR seek to operationalise its aims by means of category management, product replenishment and enabling technologies.

- Collaborative planning, forecasting and replenishment (CPFR) is aimed at 'making inventory management more efficient and cost-effective, while improving customer service and leveraging technology to significantly improve profitability'. CPFR focuses on the process of forecasting supply and demand by synchronising the plans and projections of both the supplier and customer. Replenishment of needed products is then more accurate and timely.

Discussion questions

1 What is the purpose of collaboration in the supply chain, and why should it lead to value added from the customer perspective?

2 In the Procter & Gamble case study, the advice is to cut down on the number of skus on offer in order to improve replenishment. Is this collaboration or defeatism?

3 Compare and contrast the aims of ECR and CPFR. Is CPFR a more advanced set of logistics concepts?

4 'You can talk collaboration as much as you like: at the end of the day, it's a raw struggle for power, and the retailers are winning hands down.' Discuss the relative merits of the factors in forming supply chain relationships (section 8.4) from both the suppliers' (manufacturers) and retailers' viewpoints.

5 Discuss critically the six building blocks of supply chain management in section 8.5.

6 Compare the proposals for key performance measures in block 6 of the framework for managing supply chains (section 8.5.6) with the principles of the balanced scorecard (Chapter 3, section 3.4).

References

Barratt M. and Oliveira A. (2002): 'Supply chain collaboration: exploring the early initiatives', *Supply Chain Planning*, Vol. 4 , No. 1, pp. 16–28.

Boitoult, L. (1997) *Building the Foundations: An introduction to total supply chain management.* Watford: Institute of Grocery Distribution.

Chappell, G. (2001) 'Agility on the Catwalk', in Lewis, C. (ed.) *Logistics Europe*, June, pp. 20–4.

Coopers & Lybrand (1996) *European Value Chain Analysis Study: Final report.* Utrecht: ECR Europe.

Derocher, R. and Kilpatrick, J. (2000) 'Six supply chain lessons for the new millennium', *Supply Chain Management Review*, Vol. 3, No. 4, pp. 34–40.

Fernie, J. (1998) 'Relationships in the supply chain', in Fernie, J. and Sparks, L. (eds), *Logistics and Retail Management: Insights into current practice and trends from leading experts*, pp. 23–46. London: Kogan Page.

Frohlich M. and Westbrook R. (2001) 'Arcs of integration: an international study of supply chain strategies', *Journal of Operations Management*, Vol. 19, No. 2, pp. 185–200.

Holweg M.and Miemczyk J. (2002) 'Logistics in the "three-day car" age: assessing the responsiveness of vehicle distribution logistics in the UK', *International Journal of Physical Distribution and Logistics Management*, Vol. 32, No. 10, pp. 829–50.

Lamming, R. (1993) *Beyond Partnership: Strategies for innovation and lean supply.* New York: Prentice-Hall.

Kirby, J. (2003) 'Supply chain challenges: Building relationships', *Harvard Business Review*, July, pp. 65–73.

Kuhel, J. S. (2002) 'Clothes call', *Supply Chain Technology News*, Vol. 4, No. 2, pp. 18–21.

Mitchell, A. (1997) *Efficient Consumer Response: A new paradigm for the European FMCG sector.* London: Financial Times/Pearson Professional.

Oliveira, A. and Barratt, M. (2001) 'Exploring the experience of collaborative planning initiatives', *International Journal of Physical Distribution and Logistics Management*, Vol. 31, No. 4, pp. 266–89.

PE International (1997) *Efficient Consumer Response: Supply chain management of the new millennium.* Corby: Institute of Logistics.

Salmon, K. (1993) *Efficient Consumer Response: Enhancing consumer value in the supply chain.* Washington, DC: Kurt Salmon.

Skjoett-Larsen, T., Thernøe C. and Andresen C. (2003) 'Supply chain collaboration: Theoretical perspectives and empirical evidence, *International Journal of Physical Distribution and Logistics Management*, Vol. 33, No. 6, pp. 531–49.

Stank, T.P., Daughtery, P.J. and Ellington, A.E. (1999) 'Marketing/logistics integration and firm performance', *International Journal of Logistics Management*, Vol. 10, No. 1, pp. 11–24.

Suggested further reading

GEA Consultia (1994) *Supplier–Retailer Collaboration in Supply Chain Management.* London: Coca-Cola Retailing Research Group Europe.

McGrath, M. (1997) *A Guide to Category Management.* Watford: IGD.

O'Sullivan, D. (1997) 'ECR: will it end in tears?', *Logistics Focus*, Vol. 5, No. 7, pp. 2–5.

Sharp, D. and Hill, R. (1998) 'ECR: from harmful competition to winning collaboration', in Gattorna, J.L. (ed.), *Strategic Supply Chain Alignment*, pp. 104–22. Aldershot: Gower.

CHAPTER 9

Partnerships in the supply chain

Outcomes

The planned outcomes of this chapter are to:

- introduce a range of options for intercompany relationships;
- describe the nature of partnerships;
- describe the implications for suppliers of entering into partnerships.

By the end of this chapter, you should be able to understand:

- the range of intercompany relationships;
- the benefits and difficulties of operating supply chain partnerships;
- ways of approaching implementation issues.

Introduction

A number of different supply chain structures have emerged, based upon networks and interfirm collaboration. Optimising the supply chain process inevitably leads to a growing interdependence among supply chain partners. With this interdependence has come a realisation that cooperation and partnership are necessary to achieve long-term mutual benefit. The implications for competitive strategy of this growth of collaborative supply chains are considerable – in particular the need to develop those skills that enable a company to re-engineer established buyer–supplier relationships and successfully manage them on a day-to-day basis.

The overall aim of this chapter is to introduce the concept of 'partnership' and to present the context in which partnerships can be beneficial.

Key issues

This chapter addresses six key issues:

1 **Choosing the right relationship:** which relationship is appropriate in different circumstances – bottleneck items, strategic items, non-critical items and leverage items.

2 **Partnerships in the supply chain:** cooperative, coordinated and collaborative relationships; their advantages and disadvantages.

3 **Supply base rationalisation:** dealing with a smaller number of suppliers to enable high-intensity relationships to develop.

4 **Supplier networks:** the development of supplier associations, and the Japanese equivalent, *keiretsu*.

5 **Supplier development:** managing upstream suppliers through integrated processes and synchronous production.

6 **Implementing partnerships:** the potential pitfalls in moving from open market negotiations to collaborative relationships.

9.1 Choosing the right relationships

Key issue: **What types of relationships can be observed in supply chains? How can each type of relationship be tailored to different types of product?**

There are many possible types of relationship in the supply chain. The different options can be viewed in the form a continuum ranging from *arm's length*, where the relationship is conducted through the marketplace with price as its foundation, to *vertical integration*, where the relationship is cemented through common ownership. Vertical integration can *extend* for one or more tiers and its *direction* may be upstream, downstream or both. The continuum of relationship options is shown in Figure 9.1. Each of these relationship styles has motivating factors that drive development, and which govern the operating environment. The duration, breadth, strength and closeness of the relationship vary from case to case and over time.

A focal firm may not have the same type of relationship with all of its customers and suppliers. The firm may adopt a range of styles: choosing which type of relationship to adopt in a given supply chain situation is an important strategic issue. For example, grocery retailers often adopt an arm's length style for 'own brand' goods like kitchen paper, and use on-line auctions (Smart and Harrison, 2003) to obtain lowest price solutions. Elsewhere, they may use a strategic alliance to develop petrol forecourts, such as the Esso–Tesco Express alliance referred to in case study 1.1.

Companies tend to deal with a large number of suppliers, even after the supply base has been rationalised. Treating them all in the same way fails to recognise that some have different needs to others. Differentiating the role of suppliers and applying appropriate practices towards them allows a focal firm to target purchasing and supply chain management resources to better effect.

A popular view is that Japanese companies consider all of their tier 1 suppliers as partners. This is not really true: for example, Japanese automotive manufacturers do not regard all of their suppliers as equal. In fact among the typical 100–200 tier 1 suppliers to an OEM only about a dozen will enjoy partnership status. Typically, these elite few tend to be large organisations.

A number of approaches seek to segment suppliers into categories. The *purchase portfolio matrix* presented in Figure 9.2 is based on the notion that a customer will seek to maximise purchasing power when it can. This approach assumes that the key factors that affect the relationship are the strength of the buying company in the buyer–supplier relationship, and the number of suppliers able and willing to supply a product in the short term.

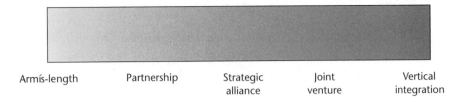

Figure 9.1 Relationship styles continuum
(Source: After Cooper and Gardner, 1993)

Strategic items

Strategic items are those for which the buyer has strength but there are few available suppliers. In this situation, purchasing should use its strength carefully to draw suppliers into a relationship that ensures supply in the long term.

Bottleneck items

Where the buyer has little power and there are few alternatives then these items are termed *bottlenecks*. The aim of purchasing in this situation is to reduce dependence on these items through diversification to find additional suppliers, seek substitute products and work with design teams to ensure that the bottleneck items are avoided in new products where possible.

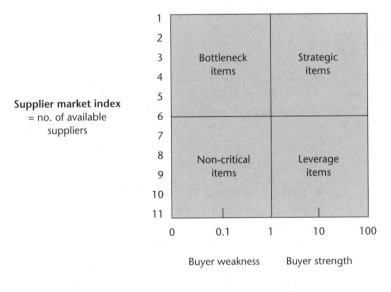

Figure 9.2 Purchase portfolio matrix
(Source: Syson, 1992)

Non-critical items

With a good choice of suppliers, possibly through following a strategy of using standardised parts, the traditional buying mechanism of competitive tendering is most valid for non-critical items. Such items are the ones with the following characteristics:

- not jointly developed;
- unbranded;
- do not affect performance and safety in particular;
- have required low investment in specific tools and equipment.

Leverage items

Where there are a large number of available suppliers and the buyer has high spending power then the buyer will be able to exercise this power to reduce prices and to push for preferential treatment. Naturally, care should be taken not to antagonise suppliers just in case these favourable market conditions change.

This approach is heavily weighted towards the buyer's viewpoint. It is also a little unfashionable because it uses the term 'power' in supplier relationships, and assumes that traditional market-based negotiations will be used for some product groups. However, it applies to many firms today, and reflects the tough approach taken by purchasing teams in some of their customers. Accepting that these sorts of conditions are likely to prevail, it is clear that suppliers need to work on their relative strategic importance to a focal firm in order to strengthen their position in a supply relationship.

Activity 9.1

Selecting an organisation of your choice, use a copy of the purchase portfolio matrix (Figure 9.2) and plot on it the names of its top 10 customers and top 10 suppliers. Which position would your chosen company prefer to be in? Suggest actions that would make the situation better.

Research in the automotive industry has predicted the emergence of two types of supplier (Lamming, 1993):

- *Type 1*: local companies that are flexible and responsive;
- *Type 2*: companies that would supply to customers on a global basis, possibly through establishing a local presence next to each customer site. These multinational companies would typically have a high level of value adding, possess technological expertise, and undertake their own R&D.

Both of these company types align themselves closely to customer needs and reduce the number of alternative suppliers they compete against. As a result, each has a high company index with its customer's individual sites. Plotting these factors on the grid in Figure 9.2, both of these types of firm are likely to be in a position to form partnerships with their customers. These are the companies that are likely to survive as tier 1 suppliers.

This leads to the development of a third type of supplier in addition to world-class product/service companies. This is the group of firms which have been 'demoted' to the second tier. Here, they will have to compete against global players on price, delivery and flexibility. Case study 9.1 explains some of the dynamics in automotive inbound supply chains and the changing roles and responsibilities of suppliers.

CASE STUDY
9.1

Automotive supply chains: a range of inbound logistics solutions

Automotive assemblers and their inbound supply chains have developed many solutions to orchestrate the manufacturing and delivery of the thousands of parts that go to make up a vehicle. The many potential inbound logistics solutions are summarised in Figure 9.3.

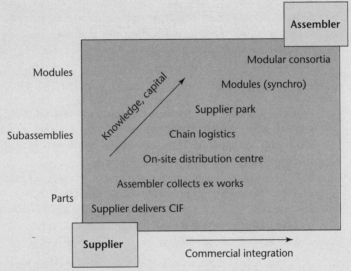

Figure 9.3 **Evolving inbound relationships**

These changes are of increasing value to the assemblers. The complexity of the logistics operation has been greatly downsized by slashing the number of tier 1 suppliers by broadening their responsibilities. Yet the ability of the assemblers to customise their finished products has increased. Quality consistency increases towards 50 ppm, while tough price reduction targets are demanded.

Supplier delivers CIF (carriage, insurance and freight)

The supplier delivers the ordered parts to the assembler's factory, and includes the distribution costs in the piece part price.

▶

Assembler collects ex-works

The assembler subcontracts the process of parts collection from a number of suppliers, who are visited at a predetermined frequency (e.g. daily). The parts are taken to a consolidation centre, where they are decanted into trailers destined for different assembly plants. An example of this is the Ford operation that is run by Exel at Birmingham in the United Kingdom. Parts collections are made from the Midlands region of the United Kingdom, and dispatched to 22 Ford plants around Europe.

On-site distribution centre

Instead of delivering parts directly into the assembler's plant, the logistics partner may instead deliver into a distribution centre positioned close to the assembler's plant. The advantages are much more controlled inbound parts movements into the plant. The assembler is able to call up loads of parts that are needed for a relatively short time period, and thus greatly improve material flow into the plant and reduce vehicle congestion. Additional value-adding activities may also be carried out in the DC. Thus, for example suppliers carry out some final assembly and sequencing tasks in the new Integrated Logistics Centre at BMW, Cowley, UK.

Chain logistics

Here the objective is to increase the *speed* of the inbound supply chain. If not planned and managed, drivers' hours regulations across Europe can lead to waste as the supply chain stops to allow for rests. The higher the speed of inbound supply, the lower the stock that needs to be held at the assembly plant. A useful further advantage is that the higher the speed, the less packaging and containers are needed in the supply chain. An example of chain logistics is the ALUK operation that supports the Toyota plant at Burnaston in Britain. Parts movements from a supplier in southern Spain are planned in four-hour stages, where the full trailer is swapped for an empty one in a similar fashion to the Pony Express in the days of the Wild West!

Supplier park

Major tier 1 subassembly manufacturers are positioned on a supplier park close to the assembly hall. Major subassemblies are then sequenced into the assembly hall in response to a 'drumbeat' (based on the master schedule – see Chapter 6), which identifies the precise specification of the next body to be dropped onto the trim and final assembly track. Suppliers then have a finite amount of time to complete assembly and deliver to the point of use on the track. An example here is the Exel operation at the VW–Seat plant at Martorell near Barcelona, where material movements on the supplier park are specified and orchestrated by means of Exel's IT systems.

Modules

The VW–Seat plant at Martorell demonstrates a further advance in logistics thinking. Instead of delivering a large number of subassemblies, why not get the tier 1 suppliers to coordinate all the parts needed to produce a complete module that can then be simply bolted onto the car? Product variety can be increased by customisation of the modules. The advantages are shown in Figure 9.4.

Modular designs offer less work in progress (WIP) and a considerably downsized process for the assembler, and greater variety for the customer. Downsizing of the assembly process means that it is shorter, and can be positioned closer to customer demand. Complexity can then be added later in the pipeline between customer order and delivery of the specified car into the customer's hands – a concept called postponed variety. The term *synchro supply* has been used to describe the delivery of modules not just at the correct quality and correct time, but on a real-time basis with the assembler and with the added challenge of zero safety stock.

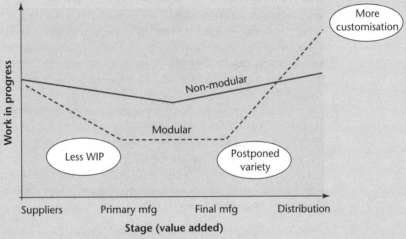

Figure 9.4 Modularisation: doing more with less
(Source: After van Hoek and Weken, 1998)

Modular consortia

The VW bus and truck plant in Brazil is an experiment in the further development of the modular concept. The truck assembly operation has been divided into seven modules, with a supplier responsible for each. All the direct workers are on the supplier's payroll, and the supplier not only assembles the module, but also performs final assembly of the vehicle. The assembler's task has been downsized to engineering, design, supervision and administration. The Mercedes plant at Hambach in France, which produces the micro-compact Smart car (see case study in Chapter 7), divides the vehicle into five main modules. Seven suppliers are fully integrated into the final assembly plant, while 16 non-integrated suppliers deliver submodules and parts. The whole information system – which supports manufacturing, logistics and distribution – is outsourced to Accenture.

Implications for suppliers

The demands on tier 1 suppliers increase in proportion to the various logistics solutions described earlier. A clear trend towards supplier parks and modularisation can be seen in the logistics strategies of automotive assemblers. Increasingly, tier 1 suppliers are being expected to control subsequent tiers in the supply chain, while ensuring delivery and quality to the assembler. At the same time, challenging cost reduction targets are being set, while the whole process is facilitated by tier 1 outbound defect levels that are less than 50 ppm. Many suppliers question whether the draconian demands for 'cost down' targets are compatible with such defect levels.

Three distinct stages can be seen in the development of capabilities by tier 1 suppliers:

- *Tier 1 basic*: suppliers with in-house design capability and project management capability who can ensure timely delivery and reasonable quality reliability (50 ppm). An example would be a tyre manufacturer who holds 4–5 days' stock and who delivers to set time windows: that is, limited logistics capability.
- *Tier 1 synchro*: suppliers who provide all of the basic capabilities, but with virtually no safety stock. Additional capabilities for the supplier are synchro logistics and IT expertise which is closely integrated with the assembler, greater flexibility and more secure emergency procedures. They operate through 'clone' plants that are situated on supplier parks no more than 10 minutes' travel time from the assembler's production line.
- *Tier 0.5*: full service providers, who integrate component manufacturing through supply chain management to achieve the optimum design of a given module. They carry out pre-emptive market research and develop innovative designs through shelf engineering (designs that are prepared proactively in advance of need and placed 'on the shelf', thus saving time in the event that the need does arise). They are partners in major cost reduction projects at each model change, and in continuous improvement projects in between.

There is a substantial passing of risk from the assembler to the tier 1 supplier at each stage. Increasingly, the supplier takes responsibility for designing and developing new products of increasing complexity in advance of new model programmes. And there is no guarantee that the supplier will get the work, because competitive tenders are issued for each new model. This forces suppliers to keep primary manufacturing and core business at a 'home' location, and to construct low-cost, late-configuration 'postponement' plants near the OEM's assembly hall to enable synchro deliveries. The decision by BMW/Rover to switch R50 (Mini) assembly from Longbridge to Cowley left a number of suppliers with £2m synchro assembly units in the wrong place.

The strategic dilemma for tier 1 suppliers who currently supply the assemblers directly is whether to expand into system integrators ('tier 0.5'), or to become indirect suppliers to such organisations. Siegfried Wolf of Magna International described the tier 0.5 transition as follows:

> To become part of this new tier, companies will require a worldwide presence, global sourcing, programme management, technology, JIT and JIS know-how and specialist production knowledge. They will also require a high level of R&D spend.

(JIS = just in sequence: the capability to supply a module in accordance with the drumbeat requirements of an assembler.) So, after tier 0.5, where do the competitive challenges lie? Tier 2 suppliers will still be largely low-overhead, product-based companies who have limited service capability. Price pressure will continue to be severe, and return on sales often little above break-even. Tier 2 suppliers often cannot afford expensive inspection and test resources, so defect levels will continue to be relatively high, often in the range 1,000–2,000 ppm (i.e. 1–2 per cent). This will present challenges for tier 0.5 suppliers, who must also guarantee delivery reliability to the assembly track, and a module that fits perfectly at all times.

As an example of tier 0.5 evolution, the joint venture between Canada's Magna International and Japan's CalsonicKansei ('Magna Kansei') produces the complete fascia ('cockpit module') for the Nissan Micra at a new facility close to Nissan's Washington plant in northeast England. Sales of the joint venture have almost trebled as it assumes responsibility for fixed assets and capital employed. CalsonicKansei designed, developed and tested the Micra from a Nissan-engineered concept design. Co-location of supplier engineers at the Nissan development HQ in Atsugi City meant that Nissan product development teams supervised the design and development process. Magna Kansei assumes responsibility for parts it makes itself, for sourcing externally made parts, and for final module assembly and shipment JIS to the Nissan plant. There are 32 tier 2 suppliers: 18 are *imposed*, where Nissan sets the price and commercial details. The rest are *nominated* by Magna Kansei. This effectively limits the amount of integration that can take place at the design stage. Imposed suppliers that have been selected mainly on price act as barriers for improvement of quality capability. The process of module production has in reality changed little from that originally used by Nissan.

(Source: Harrison, 2000 and 2004)

Question

1 Summarise the advantages and risks to suppliers who want to achieve 'tier 0.5' status.

9.2 Partnerships in the supply chain

Key issues: What are partnerships, and what are their advantages and disadvantages?

Generally, cooperative relationships or 'partnerships' have been characterised as being based upon:

- the sharing of information;
- trust and openness;
- coordination and planning;
- mutual benefits and sharing of risks;
- a recognition of mutual interdependence;
- shared goals;
- compatibility of corporate philosophies.

Among these, perhaps the key characteristic is that concerning the sharing of information. This should include demand and supply information. Chapter 8 showed how collaborative planning is being used to share information between retailers and manufacturers.

Contained within the term 'partnership' are a number of types of partnership 'styles'. Three such types of partnership are cooperation, coordination and collaboration. These types of partnership are characterised in Table 9.1.

9.2.1 Economic justification for partnerships

Entering into a partnership with a company, to whatever extent, implies a transition away from the rules of the open marketplace and towards alternatives. These different structures must demonstrate benefits otherwise they will not deliver competitive advantage.

Open market relationships are typified by short-term contracts, arm's length relations, little joint development and many suppliers per part. Observing that Japanese practice – and consequently the 'lean' model of supply differs significantly from this – indicates that other, non-market mechanisms must be operating.

The Japanese tend to infuse their transactions with the non-economic qualities of commitment and trust. These characteristics are important in successful partnerships. While this may increase transaction costs and risks, it appears that the 'non-economic qualities' help to secure other economic and strategic advantages that are difficult to achieve though the open market system.

9.2.2 Advantages of partnerships

Within partnerships, savings come in the form of reduced negotiations and drawing up of separate contracts, reduced monitoring of supplier soundness, including supply quality, and increased productivity. These are accompanied by strategic advantages of shortened lead times and product cycles, and conditions amenable to longer-term investment.

These advantages, however, need to be set against the problems that can be associated with the introduction of commitment and trust.

Table 9.1 Characteristics of partnership types

Partnership type	Activities	Time horizon	Scope of activities
Cooperation	Fewer suppliers Longer-term contracts	Short-term	Single functional area
Coordination	Information linkages WIP linkages EDI exchange	Long-term	Multiple functional areas
Collaboration	Supply chain integration Joint planning Technology sharing	Long-term with no fixed date	Firms see each other as extensions of their own firm

9.2.3 Disadvantages of partnerships

Some of the examples of potential disadvantages of partnerships include the following:

- the inability to price accurately qualitative matters such as design work;
- the need for organisations to gather substantial information about potential partners on which to base decisions;
- the risk of divulging competitively sensitive information to competitors;
- potential opportunism by suppliers.

In the long term, additional factors occur when companies enter into partnerships. With the outsourcing of the R&D of components and subsystems, buyers benefit from the decreased investment they have to make. Working with suppliers who fund their own R&D leads to their earlier involvement in new product development where buyers benefit from suppliers' ability to cut costs and develop better-performing products. This scenario leads to greater buyer risk owing to dependence on a smaller number of suppliers for designs, and also the potential for opportunism through the smaller number of other companies able to compete with the incumbent suppliers for their work.

Activity 9.2

Consider the reasons why a company would wish to enter into a partnership with a customer or supplier. List the advantages and disadvantages you can think of.

9.3 Supply base rationalisation

Key issue: **What are the drivers for reducing the numbers of direct suppliers?**

Integrating a supply chain means that a focal firm's processes align with those of its upstream and downstream partners. It becomes impractical to integrate processes of the focal firm with the processes of a substantial inbound network of suppliers. Instead, high-intensity relationships can be managed with a limited supplier base. Such considerations argue for the appointment of a limited number of lead suppliers, each responsible for managing their portion of the inbound supply chain. Clearly one of the concerns for logistics management is the criteria by which lead suppliers are chosen.

9.3.1 Supplier management

Supplier management is the aspect of supply chain management that seeks to organise the sourcing of materials and components from a suitable set of suppliers. The emphasis in this area is on the 'suitable set of suppliers'. The automotive case study above explains some of the considerations in this process, as does the Global Lighting case in Chapter 2 (case study 2.3).

Generally, companies are seeking to reduce the numbers of suppliers they deal with by focusing on those with the 'right' set of capabilities. The extent to which companies have undertaken this and have tiered their supply chains is exceptional. Even in the early 1990s, two-thirds of companies were reported to be reducing their supplier base. Anecdotal accounts of the reductions abound. For example, Sun Microsystems was reported to have consolidated the top 85 per cent of its purchasing spend from across 100 suppliers in 1990 to just 20 a few years later.

Activity 9.3

Consider an organisation of your choice: have its major customers consolidated their supply base over the past five years? If so, by how much? What criteria did these customers use to decide which companies to keep and which to 'demote' to a lower tier?

9.3.2 Lead suppliers

While true single-sourcing strategies are the exception rather than the rule, the concept of the *lead supplier* is now widely accepted. Over the past 10 years many large companies have consolidated their supplier base. In some cases, the number of direct suppliers has been reduced by more than 1,000. However, many of the original suppliers still contribute to the OEM's products, but they now do so from lower tiers. The responsibility for managing them now lies with the suppliers left at the first tier. In some cases this responsibility is new and has had to be learnt.

Activity 9.4

Has the position of your selected organisation changed in the supply chain? If it has risen up the supply chain, or remained at the same tier while others were 'demoted', what new capabilities had to be developed? If it was demoted, why did this happen? Was it a good thing or a bad thing to happen?

9.4 Supplier networks

Key issue: What are supplier associations, and the Japanese keiretsu?

Supplier networks can be formal or informal groups of companies whose common interest is that they all supply a particular customer, usually an assembler or tier 1 supplier. Three such networks are considered here:

- supplier associations;
- Japanese *keiretsu*;
- Italian districts.

9.4.1 Supplier associations

Aitken (1998) defines a supplier association as:

> **the network of a company's important suppliers brought together for the purpose of coordination and development. Through the supplier association forum this company provides training and resource for production and logistics process improvements. The association also provides the opportunity for its members to improve the quality and frequency of communications, a critical factor for improving operational performance.**

Supplier associations may be traced back to the late 1930s with the oldest known group being one linked to Japanese automotive manufacturer Toyota. This early group consisted of 18 suppliers producing basic commodity items such as screws, nuts and bolts. These suppliers formed the group for the benefit of themselves. The Toyota organisation itself did not perform an active role in the beginning of the association. However, the distant role of Toyota was to change, as raw materials became scarce during the Second World War. As part of wartime control by the Japanese government, small and medium-sized firms were directed to supply larger firms, which were being utilised as distributors of raw material by the government. Prescribing the flow of materials forced the movement of scarce raw materials to key manufacturers. Through this direct interventionist approach the government tried to force assemblers and the subcontractors to work together to increase the efficiency of the supply chain.

The policy employed by the government therefore encouraged assemblers to establish links with suppliers to ensure component supplies. The carrot and stick approach of the government assisted the foundation of several associations. The institutionalist approach by government succeeded in determining the future structure of the supply chain for Japanese automotive companies. Japanese car assemblers changed their *modus operandi* to align with the prevailing governmental coercive isomorphic forces, thereby obtaining social legitimacy. However, it was not until the early 1940s that assemblers began to recognise the potential benefits of becoming active members of the associations. In 1943 Toyota became interested in the management of the association. Through the provision of management support Toyota started to develop and improve confidence and trust between members and itself.

There can be many improvement objectives of a supplier association, and these will vary between associations and industry sectors. Research has identified 10 primary objectives for establishing and developing an association, as shown in Table 9.2.

Table 9.2 Primary objectives for establishing and developing supplier associations

Objective	Rationale
The provision of manufacturing tools and techniques such as JIT, *kanban* and TQM	*Improve knowledge and application of best-practice tools and techniques within the supply base*
Produce a uniform supply system	*Remove muda (waste) from the system, then standardise process management in all parts of the supply chain*
Facilitate flow of information and strategy formulation	*The assembler assists the suppliers in formulating an improvement strategy by providing best-practice information*
Increase trust between buyer and supplier	*The result of gaining improvements in the first three objectives is an improvement in trust*
Keep suppliers and customers in touch with market need	*Assemblers aid their suppliers in understanding the needs of the customer through sharing market intelligence, sales plans and development opportunities*
Enhance reputation of assembler within supply base	*Assemblers attempt to prove to their suppliers that they are worth dealing with*
Aid smaller suppliers	*Some supplier associations are established to aid smaller associations who could not support the development or improvement programmes necessary to achieve world-class manufacturing standards from their own internal resources*
Increase length of trading relationship	*Through supporting suppliers in the development of their operations the assembler needs to invest resource. Through committing resource the assembler increases the asset specificity of the supplier and it is therefore important that the relationship is maintained*
Sharing development benefits	*The association forum supports not only supplier–assembler improvements but also supplier–supplier knowledge sharing*
Providing examples to suppliers of how to develop their own supply base	*The performance of the entire supply chain is improved by cascading supply chains management techniques into it*

CASE STUDY 9.2   Supplier association

A major supplier of digital telecommunications systems, which we shall call 'Cymru', had established a successful manufacturing plant in Wales. The European region had been restructured into five customer-facing divisions, which would provide large customers with a single point of contact for integrated solutions. This would in turn focus operations by key account, and boost Cymru's commitment to quality and customer satisfaction. Cymru's big customer was TELE, a national telecommunications service provider. Following deregulation of markets in Europe, TELE started to buy telephone handsets in the global market at prices that were well below those of Cymru. A two-year contract was replaced by a four-month contract, and call-off quantities became much more uncertain for Cymru and its suppliers.

In order to compete, Cymru decided that it would have to improve customer service in terms of availability, speed of new product introduction and cost. A new logistics programme was conceived whereby Cymru bypassed TELE's internal distribution structure and delivered direct to TELE's customers. This meant that TELE carried no inventories and that Cymru took over the distribution task with superior service levels. TELE signed a five-year deal with Cymru, and both parties enjoyed better margins.

In order to support the better service levels, it was essential that Cymru's supply base was integrated into the new logistics programme. This meant that the relationship style (Figure 9.1) would need to be moved from arm's length to strategic. As the procurement manager commented:

> I quickly realised that the old way of communicating on a one-to-one basis would no longer work. I'd never get round the suppliers quickly enough to get them all in a mindset of what had to change and when.

Suppliers had previously been informed of future plans on a 'need to know' basis through their organisational 'gatekeepers' in the purchasing department at Cymru. New work was put out to tender, and the lowest-price bid secured the business.

Setting up a supplier association was viewed as the best way to address the needs and timescales for changing the supply chain. Suppliers could be involved simultaneously in reducing lead times from two weeks to two days (receipt of order from TELE to delivery at end user's site). This would be achieved through improved responsiveness, both inbound and outbound. Far Eastern competitors would be unable to match such service levels and total logistics costs.

In setting up the supplier association, priority was given to suppliers who provided parts for final assembly of the telephone, especially those who made colour-related and mechanical parts which would have maximum impact on lead-time reduction. Seven tier 1 suppliers and one tier 2 supplier agreed to take part, and the network is shown in Figure 9.5.

The Cymru supplier association was therefore formed from a wide variety of companies, in terms of both size and industry sector. In a marked break with the past, Cymru kicked off the association with an inaugural meeting that presented confidential product development and market information. The aim of the association was 'to promote best practice, improve overall supply chain performance and support product development'. This was to be achieved by self-help teams committed to sharing knowledge and experience in an open and cooperative manner. Many suppliers were concerned that the association was being formed 'as a disguise for margin reduction', and were reassured when Cymru insisted that the main task was cost reduction. More open communications and an emphasis on mutual cost reduction were seen by suppliers as essential foundations for the new association.

The initial activity was to benchmark all members to 'gain an understanding of the strengths and weaknesses of current processes and practices relative to a best practice model'. Areas for benchmarking were those that Cymru had itself established already as competitive priorities. They were:

- *quality*: ppm of components received, goods produced and goods shipped;
- *productivity*: value added per employee, throughput and operation times;

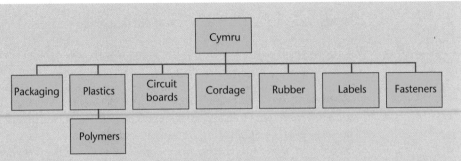

Figure 9.5 Cymru supplier association

- *delivery*: percentage of deliveries on time to customer and from suppliers;
- *stock turns*: stock turn ratio;
- *continuous improvement*: improvement plans, team activities and employee development programmes.

The results of the benchmarking process stimulated much interest among the suppliers. The account manager of one of them commented:

> Benchmarking is very important. We need to know from the customer what he thinks of us. How do we rate against other suppliers in the association? I want to know because it could be I've got something to learn from another supplier.

Following the benchmarking phase, suppliers met every quarter to formulate strategy, share market and product development information, and share plans for implementing best practice. The new plans were then deployed within individual supplier companies by training workshops. In turn, these plans spawned improvement projects aimed at achieving the competitive priorities.

(Source: Aitken, 1998)

Question

1 The supplier association described above eventually collapsed. What causes do you think might have led to this collapse?

9.4.2 Japanese *keiretsu*

One of the Japanese business structures that has received interest from Western business is the *keiretsu*. *Keiretsu* is a term used to describe Japanese business consortia based on cooperation, coordination, joint ownership and control.

The *keiretsu* possesses the particular characteristic of having ownership and control based on equity exchanges between supply chain members. Despite the complexities of their ownership structure, *keiretsu* represents a supply chain model that helps to explain the organisation of most companies in the automotive and electronics sectors in Japan.

The supply chain *keiretsu* is a network in which activities are organised by a lead firm. The typical supplier networks of large automobile and electronics firms are managed and led by the major assemblers, as shown in Figure 9.6.

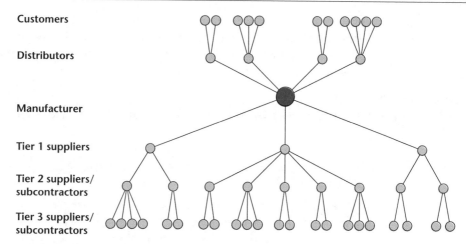

Figure 9.6 Japanese *keiretsu* structure
(Source: Aitken, 1998)

Keiretsu occurred as a result of the strategy in the 1960s of assemblers out-sourcing subassemblies to increase capacity. The *keiretsu* became instrumental in developing the pyramidal structure of the supply base with its tiered arrangement to ensure that the assembler only works directly with a reduced number of suppliers. These suppliers in turn take responsibility for managing the next level down, and so on. The tiered *keiretsu*-style of arrangement has now become the favourite supply structure in the motor industry worldwide.

Activity 9.5

Brazilian-born Carlos Ghosn was despatched to Nissan after Renault took a 36.8 per cent stake in the Japanese car maker in 1999. What he has done in turning round Nissan's €15bn of debt and chronic losses has sent shock waves through Japanese business thinking. One of his main targets for change has been the *keiretsu* system, which he described as a 'gross waste of capital'. Ghosn has broken up Nissan's *keiretsu* system, and is reducing the number of suppliers from 1,200 to 600. Masaaki Kanno, head of economic research at JP Morgan's Asian office, is quoted as saying: 'While many people in Japan realised this system should be changed, it has taken a foreigner to change it. I am not exaggerating when I say Ghosn is a hero in Japan now. People believe that he has saved Nissan from death.'

The system that has acted as a model for Western automotive inbound logistics is being dismantled by Nissan. Is this anomalous?

9.4.3 Italian districts

A third way of organising supply partnerships has been popularised and led by industrial districts in Italy (Becattini, 2002). Porter (1990: 210) commented on the strengths of the Italian ceramic tile 'cluster' in the Sassuolo district in his *Competitive Advantage of Nations*. Producers benefited from 'a highly developed set of suppliers, support industries, services and infrastructure', and the geographic concentration of firms in the district 'supercharged the whole process'. Districts are characterised by hundreds or even thousands of small, family-owned firms with a handful of employees working single shifts. The great majority of firms are led by entrepreneurs who are craftsmen, often relying on the most basic planning and control tools. Concern currently focuses on the ability of districts to adapt to changes in global competition, as case study 9.3 explores.

| CASE STUDY 9.3 | Supply chain internationalisation in the Macerata shoe district |

The National Association of Italian Footwear Manufacturers (ANCI – www.anci-calza-ture.com/) explains:

> The success of the footwear sector in Italy is linked to an enterprising spirit and to the structure of the sector. The structure is a 'web' of raw material suppliers, tanner-ies, components, accessories, machinery manufacturers, model makers and design-ers. This has resulted in a territorial concentration of firms and the formation of shoe manufacturing districts such as Tuscany, Venetia and Lombardy. The leading position of the Italian shoe industry is due to superior product quality and high levels of inno-vation.

Figure 9.7 shows two products from the ANCI website.

 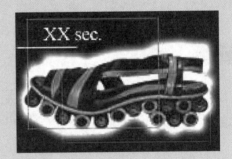

Figure 9.7 Italian style from ANCI website

The Macerata shoe district is not only the largest in Italy, but also the largest con-centration of producers of shoes and accessories in Europe. There are more than 4,000 firms employing 33,000 workers, with combined sales of over €2.5bn. The district is export-oriented, with more than 70 per cent of production going abroad – mainly to Germany, the United States and increasingly to Russia.

District firms are mostly small family businesses with maybe 15 or 20 employees, but there are also a few larger firms with internationally recognised brands. The district leader, Della Valle Group, produces high quality shoes and bags, matching a classic style design with comfort and a sporty look. Traded on the Milan Stock Exchange, it has sales of €360m, and has developed strong international brands – such as Tod's, Hogan and Fay, plus a growing network of directly owned stores. Leading positions in specific market niches are occupied by Fornari (focused on the female teenager trendy shoes with its brand Fornarina), and by Falc (specialising in children top-quality shoes under Falcotto, Naturino and Rasker brand names). Top fashion firms such as Prada, Dolce & Gabbana and Hugo Boss have signed licensing agreements with Macerata district firms for the production of their shoe collections.

The shoes district has developed as an integrated supply network, offering the vast and competitive range of components and equipment required for making shoes – from leather processing to soles, from cutting machinery to packaging. Logistics is simplified by the geographical concentration of firms in the district and the personal knowledge and trust that characterises relationships among district entrepreneurs. Flexibility by the small firms enables the ups or downs of fashions to be met.

Since the 1990s, however, the network has had to come to terms with an outsourcing trend to low-labour-cost countries that is always a threat to mature and labour-intensive industries in developed economies. As a result, production of low-cost shoes has been almost fully outsourced, first to eastern Europe and then to the Far East. In low price product ranges, district companies retain only high-value activities of design, marketing and distribution in the Macerata district.

Outsourcing has also affected the core district products in medium- to high-quality footwear. Here, however, foreign partners are involved only in less complex tasks to preserve Italian style and quality. The result is an increasingly widespread network. Processed leather is brought into the district after initial processing in Asia (mainly India and China). The leather is then checked, cut and prepared to be sent to eastern Europe for further processing (mainly to Romania and Albania for sewing and hemming). Prepared leather is returned to the district for finishing and assembly. Such partial outsourcing – called outward processing traffic – preserves the high-quality standards of district shoes while cutting down on costs.

This makes logistics a critical activity. Transportation costs per unit have been increased, and responsiveness has been put at risk. This is of particular concern to a business that is linked to fashion, where season collection and sales campaign deadlines cannot be missed. Increasing inventories and lot sizes is not an effective answer to the longer lead times. Most district firms offer differentiated products based on fashion trends, and would therefore face a high risk of mark-downs at the end of season. Therefore, firms normally order only 25–30 per cent of forecast requirements for a seasonal collection from their suppliers. Orders for the rest of the collection are made in line with incoming orders from distributors and boutiques.

The new international network has become so complex that even large companies find it difficult to manage. Leading district firms are tackling logistics issues through increased information processing capabilities and through advanced services from logistics service providers. In order to manage a production network spanning from nearby district suppliers to eastern Europe (mainly for shoes) and China (for clothing), Fornari has installed SAP–AFS (Apparel and Footwear Solution). This new ERP system has allowed the company to improve visibility over production planning and to tighten control over suppliers. Fornari has outsourced outbound logistics, and is considering a logistics platform to handle information exchange for district subcontractors and foreign suppliers to reduce costs and improve responsiveness to European customers.

However, most district companies are not large enough to become attractive propositions for IT or logistic service providers. While they cannot afford to lose outsourcing opportunities, these small firms risk being unable to manage the more complex net-

▶

works that result. Therefore the District Committee is supporting development of a new logistic approach through its service company and through regional incentives. In June 2003 SCAM (a region-owned service company) activated a district portal (www.italian-mark.com) involving more than 100 companies, with a focus on B2B relationships and on order management. Under discussion is a shared logistics platform that is able to offer stock management, order preparation and transport services.

In spite of the importance of logistics, most district entrepreneurs do not fully support the potential advantages of sharing outsourced services. Since they lack the accounting tools for getting a complete picture of logistics costs, they do not perceive logistics as a competitive weapon. They do care about emergencies when a rush order is required or when a planned delivery is late, but solving such emergencies becomes more difficult when distant foreign partners are involved. A radical change in international supply chain management cannot be limited to the set-up of new infrastructures and new services but will also require cultural change that, led by larger firms, changes the mindsets of district entrepreneurs.

(Source: Professor Corrado Cerruti, University of Macerata)

Question

1 Analyse strengths and weaknesses of the Italian shoe district logistics model.

9.5 Supplier development

Key issue: **How can upstream supply processes be integrated to improve material flow?**

One of the keys to increased responsiveness in the supply chain is a high level of integration with upstream suppliers. Analysis of the supply chain often shows that product lead time is usually measured in weeks rather than days. This is caused by excessive inventories of raw materials, packaging materials and intermediate products being held upstream of the final point of manufacture. Not only does this represent a cost burden, it also increases the P-time of the supply chain as a whole.

Where suppliers appear unable to make improvements, or fail to do so sufficiently quickly, customers who feel their own performance is being hampered – yet remain committed to the relationship with the supplier – often seek ways to remedy the situation. Many buying firms actively facilitate supplier performance and capability through supplier development. This typically results in activities aimed at developing and improving overall capabilities and performance of the supplier towards the goal of meeting and serving the needs of the customer.

Supplier development consists of any effort of a buying firm with a supplier to increase its performance or capabilities and meet the buying firm's short-term or long-term supply needs. Unfortunately the temptation for buyers to gain short-term advantage still exists in supplier development to the detriment of long-term partnerships. Also, meeting the needs of buying firms is not necessarily linked to development that would enhance overall supply chain competitiveness.

Therefore care must be taken not to lose sight of end-customer needs in the transactions between specific pairs of companies.

Various trends are observable as leading-edge companies seek to improve their management of the upstream supply chain, including:

- integrated processes;
- synchronous production.

9.5.1 Integrated processes

A key focus of supplier development should be the alignment of critical processes: that is, new product development, material replenishment and payment. This alignment needs to consider collaborative planning and strategy development.

It is perhaps the concept of joint strategy development that distinguishes integrated supply chains from mere 'marriages of convenience'. While the customer will always be pre-eminent in the determination of joint strategic goals, involvement of large suppliers in this process benefits all parties.

Process integration can be enhanced through the creation of *supplier development teams*. The purpose of these teams is to work with suppliers to explore ways in which process alignment can be achieved: for example, seeking to establish a common 'information highway' between the vendor and the customer, or working to establish common product identification codes. Nissan in the United Kingdom reports that supplier development teams have been a significant element in its success in creating a more responsive supply chain.

9.5.2 Synchronous production

Linking upstream production schedules with downstream demand helps to improve material flow. The creation of a 'seamless' network of processes aims to dramatically reduce inventories while greatly enhancing responsiveness. The Japanese concept of *heijunka* seeks coordination of material movements between different processes in the supply network. Transparency of information upstream and downstream is essential for synchronisation to work. For example, the supplier must be able to access the customer's forward production schedules, and the customer must be able to see into the supplier's 'stockroom'. The *virtual supply chain* envisages partners in the chain being linked together by a common information system, so that information replaces the need for inventories.

Another approach that seeks to improve synchronous supply chain processes is that of *vendor-managed inventory* (VMI). Here, the supplier takes responsibility for the management of the customer's inventory (see section 6.3, Chapter 6). The advantage is that a large element of uncertainty in the supply chain is removed through shared information. The need for safety stock can thereby be dramatically reduced.

9.6 Implementing partnerships

Key issue: **What are the barriers to achieving partnerships in the supply chain?**

The goal of 'partnership' often proves to be elusive to individual customer–supplier links within supply networks. Despite a recognition of the need for partnership, there are many obstacles to overcome if the concept of process alignment is to realise its full potential within a given network. It is therefore helpful to understand the inherent difficulties in order to gauge how the goal of 'partnership' might be achieved.

A transition route from open market negotiation to collaboration, along which relationships evolve, is shown in Figure 9.8. Before seeking to develop a partnership it is necessary to determine where the most appropriate point along this path is for your relationship with another company. There is no point in pursuing a partnership just because this is further along the scale. In some cases, as described earlier, open market negotiations will be most appropriate anyway.

The transition from multiple sourcing and arm's length negotiation of short-term, purchase-price-allocated contracts to one based on cooperation, collaboration, trust and commitment requires a supply chain process to be put in place which needs designing, developing, optimising and managing. A vital step in achieving this is to ensure that supplier development and purchasing teams are fully involved in the change.

Failure to do this often leads to purchasing executives undertaking behaviour incompatible with fostering successful supply chain partnerships. While many are familiar with – and voice support for – partnerships, in practice their approach and practices are not supportive. Barriers that have been identified include the following:

● There is an inappropriate use of *power* over the supply chain partner.

● Buyers focus on their own company's *self-interest*.

● There is a focus on the *negative implications* of entering into partnership.

● While buyers value trust, commitment and reliability, they continue to be *opportunistic* and seek gains at their partner's expense.

● *Price* is viewed as the key attribute in evaluations of suppliers.

These barriers, which are explained below, show that the decision criteria used by buyers retain a legacy of the traditional approach where the choice of lowest price remains the most defining characteristic. Unless such behaviour is changed, it prevents supply chain relationships from developing beyond a crude application of commercial power, where the free market is used to instil discipline and promote a supply base in which it is assumed that the fit survive. An explanation of the above barriers is as follows.

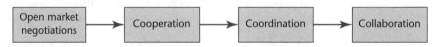

Figure 9.8 The transition from open market negotiations to collaboration

Power

The ability of one member in the supply chain to control another member at a different level can be detrimental to the overall supply network, and can provide a source of conflict. Conflict is clearly associated with power, arising when one organisation impedes the achievement of the goals of another. For example, in retailing, shelf space is a resource that has potentially conflicting implications for the retailer and for its suppliers. The retailer looks for maximum return on space and contribution to its image, while the supplier seeks maximum shelf space, trial for new products and preference over competitors.

Self-interest

Companies face difficulties in establishing and maintaining supply chain partnerships. Even in the automotive industry, often considered the supply chain exemplar, companies keen to implement single sourcing still continue to multi-source, particularly for non-critical items and commodity items. They rarely enter into collaboration even when the customer is dependent on the supplier – that is, when the product is strategically important and alternatives are limited – and instead set their self-interest higher than the need to act according to common best interest.

Focus on negative implications of partnership

Buyers consider the benefits gained through heightened dependence on a smaller number of suppliers less favourably, and tend to highlight the risks. Buyers also consistently view the cost-saving aspects of supply chain management as more important than the revenue-enhancing benefits.

Opportunism

An issue that prevents partnerships from enduring appears to be the gap between the strategic requirements of long-term partnerships and tactical-level manoeuvring – in particular, opportunism. It is a problem to resolve this, given that the dimensions that characterise close working relationships also provide both opportunity and increased incentive for opportunistic behaviour. This is caused when partners cannot easily obtain similar benefits outside the relationship and when specialised investments have been made. Buyers often assume that suppliers will take advantage if they become too important, and as such act to prevent this. The consequences for the partnership relationship come second in their considerations.

Focus on price

The focus on price may be due in some part to buyers having trouble valuing matters such as know-how, technological capability, a particular style of production or a spirit of innovation, and therefore being unable to price them accurately. Their concern that suppliers may act opportunistically tends to lead them to avoid entering into areas where these factors prevail. Significantly, one of the areas that feature these traits is that of design and development. It seems that, in this area, buyers find it extremely difficult to measure designer performance or the amount of productive time spent during design, and therefore feel the need to guard against high bids from suppliers.

Summary

What are the different types of relationship in the supply chain?

- Supply chain relationships can vary from arm's length (characterised by a focus on price, and by few points of contact between the organisations concerned), to vertical integration at the other (characterised by integration of processes and by contacts at all levels).

- The choice of the appropriate relationship is helped by recognising that some suppliers are more important than others. One way to segment the supplier base is to use the purchase portfolio index, and to divide suppliers according to strategic, bottleneck, non-critical and leverage characteristics.

- The role of partnership in the supply chain has been described using seven factors: the sharing of information, trust and openness, coordination and planning, mutual benefits and sharing of risks, a recognition of mutual interdependence, shared goals and compatibility of corporate philosophies.

- Three stages of the development of partnerships have been defined: cooperation, coordination and collaboration. The move towards collaborative partnerships is characterised by increases in the time horizon and the scope of activities involved.

How can closer supply chain relationships be implemented?

- Supply base rationalisation seeks to reduce the suppliers with whom an organisation deals directly to a smaller number of strategic suppliers. Rationalisation involves re-tiering the supply chain so that other suppliers are placed under a lead or 'tier 1' supplier.

- Supplier associations bring suppliers to an OEM or tier 1 supplier together for the purpose of coordination and development. They also aim to improve the quality and frequency of communications between members. In practice, association companies benchmark each other and formulate improvement projects aimed at increasing the competitiveness of the overall network.

- *Keiretsu* is the term used to describe the supplier association in Japan. Here, the additional characteristics are that ownership and control of the network are based on equity exchanges between members. *Keiretsu* structures have attracted much recent criticism owing to their relative inflexibility and high cost.

- Districts are a distinctly Italian solution to competitive advantage that involve the clustering of numerous SMEs in a focused network with close geographic distances between partners. Again, flexibility to respond to globalisation issues is proving to be a challenge.

- Improved responsiveness from supply chains is facilitated by integrated processes (including joint strategy determination) and synchronisation (co-ordinated flow facilitated by transparency of information upstream and downstream).

- Barriers to implementation include the inappropriate use of power, self-interest, a focus on negative implications, opportunism and a preoccupation with price.

Discussion questions

1 Consider the use of partnerships with customers to improve competitiveness. Discuss this within a group using the following guidelines:

   a Make a list of companies in your chosen company's industry known to undertake supplier development. This should include all its customers and other companies that are potential customers.

   b Make a list of all the types of development and improvement that your chosen company would like help with.

   c Assemble these lists along the two sides of a grid, following the example shown in Figure 9.9. Mark on the grid where each of the companies is able to provide the necessary help.

   d Examine the grid you have constructed and identify the following:
   - issues requiring help that current customers provide;
   - issues requiring help that only potential customers provide;
   - issues requiring help that no-one provides;
   - customers (current or potential) that provide a great deal of help;
   - customers (current or potential) that provide little or no help.

   e Use these five criteria as the basis for identifying companies that should be valuable in ensuring your company's long-term success. These companies are the ones that should be considered as likely partners.

   f Having identified the likely partners, identify the difficulties in establishing partnerships and the problems in maintaining them.

   g Conclude with the actions that you would undertake to overcome the problems associated with partnerships in order to achieve their advantages.

2 'Supply chain relationships do not mean anything. At the end of the day, it depends entirely on who has the most power. It is the big boys in the supply chain who decide just how much of a relationship there is going to be.'
   Discuss the implications of this statement.

References

Aitken, J. (1998) 'Integration of the supply chain: the effect of interorganisational interactions between purchasing-sales-logistics'. PhD thesis, Cranfield School of Management.

Becattini G. (2002) 'Industrial sectors and industrial districts: tools for industrial analysis', *European Planning Studies*, Vol. 10, No. 4, pp. 483–93

	Companies that help suppliers			
Improvement help required	Company A	Company B	Company C	Company D
ISO 9000	●			
Process improvement		● 	○	
Communication systems		●	●	
Environmental legislation		○	○	●

Key

● Strong positive link

○ Weak positive link

Figure 9.9 **A supplier development grid**

Cooper, M. and Gardner, J. (1993) 'Building good business relationships – more than just partnering or strategic alliances?' *International Journal of Physical Distribution and Logistics Management*, Vol. 23, No. 6, pp. 14–26.

Harrison A.S. (2000) 'Perestroika in automotive inbound', *Supply Chain Practice*, Vol. 2, No. 3, pp. 28–39.

Harrison A.S. (2004) 'Outsourcing in the automotive industry: the elusive goal of tier 0.5', *Manufacturing Engineer*, February/March, pp. 42–5.

Lamming, R. (1993) *Beyond Partnership Strategies for Innovation and Lean Supply*. New York: Prentice-Hall.

Porter, M. (1990) *The Competitive Advantage of Nations*, London and Basingstoke: McMillan Press.

Smart A. and Harrison A. (2003) 'On-line reverse auctions and their role in buyer–supplier relationships', *Journal of Purchasing and Supply Management*, Vol. 9, pp. 257–68.

Syson, R. (1992) *Improving Purchase Performance*. London: Pitman.

van Hoek, R. and Weken, H.A.M. (1998) 'The impact of modular production on the dynamics of supply chains', *International Journal of Logistics Management*, Vol. 9, No. 2, pp. 25–50.

Suggested further reading

Das T.K. and Teng, B.S. (1998) 'Between trust and control: developing confidence in partner co-operation in alliances', *Academy of Management Review*, Vol. 23, pp. 491–513.

Scarborough, H. (2000) 'The HR implications of supply chain relationships', *Human Resource Management Journal*, Vol. 10, pp. 5–17.

Storey, J. (ed.) (1994) *New Wave Manufacturing Strategies: Organisational and human resource management dimensions*. London: Paul Chapman Publishing.

Part Four

CHANGING THE FUTURE

The final part of this book takes a somewhat different approach. It takes the lessons learned in the previous nine chapters and considers how progress can be expected based upon those combined with current leading-edge thinking on logistics. Chapter 10 assesses current approaches to the supply network, and their impact on logistics in several areas such as postponement, modern planning tools and the Internet. The chapter ends with a section on managing change, which is 'where the rubber meets the road'. The management of change is also where many ambitious visions founder, and where every logistics manager should have at least a basic understanding. Finally, a set of diagnostic questions is offered in the Appendix for reflection upon further improvement opportunities in practical environments and logistics thinking. We hope that this will provide input to the process of taking the lessons learned in this book off the page and into practice.

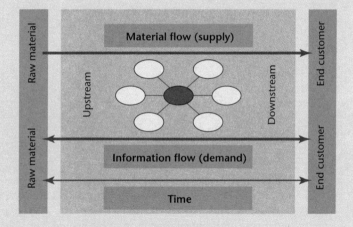

CHAPTER 10

Logistics future challenge

Outcomes

The intended outcomes of this chapter are to:

- collect together the major changes that are affecting supply chain strategies;
- identify how management of the supply chains of the future will be affected by the advance of new structures and reconfiguration of material and information flow;
- explain the role of the Internet in evolving new supply chain strategies;
- list key issues in managing the transition process towards future state supply chains.

By the end of this chapter, you should be able to understand:

- key issues that will affect the way supply chains of the future will be structured;
- the different ways in which supply chains may compete in the marketplace;
- ways of approaching implementation issues.

Introduction

Having reviewed the principles and practices of management and strategy for logistics in the supply chain, this final chapter concludes by considering logistics developments that will challenge our thinking in the years to come. While these developments have an impact now, their significance extends beyond our current capabilities. As a result this chapter has a more forward-looking and exploratory outlook.

The chapter begins by listing principles of the supply network of the future. These are not entirely new; they are principles that have been developed in previous chapters. But taken together as a new way of working they form a formidable challenge. Overall, they have the potential to change the way that supply chains and logistics operations are structured, and place new challenges on the management task.

The overall aim of this chapter is to inform you of advances in thinking that are shaping management and strategy for logistics in the supply chain.

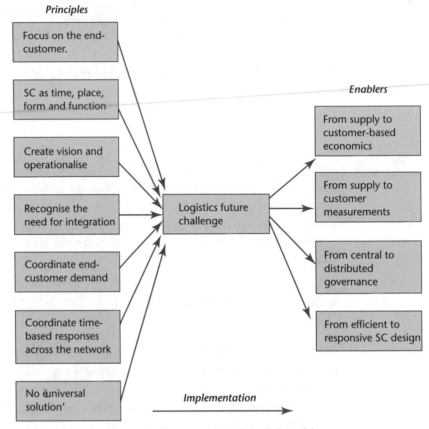

Figure 10.1 Logistics future challenge: principles and enablers

Figure 10.1 summarises the principles which will form logistics future challenges. Realisation of this vision will, we propose, be implemented by means of four enablers. The transformations in the supply chain environment are compared with market challenges leading towards the creation of the agile supply chain. The transition process from left to right is driven by a set of forces that are explained in section 10.4 of this chapter.

Key issues

This chapter addresses four key issues:

1 **The new supply chain environment**: examines three developments that are transforming the flow of materials and information in supply chains.

2 **Management challenge**: organisational alignment (internal integration) and enabling technologies for external integration.

3 **Implementation issues**: considers the forces at work in managing the transition process.

10.1 The new supply chain environment

Key issues: **Seven principles to characterise the new environment of customer responsive supply chains and the four transitions that will help to get us there.**

The single most important set of changes in the supply chain that is already under way is a fundamental shift towards customer-responsive supply chains. Drivers of change in developing the supply network of the future will be customer demand for greater choice and improved value. In parallel, competition between supply chains and the organisations participating in them will increase. Product and technology life cycles are likely to continue to shorten, while demand will be increasingly difficult to forecast. For most product-service propositions, the marketplace will be increasingly turbulent, placing greater pressure on supply chains to respond in an agile manner.

Demand for new products will lead organisations to introduce new products – and to promote existing ones – more frequently in order to maintain or to increase sales. Customers are also likely to demand delivery of goods and services through innovative channels alongside traditional ones.

Competition among organisations will increase due to a combination of factors, notably:

- *Globalisation of supply chains*: while localisation of service, products and distribution remains important.
- *Convergence of low cost computing and low cost communications*: making information integration in the supply chain a more feasible proposition and the achievement of it really a management, rather than a technology, challenge.
- *Increased capability to extend product variety and reduce product life cycles* while remaining cost competitive.

These competitive factors are changing the means by which organisations compete.

These changes in the competitive environment are likely to have a number of consequences. Based on previous chapters, a set of supply chain principles can be put forward as a basis for the future organisational landscape.

Principle I: The supply chain exists to serve the end-customer, not the other way around. Therefore, responsiveness across functional, organisational and geographic boundaries, and speed of flow of goods and information, are key capabilities.

Principle II: The output of supply chain management is not just a physical product, but a combination of time, place, form and function of a product/service proposition.

Principle III: Moving beyond the strategic vision established by the top team is a key challenge for logistics management. Implementing and operationalising the vision are just as important as the vision itself.

Principle IV: A linear view of the supply chain is too simple because it relies on an outdated, internal concept – the focal firm and its immediate neighbours. It fails to engage with the integrated needs of today's market environment.

Principle V: Immediate customers in the supply chain have an essential role to play in communicating, translating and coordinating end-customer demand. They must stop obscuring that demand by batching rules and the like which serve their own selfish ends.

Principle VI: Supply chain priorities are constantly changing and lead to an ongoing need for co-ordinated, time-based responses.

Principle VII: There is no universal 'solution' to supply chain challenges and opportunities.

Putting these principles into place involves four 'transformations', which are shaping the future of supply chain management as more customer-responsive:

- product to customer-based economics;
- supply to customer measurement;
- central to distributed governance;
- efficient to responsive supply chain design and operation.

10.1.1 Product to customer-based economics

Despite all the progress in the last few years on moving from functional organisations to process and supply chain organisations, most firms today are still focused on managing efficient supply of products against customer demand. Cost rationalisation efforts centre on using global sourcing and purchasing to reduce material costs. As a result, supply chain cost reduction has been executed in isolation of customer value and revenue generation. The undesirable outcome is to rationalise service to the most valuable customers. This has been brought about by lack of a clear sense of customer relationship investment opportunities, and the inability to have a constructive discussion with sales and customer service about what services are valuable for which customers and which are not. Figure 10.2 shows how costs and revenue have been spinning in opposing directions. Customer profitability analysis helps dispose of that shortcoming. Customer profitability analysis assesses an organisation's ability to profitably fulfil individual customer orders, and to serve individual customer accounts and distribution channels with current supply chain design and customer service systems. Essentially, this analysis changes the economic starting point from internal costs to working from customer orders upstream.

Figure 10.2 also shows how customer profitability analysis can reveal how 150 per cent of profits are generated by 50 per cent of the customer base, and how 50 per cent of current customers are currently unprofitable. This finding assumes that most traditional accounting systems are very accurate in tracking cost of goods sold (*source* and *make* costs) but underperform in tracking logistics costs to individual customers (*deliver* costs). Once shipment, service and customisation costs are added on a 'per customer' basis, a different profitability curve emerges.

This analysis has several implications, such as:

- service terms and conditions for unprofitable accounts need to be changed, and converted into profitable alternatives;
- the most important customers need more attention, by focusing more customer service efforts on these customers;
- prices should be increased for unprofitable customers, or they should be gradually removed from the focal firm's sale portfolio altogether.

Most importantly, customer profitability analysis enables focal firms to link supply chain efforts to customer value and market opportunity in a way that improves customer relations and revenues in a profitable manner.

10.1.2 Supply to customer measurement

Although there has been progress in moving towards process-based and cross-functional measurement, there is still an overriding focus on measuring supply chain response – as distinct from accuracy in customer response. The fundamental shortcoming in measuring supply chain response is that delivery reliability may be 100 per cent using traditional measurements, but customer value remains unchanged. The key point is that delivery reliability is measured against supplier commitment, not against customer request. In other words, we may deliver exactly when we said we would – but that may not be when the customer wants it! Figure 10.3 shows an example from our research (Godsell and Harrison, 2003), where a fourth-party logistics operator collated and sorted deliveries from suppliers around the world and despatched completed orders to global customers.

Cost and revenue spinning in opposite direrctions

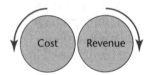

... lead to an unfavourable profit distribution

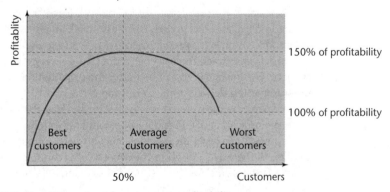

Figure 10.2 **The dynamics of customer profitability**

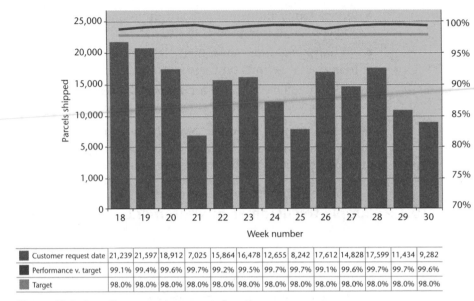

	18	19	20	21	22	23	24	25	26	27	28	29	30
Customer request date	21,239	21,597	18,912	7,025	15,864	16,478	12,655	8,242	17,612	14,828	17,599	11,434	9,282
Performance v. target	99.1%	99.4%	99.6%	99.7%	99.2%	99.5%	99.7%	99.7%	99.1%	99.6%	99.7%	99.7%	99.6%
Target	98.0%	98.0%	98.0%	98.0%	98.0%	98.0%	98.0%	98.0%	98.0%	98.0%	98.0%	98.0%	98.0%

Figure 10.3 Supplier commitment and customer request

(Source: After Godsell and Harrison (2003) 'Supply chain management: putting the end-customer first', *Proceedings of the Eighth International Symposium on Logistics*, Seville)

Customer request in terms of total parcels shipped each period is shown as the vertical columns. However, the 4PL operation measured its performance against its own internally measured delivery target (when parcels *could* be shipped to customer – given current loading), and not against the customer *requested* dates. Internally, its performance was better than target of 97 per cent: externally, performance was about 85 per cent. Who's kidding whom?

Performance reflects adherence to the *internal* delivery schedule that is forced upon customers. Measuring accuracy in responding to customer requests ('when you need it where?') forces a supply chain to be aligned from the customer upstream rather than the other way around. General Electric offers a role model with its Span measurement, as summarised in case study 10.1.

CASE STUDY 10.1

General Electric Span

General Electric is using 'span' measurement across all of its business, ranging from plastics to consumer electronics. Span essentially measures the variation of actual delivery around customer requested delivery; how often were we late or early, how closely do our deliveries track to customer requested delivery dates, in any time window and location? The lower the span, the better the organisation is in meeting exactly the customer requested delivery date. Zero span is the goal.

With span, the measurement is based on the day the customer wants the product. When the order is taken, that date becomes known to everyone – from the first person in the process receiving the castings, circuit boards or any other components from the supplier, all the way through to the service reps who stand next to the customer as the product is started up for the first time. Every single delivery to every single customer is measured and in the line of sight of everyone; and everyone in the process knows he or she is affecting the business-wide measurement of span with every action taken.

The object is to lower the two sides of the delivery span, days early and days late, ever closer to the centre: the exact day the customer desired. Plastics has reduced its span from 50 days to five; Aircraft Engines from 80 days to five. Driving this variation down means that customer service improves and that the supply chain is truly responding to customer requests. It also provides a way to measure contribution of all functions to customer service, forcing alignment internally, from the customer back.

(Source: Company Annual Report)

10.1.3 From central to distributed governance

An organisational governance structure and systems need to support the creation of customer responsive supply chains. As discussed in Chapter 4, one of the key decisions in organising supply chains is whether to centralise or decentralise. Overall management of the supply chain has been approached with a similar trade-off in mind – central control and monitoring or local autonomy and execution. A modern approach to global supply chain governance is that of a centre-led or *governance council* approach. This means sustaining local market or individual business decision making to support responsiveness where needed. It also means that a global council is appointed – in which key decision makers from major regions and businesses come together to craft overall strategy, set direction and coordinate initiatives and services. Very often these councils are supported by head office staff and chaired by a corporate head of supply chain.

CASE STUDY 10.2

Hewlett Packard's supply chain governance council

In order to find a way to balance proliferation of businesses and divisions, high divisional autonomy and complexity in organisation, operations (including redundant operations) and key support processes such as procurement and customer support, HP launched a governance council. The charter that its executive committee set was to implement pan-company efficiency initiatives and uncover supply chain-based revenue opportunities. Goals include: establish and drive a coordinated approach to investments pertaining to opportunities that have a pan-enterprise scope and impact and supporting executive awareness of key initiatives to avoid reinventing the wheel.

This means that the council explicitly does not get involved with initiatives that are specific to an individual business or region; it does not centrally supply chain governance but it does support larger initiatives from which many parts of the organisation can and should benefit. It also provides senior management with a method for signalling, supporting and steering direction on most important opportunities and directions.

Four key operating rules at the council are:

● mandated senior participation;
● focus on enterprise-wide initiatives;
● driving initiative development through divisional sponsorship;
● fund initiatives from divisional budgets.

The latter two are particularly interesting as they help avoid creating a corporate centre approach that can dictate without the businesses caring or paying for it.

(Source: www.hp.com/hpinfo/globalcitizenship/geneport/supplychain/supplyapproach.hjtml)

10.1.4 Efficient to responsive supply chain design and operation

Agility is in many respects the operational and supply chain response to the need to create customer responsive supply chains. It signifies the migration from a focus on internally efficient to customer responsive supply chains. Postponement is a widely used approach to increase responsiveness. Postponement is defined as:

> the delay of value adding activities in the supply chain until customer orders are received. Fulfillment is then executed with the intention of customising product/service combinations when the product is on the way to the customer.

Postponement can be applied at various levels in the supply chain. Based upon a large scale survey of companies in Europe (van Hoek, 2000), Figure 10.4 presents average application levels for postponement along given supply chain operations aggregated across various sectors, countries and supply chain positions. What the overall pattern indicates is that the application of postponement decreases when moving further upstream and away from the end-customer. Downstream, post-ponement applications are ahead of those upstream, with over one-third of pre-delivery packaging activities performed according to end-customer specifications and needs. Obviously, these activities do not generate the greatest level of cus-tomisation but in addition to delivery services (time-tables, etc.) they can tune the logistics link with the end-customer. Further, over one-third of final manu-facturing activities, which lead to further customisation of form and function of products, are also postponed. The overall pattern as displayed confirms the cross-functional relevance of postponement, since it is practised across different func-tions ranging from engineering through supply, through production to pre-delivery activities.

The applicability of postponement differs depending upon operating environ-ments that differ by industry. Figure 10.5 presents the application of postpone-ment across industry sectors from the same study. Respondents were divided into three groups: those who did not apply postponement or applied it to 10 per cent

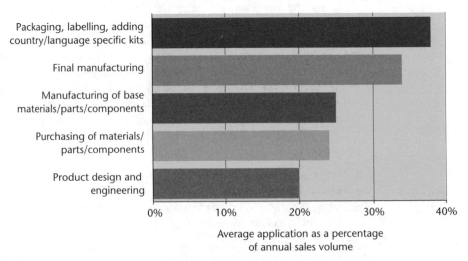

Average application as a percentage
of annual sales volume

Figure 10.4 **Postponement applications across supply chain operations**

or less of sales volume, those with medium-level postponement applications (defined as 11–50 per cent of sales volume), and those with high-level postponement applications (defined as greater than 50 per cent of sales volume). The scores used here are averages across all of the postponement applications listed above.

Overall, postponement applications are highest in the automotive sector, followed by electronics, while food and other industries lag behind. This can be explained by different operating circumstances in these industries, which do not favour high levels of postponement across the supply chain. Food products can be packaged and adjusted to orders but manufacturing, if involved, is more pressured for time and more difficult to organise around standardised discrete modules that can be assembled into customised finished products, as is possible in the other industries. It is more difficult to delay process steps in food production given the continuous nature of most of the processes. In comparison, the discrete nature of production in electronics and automotive is better suited to postponement applications. Automobiles are also sold at a higher level of customisation (through the specification of options, etc.) than electronics products – particularly in consumer electronics where the level of standardisation is higher.

Companies implement postponement for various reasons, several of which are force-order-ranked in Figure 10.6, based upon the same study. Service considerations are most important but in addition to responsive distribution and logistics systems and customisation, continued lowering of integral logistics costs remains important as well.

Postponement was found to be correlated to dimensions of the agile supply chain, which further substantiates its contribution to creating the agile supply chain.

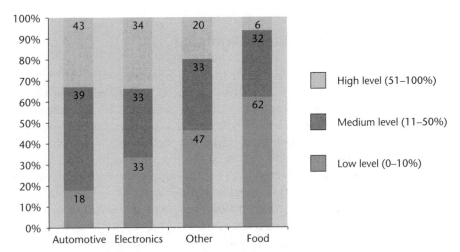

Figure 10.5 Postponement applications by industry

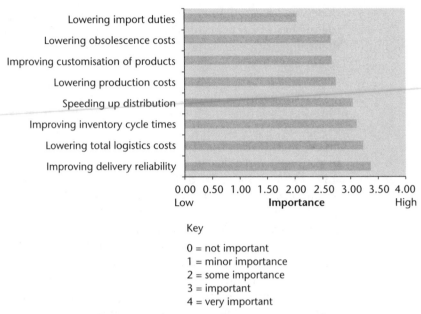

Key

0 = not important
1 = minor importance
2 = some importance
3 = important
4 = very important

Figure 10.6 **Why implement postponement?**

10.2 Two management challenges

Key issues: **Organisational alignment, enabling technologies**

While the new environment of customer responsive supply chains will be shaped on challenging principles, the third of these states that 'implementing and operationalising the vision are just as important as the vision itself'. Here, we review two key management challenges that are central to implementing and operationalising the vision. The first addresses the alignment of the organisation to supply chain goals. The second addresses enabling technologies.

10.2.1 Organisational alignment

Beyond the need to distribute governance within the supply chain, supply chain managers and executives also need to align with peer functions. This however is a formidable and long-lasting challenge. Consider the role of the sales function in the supply chain. Sales generates orders and the supply chain fulfils them – a clear interdependency that requires effective cooperation for success. However, sales often request special services, promotions and new product introductions without first checking that the supply capabilities are in place. For supply chain executives, this means additional costs of complexity and risks of lower efficiency. Such 'surprises' may increase the risk of missing orders due to lack of responsiveness. Again, customer profitability analysis (Figure 10.2 above) is a way to address this challenge. The supply chain also needs to align with other business functions – IT for enabling technologies, R&D for preparing for market introduction of new products and marketing for segmentation. Customer profitability analysis suggests that customer segmentation cannot solely be based on marketing criteria, because customer ordering behaviour has a major impact on fulfilment and ultimately on profitability. Marketing and logistics functions therefore need to align around segmentation schemes that are informed by logistics considerations.

Table 10.1 proposes key considerations in order to move the focal firm towards a differentiated supply chain strategy that aligns supply capabilities to major market segments. Note that achievement of the 'common objectives' of inventory, quality of service and unit cost forces organisational alignment.

Organisational alignment has less to do with supply chain technology and specialist functional expertise. It has much more to do with communication, engagement and management skills. Launching into a technical conversation with sales may be the worst thing to do when the objective is to gain the commitment of a busy sales person. This implies a need to focus on development of effective supply chain managers of the future.

Table 10.1 Organisational alignment considerations

Focus on the end-customer	Organisational issues	Common objectives
Understand the needs of the end-customer. Revisit regularly	Enhance knowledge of the supply chain within the organisation	Incentivise purchasing, operations and logistics on: – Total inventory – Quality of service to end customer (e.g. on shelf availability) – Unit cost
Define customer segments jointly between marketing and logistics	Develop human capabilities through selection cross training and switching between functions	Incentivise sales, marketing and logistics on forecast accuracy and quality of service
Process integration is driven by quality of service to the end-customer. Forecasting and planning are tools to this end	Redesign business processes for flexibility and visibility – IT systems – Logisitics	Ask people to take more risk by continuous stock reduction
Extend integrative thinking to tier 1 customers and suppliers (Figure 8.1) through relationship management	Align the organisation to major end-customer segments to strengthen horizontal business processes	Combine internal measures to drive efficiency with external measures (especially quality of service) to drive effectiveness

10.2.2 Enabling technologies

E-business, ERP and RFID are among dominant enabling technologies. None of these will structurally alter the supply chain, they will, however, need to be used to enhance and enable its effectiveness.

E-business

Electronic business has generated new ways of working, allowing companies to react in real time to changes in the market by:

- gaining more knowledge about their customers;
- increasing the visibility of demand across their supply chains.

The term e-commerce is usually used by the media to mean businesses trading with customers via the Internet, i.e. business to consumer. The hype surrounding 'e-commerce' has resulted in organisations stampeding to have a website and then asking themselves 'what do we do next?' If they are managing to sell to customers then there is the sudden realisation that the organisation's back-office processes and supply chains have to be aligned to meet a new set of customer expectations.

E-business is a term used to cover trading with an organisation's suppliers and business customers, i.e. business-to-business, by electronic means. A feature of B2B is the formation of online trading communities (see for example Ariba (www.ariba.net) and electronic marketplaces. Such structures have been enabled by the explosion of Internet technology and seek to offer cost reductions in procurement of both direct and indirect goods and also in the processing of such transactions. The relationship of these terms in the context of the 'e-supply chain' is shown in Figure 10.7.

Rather than define e-business by the technology, it is more useful to define it by its intent to allow the flow of accurate, timely and rich information. This flow of rich information starts with the customer and is shared with all organisations in the supply chain. It is therefore imperative that managers take every opportunity to understand the implications of electronic business for their own companies and how they can develop an effective strategy to harness it together with an agile supply chain that will support this approach.

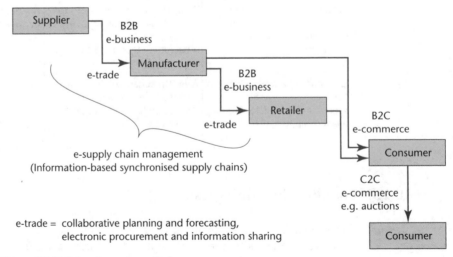

Figure 10.7 E-business terminology

The benefits of *B2B exchanges* to support a focal firm's supply strategy have been somewhat over-promised, but will nevertheless still have a major role to play in future. The theory is that companies can place orders through online exchanges on the web and get interested suppliers from around the world to bid for that order. This enables companies to find capacity in the supply market immediately – possibly from previously unknown suppliers. The very fact of introducing a larger sample of suppliers than would usually bid for the business (Smart and Harrison, 2003) was the main factor in helping the buyer to reduce prices. The bidding mechanism also lowers costs. Exchanges have a low participation threshold as they are web-based – member companies can simply log on.

However, there has been a very fast growth of the number of exchanges. There are many exchanges for each industry, which reduces transparency for that industry. In fact many companies have involved themselves in multiple exchanges, thereby 'spreading their bets' but still leaving some coordination tasks to themselves.

Additionally, the buying behaviour leads to transactional relations, not partnerships. And the auctioning only really works if there are multiple suppliers bidding, this mechanism is typically best used for commodities. Such products are widely available from multiple suppliers as they are broadly specified, and supplier evaluation is more concerned with price than with technological capability – or any other complex metric that might require off-line interaction.

As a result there are two expected future avenues for exchanges; that of low cost or collaborative relations. The first is close to the current role of exchanges, but recognises that it only plays a limited role (perhaps 10–15 per cent) as a part of the supply efforts and does not replace others. The revenue model for these exchanges will have to be reconsidered because of the proliferation of exchanges (challenging scale and coverage of the market) and the focus on one-off orders (that may not generate a sustainable constant revenue stream). The second approach, that of supporting collaborative relationships is a model that requires a migration of the exchange. To support collaboration, different mechanisms other than online reverse auctions (ORAs) with a large supply base are needed. Co-design, joint forecasting and sharing of confidential demand information are amongst functionalities to be developed. The establishment of private networks is currently thought to be more appropriate for that. Case study 10.3 provides a summary of the conclusions of our study into the future of B2B exchanges, which was based on expert opinion for developments up to the year 2010.

CASE STUDY 10.3	The future of B2B exchanges

The future of exchanges as major enablers of supply chain integration is not in dispute. Benefits are already accruing in terms of reduced transaction times and costs, and of facilitation of links between buyers and suppliers in areas like new product introduction, procurement and supply chain management.

However, a number of significant barriers remain to achievement of a 2010 nirvana of IT-enabled supply chains. The e-auction facility promoted in the early days of market places presented buyers with the ability to be able to compare many suppliers and

▶

switch between them. This in turn deterred suppliers from joining such marketplaces and undermined their viability. Our study finds that marketplaces will improve the relationship between buyers and suppliers. Therefore it is important for sellers to join such marketplaces and so help create the critical mass of business that insures viability earlier rather than later. Without such an understanding of how electronic trading can improve relationships with customers, suppliers will continue to be reluctant to participate. The use of IT to support supplier relationship management (SRM) is rapidly gaining in currency, and is expected to become as significant as customer relationship management (CRM). Our study demonstrates how B2B exchanges are starting to form a key part of such an IT-enabled SRM stategy. Current trends towards supplier reduction in many networks are being accelerated by the growth of exchanges, but consolidation would have happened anyway.

Our findings also probed the speed of take-up of B2B exchanges. A key factor was found to be the relative maturity and hence relative consolidation of a given industry. If an industry has a small number of large players – either buyers or suppliers – these players are considered to have a high degree of market power. Players with a high degree of power can influence whether a marketplace is sustainable. For example, if a large buying organisation participates in a marketplace, it is likely that the suppliers to that organisation will also consider participating in that marketplace. Indeed, such suppliers may be required to participate if they wish to continue trading with the buyer, as occurred with adoption of EDI in some industry sectors in the 1970s and 1980s.

The presence of powerful players in an industry is also likely to influence the type of marketplace that will evolve. In industries where the suppliers and buyers are small and fragmented, no individual player is large enough to form their own private marketplace. Third-party public marketplaces or consortium marketplaces are therefore likely to dominate such industries. In industries where there are large players, these may, depending on the influence of the other factors discussed here, form a private marketplace which they use to connect to their own supplier or customer base.

Considerable benefits are forseeable in the area of supply chain integration. Exchanges that were initially procurement-based have developed broader suppy chain management services. In places, it is already evident that exchanges are adopting a '4PL' role, for example by increasing visibility of inventory and demand across supply networks. Greater levels of information sharing and visibility act as a spur to joint problem solving, all of which helps to broaden the relationship between supply chain partners. Trust levels can be expected to increase as exchanges promote a virtuous cycle of problem solving and enhanced relationships.

(Source: Daniel *et al.*, 2003)

Next generation enterprise-wide resource planning systems

Legacy IT systems can lead to fragmentation of information which in turn impedes supply chain performance and the integration company-wide processes and information systems. The main problems with legacy systems are the cost of maintaining them, the risk of turnover amongst key staff who have evolved the system over the years and the invisible costs of not being able to share information up and down the business. Accordingly, software suppliers such as SAP and Manugistics have developed Enterprise Resource Planning (ERP) systems that bring several benefits compared with the legacy systems that preceded them.

ERP system benefits include improved control of the business and reduced costs arising from a faster flow of data and virtual integration across processes. To date, ERP systems have focused on connecting back-office operations such as manufacturing, financial accounting and human resource management into one system. Part of the future for ERP is to expand its capability to incorporate functionality in front-office applications such as sales force automation and customer care. An example of this is the trend to centralisation of customer-care activities into service centres. Standardisation of processes, procedures and data on one site using ERP as a backbone allows the realisation of higher levels of service alongside cost savings through economies of scale.

The challenge for organisations over the next decade does not rest with implementing transactional-based ERP systems. Achieving true enterprise planning with more informed decision in the supply chain requires the implementation of additional Advanced Planning and Scheduling, APS, systems. APS seeks to carry out material requirements planning (MRP – see Chapter 6, section 6.1.4) in ultra-short time frames, and to extend the planning process to scheduling of bottle-neck operations.

Achieving visibility throughout the supply chain is of paramount importance in the search for competitive advantage. The exponential development of Internet technology together with the increased power of the personal computer offers organisations a relatively cheap means of integrating information systems across the supply chain.

The Internet provides a platform-independent communications highway that can be used as a cross-company interface to enable electronic commerce. Thereby, it fosters operationally efficient, connected and cooperative relationships among manufacturers, suppliers and distributors. Using the Internet can provide an easy and cost-effective answer that is available to all organisations in the supply chain. The need for a dedicated electronic link between each partner is thereby made unnecessary.

Technology-driven improvements tend to favour larger companies, concentrating power in the hands of the bigger retail, distribution and manufacturing companies. Classically 80 per cent of volume is channelled through only 20 per cent of suppliers/customers, all handled by automated EDI links with much lower unit processing costs. The remaining 80 per cent of suppliers/customers represents only 20 per cent of volume and yet a massive 50–75 per cent of sales order processing costs (see Activity-based costing in Chapter 3, section 3.3). The vision for the Internet is that this technology could in fact encourage more equitable roles for smaller players and ultimately improve choice, price and availability for customers.

| CASE STUDY 10.4 | Sharing information in the grocery supply chain |

Lack of visibility in the supply chain is a significant barrier to reducing costs and improving service levels, and a major inhibitor of supply chain agility. Major European grocery retailers have sought to overcome these barriers by sharing demand, promotional and ▶

stockholding information with its suppliers via Extranets, limited access Internet-based systems.

Through enabling joint planning, product tracking and more efficient promotions management these systems allow suppliers to replenish more efficiently while improving in-store availability. This makes supply chains more responsive and provides opportunities to reduce lost sales caused by stock-outs.

Tesco and Sainsbury are amongst the companies rolling out such systems to large and small suppliers alike. However, one problem arising from this is the lack of an industry standard resulting in manufacturers having to deal with multiple systems. Although initial work in the area of standard communication protocols, interface standards and data definitions has begun there is still a long way to go before the benefits of such a standardised approach are realised.

Question

1 Visit a supermarket web site such as www.tesco.com and find out about the policy for information exchange with suppliers in that organisation. Is the organisation sensitive to the needs of smaller suppliers?

Radio Frequency Identification devices (RFIDs)

Radio Frequency Identification (RFID) is a product tracking technology that will soon become nearly universally applied. An RFID device, often called a *tag*, can be attached to a piece of merchandise and inform a reader about the nature and location of what it is attached to. Figure 10.8 shows how the reader can relay this information to a management system that can create a picture of what merchandise is where at a level of detail that has not previously been possible.

An active tag has a power source, a passive tag does not. Active tags use a battery, have a limited life and cost far more. The *antenna* is a device that uses radio waves to read and/or write data to the tags. The *reader* manages the interface between antenna and management system. A big advantage of RFID technology over bar-codes is that the tag does not have to be directly in the line of site of the face of the reader. Tags can be detected by readers remotely because the radio

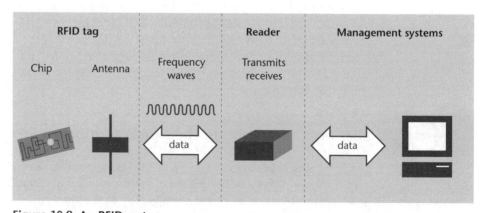

Figure 10.8 An RFID system
(Source: After Beck, 2003)

waves can pass through many materials (see for example www.ems-rfid.com). Experiments are being conducted across a broad range of frequencies – 125 kHz to 2.45 GHz for chip-based tags – but standards have yet to be agreed as this edition goes to press. The *management system* enables data from tags to be collected and sorted for the purposes of management information and action.

The key piece of information held on a tag is the *electronic product code* (EPC, standards for which were developed by the Auto-ID Center). This 'number plate' is unique to each tag. The unique number can then be linked to information about the product to which it is attached, for example about when and where the product was made, where its components came from and shelf-life details. Some tags may hold this additional information on board however the intention is most tags will only hold the EPC and additional information will be stored remotely, on a database linked to the management system.

Readers tell us *what* the product is and *where* it is located in the supply chain. The management system compiles this information and allows us to know *how many* products are present at that location for each time bucket. This translates into dynamic data that allows us to know rates of consumption, and stock data at a given point in time – together with what needs to be done. One can already imagine that such data could enable supply chain planning and control to be transformed.

Product tagging allows for several interesting applications including:

- tracking products throughout the distribution pipeline ('asset tracking') to provide continuous quantities and position by sku in the supply chain;
- tracking products through back of store to the shelf;
- intelligent shelves, whereby 'sweeping' of product by thieves from shelves in store shows up automatically and raises alarm signals;
- registering sales without involving a cashier: a fancied future state is one where shoppers push their trolley past readers that automatically read EPCs for each item in the trolley, and present the bill for credit card payment to the shopper without the need for shop staff to be involved.

Benefits for manufacturers include the ability to understand when products are in the store but not on the shelf (a source of lost sales that manufacturers cannot control), and reducing the opportunities for theft. Retailer benefits include ability to track products in the pipeline against delivery schedules, automation of the check-out process and ability to expand customer information on buying patterns.

Technically, products can be tracked all the way to the customer's home and into it. However, when Benetton planned to track products after the sale, with an eye on returns, it was met with customer resistance on grounds of privacy. This caused Benetton to delay plans for rolling out this idea. The other major hurdle to implementation is the price of the tags. Price/margin levels in most consumer packaged goods tags need to be low enough to be affordable at the individual product level. The '5-cent tag' is widely regarded as a watershed, but doubt is expressed as to whether this is achievable in the next eight years (Homs, 2004). However, with Wal-Mart mandating tag application from its major suppliers, critical mass will be accomplished sooner rather than later. Beyond product level tagging in retail channels, many other applications are already in place at case level, and in higher value goods such as automotive parts.

Further considerations

There are a few additional considerations relating to the Internet and to IT applications in general that should be taken into account. First, technology is not the only answer to supply chain opportunities. Implementation of ERP systems for example, remains primarily within the confines of the focal firm, and does not yet extend through the supply chain. The next section will address enabling technologies in terms of application and integration. In the long run, these are more important than the technological advances themselves.

Furthermore, the Internet has not led to a new 'world order'. The bursting of the e-commerce 'bubble' and failure of many of the 'dot-coms' was largely based on lack of proven business experience and reliance on advances in technology rather than operational expertise. B2B exchanges for example have been widely used in an effort to lower costs by leveraging the bargaining power of buyers. The transactional approach is now being complemented with a stronger and more sustainable focus on using exchanges in collaborative supply efforts, including forecasting and collaborative design. Case study 10.5 is based on a view of future issues for supply chain management and logistics (Zographos, 2003).

CASE STUDY 10.5

Emerging Supply Chain Management and Logistics Concepts

E-commerce is changing the way in which businesses are organised and managed. Supply chain management and logistics functions are greatly influenced by the speed of information flow and the connectivity of supply chain partners afforded by information and communication technologies (ICT). Although a substantial amount of research activity has been accumulated worldwide on issues regarding the potential impacts of e-commerce on supply chain management and logistics operations, there is a knowledge gap concerning the technological, business and institutional implications of e-commerce. Recognising this need the European Commission supported a Thematic Network Project 'Business, Policy, and Research Implications of Logistics in the e-Economy Environment (BPR Logistics)'. The primary objective of BPR Logistics was to identify future and emerging research issues as well as the associated roadmaps for implementing the identified research and technological development (RTD) issues.

The results of this project suggest that emerging supply chain management concepts are characterised by integration, collaboration, synchronisation and the creation of virtual supply chains based on networks of businesses. These concepts impose new logistics requirements:

- integration of enterprise processes;
- information sharing and visibility across the supply chain;
- establishment of collaborative relationships and decision making;
- synchronisation of decisions to real-time events.

However, the current state is characterised by fragmented information and communication systems – both within a focal firm and along the supply chain – isolated decision making, and planning based on historical information. Sharman (2002) depicts the transitions and associated barriers as shown in Figure 10.9.

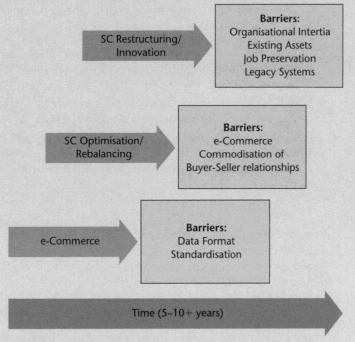

Figure 10.9 Timeframe for supply chain improvement opportunities
(Source: After Sharman, 2000)

The transition from current state to future state means breaking down barriers:

● corporate cultural differences;
● the absence of technological and process standards;
● the lack of information-sharing culture;
● the limited use and knowledge of ICT by small and medium-sized enterprises (SMEs).

The following initiatives and associated research issues were identified for inclusion in the European RTD agenda:

Initiative 1: Develop and apply technological solutions for improving the availability of reliable real time information concerning the flow of goods along the supply chain. The objective of this initiative will be to address these issues:

● Development of low-cost, robust RFID tags that will provide reliable information regarding the location and status of shipments along the supply chain, and of flexible and more advanced tag reading devices.
● Integration of shipment tracking and tracing devices, i.e., RFID tags, with automatic vehicle location and identification (AVL/AVI) systems, and real-time traffic information.

Initiative 2: Develop and apply technological solutions for improving the flow of information related to demand for products/services and availability of inventory/capacity for fulfilling demand along the supply chain. The objectives of this initiative are to:

- develop and apply interfaces that will allow the integration of heterogeneous enterprise resource planning networks (ERPs) along the supply chain.
- integrate real-time information concerning the location and status of shipments (initiative 1), with corporate ERPs across the entire supply chain.

Initiative 3: Develop and apply real time Decision Support Systems for securing flexibility, adaptiveness, and coordination along the supply chain. The objectives of this initiative are to:

- develop and apply fast and efficient optimisation methods for supporting real-time routing and scheduling decisions, taking into account the availability of real-time traffic information;
- develop and apply real-time supply chain performance monitoring systems.

Initiative 4: Develop and assess new organisational structures for efficient supply chain management:

- Identify emerging business models that will capitalise on the use of advanced technologies in order to fulfil the emerging supply chain management requirements.
- Develop and implement methodologies for identifying the impact of corporate cultural differences and new business models.
- Evaluate the effects (and the allocation of costs and benefits among supply chain partners) of technological and business modeling solutions.

Initiative 5: Identify the policy developments that are needed to support the effective and efficient implementation of e-commerce by:

- identifying the role that public bodies should play in the development and dissemination of standards in the field of e-commerce and telematics;
- identifying what is required to assist SMEs to use e-commerce and e-logistics services;
- determining the extent to which e-business logistics is being constrained by regulations governing the trading of goods and services online.

Initiative 6: Evaluate the effectiveness of policies for supporting the sustainable implementation of e-commerce, while reducing externalities to the society at large by:

- studying the likely net effect of B2B and B2C e-commerce on traffic levels and related externalities;
- studying the impacts of e-commerce on land-use and transportation planning;
- identifying the likely social implications of a sharp increase in the volume of B2C e-commerce;
- identifying how growth of online freight exchanges is likely to affect the structure and profitability of the market for freight transport services.

Question

1 Summarise the future state vision contained in this report, and the barriers to achieving this vision.

(Source: Professor Konstantinos Zographos, Transportation Systems and Logistics Laboratory, Athens University of Economics and Business, 2003)

10.3 Implementation issues

Key issues: the transition process, viability of current performance levels, perceived payoff benefits, belief and enthusiasm, the ability to manage change.

Implementing change in businesses is often frustrating and frequently produces disappointing results. The process of change is particularly difficult in supply chains as it has to be undertaken in a coordinated manner across and between a number of organisations. It is therefore important to gain agreement from the top level of all companies involved before wide-scale changes can be made. As an example of the relevance of appropriate implementation approaches, it is well-known that about three out of five third-party logistics outsourcing implementations are discontinued after a year, based upon disappointing progress and accomplishment. Poor implementation skills leads to enormous wasted efforts and stalled progress.

'Where the rubber meets the road' is also the divide between vision and reality. Operationalising for execution is a key task for logistics and supply chain managers. It is often seen as the most crucial organisational task. In the words of one manager: 'we are not short of ideas, but we are also looking for proper execution'. Implementation requires more than a technical skill set. In fact communication, negotiation and convincing skills across functional domains are part of a broader skill set, which logistics managers need to master.

Implementation of large-scale changes across supply chains benefits from the use of project management methods. At the outset, it is necessary to identify the *change objectives* (benefits, time scale) and to define the *scope* of the change project. Defining the scope clarifies the boundary of the project by identifying which areas and processes in the supply chain will be tackled.

In order to implement new ideas, a number of transitional forces need to be harnessed to give momentum to the change project. Figure 10.10 represents a structure that helps to illustrate these forces.

A viable route forward in uncertain circumstances is to initiate exploratory pilot projects, which should be viewed primarily as learning opportunities. Running these as joint ventures with other organisations will assist with the development of understanding.

Waiting for the 'mists of uncertainty' to clear may not be an option given that brave and committed organisations are learning the lessons that trading in the digital era requires being ready to compete unshackled by the vestiges of the traditional business.

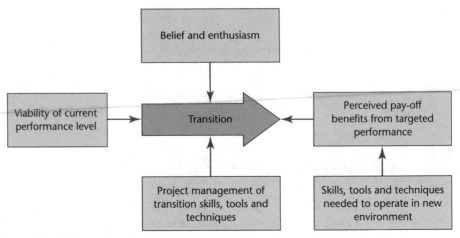

Figure 10.10 Transition forces

10.3.1 Viability of current performance level

The first priority for any organisation must be to transform the *supply* chain into a *demand* chain. This is more than mere semantics: it is a recognition that in tomorrow's marketplace, customers will be looking for even greater value and that the supply chain needs to be designed with the desired *value delivery* objectives in mind. The supply chain is concerned with efficiency. The demand chain is concerned with effectiveness and value provision to the end-customer.

Viability of the current state of performance of the supply chain should be considered in the light of a number of important market changes. These include:

- *Demographics*: for example, an ageing population with more single person households and fewer working people to support growing social costs. Value for money will increasingly be a determinant of customer choice.

- *Time-stressed customers*: as a result of pressures of work and greater commuting, there is less time to shop. The implications for home shopping and delivery are significant.

- *One-to-one marketing and mass-customisation*: the search for individual solutions to customer buying needs requires a means to postpone the final product form and location.

- *The marketplace becomes the 'marketspace'*: development of the Internet and e-commerce are transforming marketing and logistics.

The viability of current processes should be explored in light of new developments that may render them obsolete to establish whether not changing is an option. For example, competitors may be developing and putting into place the right electronic commerce strategy supported by agile supply chains capable of meeting new forms of demand from business customers that will see the demise of many existing companies.

10.3.2 Perceived payoff benefits from targeted performance

An example of a change that could be implemented in order to take advantage of developments in supply chains is to embrace electronic business. In order to gain support for implementing new practices the business must be convinced that there will be sufficient performance benefits from the investment required. While this may be calculated to a reasonable degree of accuracy, there will always be an element of perception in the investment required, the likely benefits and the risk of success. At the end of the day, it is the perception that counts.

The uncertainty inherent in any change project is particularly true in e-business projects. This is an environment of uncertainty where there are no rules or boundaries that organisations can use as references. Instead they are faced with journeys into the unknown while trying to maintain their existing business. It is clear that organisations face an enormous upheaval if they are to reap the potential benefits of electronic commerce.

Undertaking benchmarking projects is a useful way of both quantifying the potential benefits of making a change and of giving inspiration on how the new processes and systems should be designed.

What should be stressed here is that traditionally arguments for change in logistics and supply chains are justified based upon anticipated cost savings. Realising, however, that service is a more fundamental task than cost savings is not always sufficient in the context of an agile supply chain. Although service improvements are usually more difficult to quantify, their revenue-enhancing opportunities and abilities to achieve pre-emptive strikes need special consideration.

10.3.3 Belief and enthusiasm

Belief in the ability to make the transition is essential for success. Tapping into enthusiasm and developing confidence is what motivates people to 'Just do it!' and maintains their self-belief that sees the project through adversity. Key here is the ability of the project manager to communicate belief in the change process with enthusiasm.

10.3.4 Ability to manage change

In order to make the change from the current system to the new one an organisation will need to be able to undertake a number of activities. First and foremost they need to be able to manage the change project. This involves planning the change, organising the resources needed to make the change and managing the application of those resources in order to achieve the necessary outcome.

Additional skills required to change a process include:

● the ability to analyse customer needs;
● the ability to quantify the current process;
● the ability to design the process that will meet customer requirements.

These skills may be present within a company already. If not they can be acquired either through training or through 'outsourcing' them through consultants.

10.3.5 Ability to operate in the new environment

In order to embed the change from the old process to the new the people involved in the organisation must have the right skills, tools and techniques to operate it. Rather than wait until the change has been made, these should be provided in advance so the people are ready to effectively operate the new process from day one.

Managing the new process will require a new set of performance measures to be in place so its efficiency and effectiveness can be assessed. Case study 10.6 tracks the changes made in developing fourth-party logistics service provider capabilities at UPS, and their application to the European operations of Cisco Systems.

CASE STUDY 10.6

UPS Logistics

This case study presents the experiences of UPS Worldwide Logistics in developing fourth-party logistics service provider (4PL) applications. IT capabilities have been used to move the client's supply chain towards greater added value. The 4PL is a supply chain service provider that participates in supply chain coordination more than it does in supply chain operational services. It is highly information-based, and coordinates asset-based players (for example, on behalf of its clients). This implies a great focus on using information and ICT to support supply chain competitiveness. Implementation required a major transition for UPS – which has its origins in express and physical logistics services – towards the creation of supply chains based on operational and strategic applications of information.

The business model of the 4PL, as it has developed with UPS Worldwide Logistics clients, is displayed in Figure 10.11.

Traditionally, various transport and warehousing companies and third-party logistics service providers (TPLs) have provided logistics services to OEMs (phase A). Once a former TPL develops a 4PL role, the supply chain structure changes to phase B in which the 4PL takes over management of material flow on behalf of the OEM. The company takes over logistics problems and starts managing the physical supply of logistics on behalf of the client. An intermediate layer is created coordinating logistics service operations and providing the client with a single point of contact. The company may occasionally extend its role by taking over employees with expertise on the product and/or client–customer interactions in order to build up capability in supply chain processes focused on client–customer satisfaction and expectation management.

The 4PL relationship is typically information-based with few assets. Customer relations that have evolved from TPL origins may have retained some physical assets (such as trucks and warehouses). But the critical factor is a change from an inward-looking mindset based on ownership of hard assets and asset utilisation, to a broader focus on total supply chain effectiveness and process optimisation. The TPL aspects of supply chain services are outsourced to asset-based providers. The role of UPS is then to source

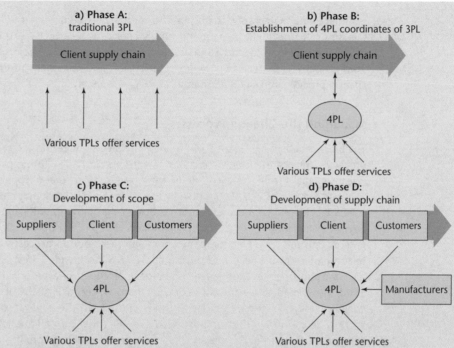

Figure 10.11 **Implementing 4PL with UPS Worldwide Logistics**

and coordinate operations on behalf of the client. The UPS business unit does not engage in day-to-day physical operations, but provides overall process management of the logistics activities being executed by the TPLs. UPS Worldwide Logistics may source services from within UPS itself, but will also source from other TPLs depending upon which provider can offer best overall value (based on service level, quality, consistency and cost) for a given aspect of the client's virtual distribution network. The TPL selection is sometimes partially based upon recommendations or stipulations from the client, but selection is then the responsibility of the client. If the 3PL performs poorly, then the client cannot hold UPS Worldwide Logistics accountable, until such time as the 3PL has been endorsed after a period of performance evaluation. Taking over the logistics problems of the clients does not involve taking over logistics personnel of the client (which competitors are sometimes prepared to do). This would transfer bad habits: removal of bad habits is a primary objective in the step-change process.

In phase C the 4PL starts to develop a supply chain focus and starts to turn into a supply chain manager for the client. The 4PL starts to engage in supplier interfaces by calling off supplies. This can be based upon call-off rules (once inventory goes below a certain level, replenishments are ordered) or on I2-based modelling. Furthermore, the 4PL starts to engage in customer-facing processes. The 4PL can receive and handle first or second level calls from the clients' customers, and order fulfilment activities.

Once the transition to supply chain management has been made, a further move (phase D) is to engage in coordinating manufacturing interfaces. Knowing customer orders and supply operations, the 4PL can coordinate manufacturing inputs, and end up in a position where the client has only a virtual or design and marketing organisation role. The 4PL integrates and runs the entire supply chain on their behalf. This could include implementation of supplementary services in the area of postponed manufacturing. Obviously, there may be battles between the 4PL and the manufacturers as to who should manage the supply chain. In the same way, there may be battles between TPLs as to who is the best player to perform the 4PL role when progressing from phase A to B. In this battle, implementation and management capabilities in the change process are key differentiators among players.

Managing the Change Process

The process outlined in Figure 10.11 is one that reflects unfreezing and re-freezing change processes. Initially the supply chain is unfrozen (phases A–D) with suppliers and different layers separated from the client. Re-freezing, at a greater level of sophistication, is then achieved around the 4PL. How should this transformation in the supply chain be managed?

UPS Worldwide Logistics does not participate in many 'traditional' tender processes anymore. It generally acts as a consultant for clients in supply chain design and re-engineering projects. The company enters into a co-design process, which moves the relation away from a sales and buying effort. UPS Worldwide Logistics will bring logistical and supply chain experience and co-develop the business model for a company. A competitive market fee for consulting is charged because of the anticipated supply chain management business opportunity. But if at the end of the process UPS Worldwide Logistics is not commissioned as a 4PL there is an additional charge to compensate for the effort. This places UPS in a more neutral position. Its initial focus is not on selling but on assisting the client in developing a business model that makes use of existing and best-of-breed capacity in the marketplace. At the same time, UPS seeks to maintain a sense of reality on the motivation of the TPLs, and how to combine them effectively into a 'seamless' collaborative supply chain.

Once the 4PL model is in place (phase B) UPS Worldwide Logistics begins to further interact with various functional areas of the client's organisation. Manufacturing and marketing units for example have to be convinced of the prospect of the 4PL model. In developing the 4PL model into phases C and D, UPS actually starts to implement supply chain management on their behalf. UPS functions as the flexible process 'glue' in the supply chain operation once it is up and running. The change of mindset within the former TPL and, more importantly, within the client's organisation may be time-consuming and demanding. Benefits such as transparency and improved communication systems achieved in phase B are used as a link with other parts of the client's organisation. Cost savings are the traditional argument in the development of logistics services, and in convincing other parts of the client's organisation. When it progresses into supply chain services however, service enhancement becomes more critical. Once the 4PL model has developed initially, moving up the scale becomes more important for sustainable improvements and longer-term relationships. In fact, client relations that do not progress into that area would quite likely terminate because of a longer-term match in joint aspirations between the supply chain owner (client) and manager (4PL).

EXAMPLE CLIENT RELATION: CISCO SYSTEMS

A UPS Logistics 'model' customer for the evolution into a 4PL is Cisco Systems. This relationship has evolved through stages A–D and currently involves both supplier- and customer-facing activities, on top of the coordination and management of all logistics flows in Europe, the Middle East and North Africa.

UPS Logistics receives notification when products are ready for shipment from contract manufacturers and Cisco plant. These products are then collected within 24 hours from one of more than 20 sites around the world, UPS books aircraft into the continent, and receives product in a dedicated 86,000 square foot European logistics centre, owned and operated by UPS.

On the outbound side, UPS selects the carrier and oversees delivery to customers throughout Europe, Middle East and North Africa. Using optimisation software developed in-house by UPS, it consolidates shipments with a common destination. Orders frequently include components from multiple origins, creating the need for a system that can minimise the number of deliveries and reduce congestion at the loading dock.

For outbound shipments, UPS acts as a neutral party with respect to carrier choice. Various carrier algorithms (e.g., service level, price and time in transit) have been populated in the system on a postal code level. The system provides a 'mini RFQ' (request for quotation) to find the best carrier from an approved vendor list every time a new shipment is being presented for a customer. Throughout the process, the order status is communicated to Cisco so that it can provide its customer with continuous access to information. Until an order is fulfilled, a customer has the opportunity to make adjustments to the order, such as changes to delivery date. Every logistics movement registered in the UPS system is also registered immediately in the Cisco system. Annually, UPS Logistics handles more than 1 million boxes for Cisco.

UPS also runs an internal call centre which answers logistics-related questions by Cisco's customer-service department. Recently, UPS has begun pick-and-pack operations, combining accessories such as power cords with Cisco orders. Beyond that, says a logistics manager from Cisco:

The opportunities of the market will drive the relationship that we have with UPS.

Question

1 Based on the UPS experience, what are the essential management of change issues in moving from TPL to 4PL service provision?

Summary

What does 'leading edge' logistics envisage in terms of the supply chain of the future?

- A combination of three factors will change the competitive landscape:
  - globalisation of supply chains;
  - convergence of low-cost computing and low-cost communications;
  - increased capability to extend product variety and reduce product life cycles.
- Seven principles will guide the development of the new competitive landscape:
  - the supply chain exists to serve the end-customer, not the other way around;

- the output of supply chain management is a combination of time, place, form and function of a product/service proposition;
- moving beyond the strategic vision established by the top team is a key challenge for logistics management;
- a linear view of the supply chain is too simple because it relies on an outdated, internal concept of 'our organisation' and its immediate neighbours;
- immediate customers in the supply chain have an essential role to play in communicating, translating and coordinating end-customer demand;
- supply chain priorities are constantly changing, and lead to an ongoing need for coordinated, time-based responses;
- there is no universal 'solution' to supply chain challenges and opportunities.

- The new competitive landscape will be formed by four transformations:
  - product- to customer-based economics;
  - supply to customer measurement;
  - central to distributed governance;
  - efficient to responsive supply chain design and operation.

How will leading edge logistics be implemented?

- Two developments that will support the creation of the customer-focused, agile supply chain are organisational alignment and enabling technologies.
- Four transitional forces help to achieve the vision of the future:
  - the pain of staying where we are;
  - the gain of achieving the desired future state;
  - belief and enthusiasm;
  - ability to manage change.

Discussion questions

1 We started out in Chapter 1 by defining supply chain management as 'Planning and controlling all of the processes that link partners in a supply chain together in order to serve needs of the end-customer'. How will leading edge logistics developments contribute to this vision?

2 Suggest how the seven principles that 'will guide development of the competitive landscape' apply to our model of the supply network (Figure 1.2) and to the integration of demand and supply shown in Figure 1.7. How will organisational alignment and enabling technologies help to achieve such ideals?

References

Beck, A. (2003) 'RFID in the supply chain', ECR Europe, Brussels. Available for download at www.ecrnet.org

Daniel, E., White, A., Harrison, A. and Ward, J. (2003) 'The future of e-hubs: findings of an international Delphi study', Cranfield University.

Godsell, J. and Harrison, H. (2003) 'Supply chain management: putting the end-customer first', *Proceedings of the 8th International Symposium on Logistics, Seville*.

Homs, C. (2004) 'Exploring the myth of the 5-cent tag', *Market Overview*, Forrester Research, 23 February, p. 15.

Sharman, G. (2002) 'How the Internet is accelerating supply chain trends', *Supply Chain Management Review*, March/April, pp. 18–26.

Smart A. and Harrison, A. (2003) 'Online reverse auctions and their role in buyer–supplier relationships', *Journal of Purchasing and Supply Management*, Vol. 9, pp. 257–68

Van Hoek, R.I. (2000) 'Postponement in European supply chains', Cranfield University working paper.

Zographos, K. (2003) 'Emerging issues for e-logistics', EUROLOG Conference, Rome, 12–14 June.

Suggested further reading

Holweg, M. and Pil, F. (2004) The Second Century: Reconnecting the customer and value chain through build-to-order. Cambridge, MA: MIT Press.

Index